Practical Palmistry

By the same authors

The Palmistry of Love
Your Hand and Your Career

David Brandon-Jones

Practical Palmistry

RIDER
London Melbourne Sydney Auckland Johannesburg

Rider and Company

An imprint of the Hutchinson Publishing Group

3 Fitzroy Square, London W1P 6JD

Hutchinson Group (Australia) Pty Ltd
30–32 Cremorne Street, Richmond South, Victoria 3121
PO Box 51, Broadway, New South Wales 2007

Hutchinson Group (NZ) Ltd
32–34 View Road, PO Box 40–086, Glenfield, Auckland 10

Hutchinson Group (SA) Ltd
PO Box 337, Bergvlei 2012, South Africa

First published 1981
© David Brandon-Jones and Veronica Bennett 1981
© Illustrations Hutchinson Publishing Group 1981

Set in VIP Sabon by
DP Media Limited, Hitchin, Hertfordshire

Printed in Great Britain by The Anchor Press Ltd
and bound by Wm Brendon & Son Ltd,
both of Tiptree, Essex

British Library Cataloguing in Publication Data
Brandon-Jones, David
Practical palmistry.
1. Palmistry
I. Title
133.6   BF921

ISBN 0 09 144830 1 (cased)
0 09 144831 X (paper)

To Veronica Bennett, who, in spite of a few conic-fingered failings, helped me to unravel the tangled skeins of my knowledge, and translated them into this book.

To Bill Atkinson, my long-suffering tutor, who patiently guided me in my first faltering steps and sowed the seeds of the book.

And to Aleph, for his foresight and for his sustaining words of encouragement during the dark days.

Contents

Part One

Introduction

1

What is Palmistry?

Theories about the origins of palmistry abound, but no one knows for certain where, when, how, or even why it evolved. The best dictionary definition is misleading and outdated – and gives no indication that hand reading in one form or another has been practised for centuries. It has a history that is both impressive and imposing.

From the very earliest times, man has sought to understand the nature of his relationship with the world around him – with varying degrees of success. His efforts to probe the secrets of the future have taken many strange forms, and still continue to this day, whether he adopts an esoteric or the more scientific and rational approach so popular now.

It is well documented that the Ancient Greeks and Romans had methods of divination using such bizarre sources as onions, eggs, cheese, the entrails of wild animals, the flight patterns of birds, the ripples formed by the movement of the wind on water, the various shapes of clouds in the sky, and the patterns assumed by fire or smoke. There was even a system that interpreted the sounds made by slapping rose petals on the back of the hand as portents or augurs for the future![1]

The human body has always been looked upon as a fruitful source of these omens and portents, hence the genesis of phrenology, physiognomy, moleosophy, necromancy and, of course, chiromancy. The latter comes from the Greek '*kheir*', meaning hand, and originally stood for divination from the whole hand. The wider implications of the word have been lost over the years and it is now understood to refer to 'fortune-telling' from the lines alone.

Traditionally, palmistry is divided into two parts. There is chirognomy, dealing with the disposition, basic character and potential, as seen in the size, shape, and outward appearance of the hand; and there is chiromancy, or the art of divining past, present and future from the signs and lines in the hand, as used (some would say abused) by the sea-front seer and fairground palmist. There is now a somewhat revolutionary third approach which owes nothing to art, and everything to science.

Dermatoglyphics is the name given to the empirical study and classification of the skin-ridge patterns found on the palms of the hand and soles of the feet. It is currently being used in America and Germany to pre-diagnose and treat latent mental and physical ill-health. We shall discuss this important subject at greater length later on in the book.

Palmistry is believed by many to have been founded in the Middle or Far East, and history records its use by the Ancient Greeks, Romans, Chaldeans, and the Egyptian priesthood at the time of the Pharaohs.

The special significance of the human hand was recognized at least as far back as the Stone Age. Hand prints made in red ochre and black pigment have been discovered in European caves, with some particularly fine examples to be seen in the famous Altamira Caves, at Santillana del Mar, Spain.

Pythagoras, Anaxagorus, Hippocrates and Aristotle were known to have used palmistry. There are references in the works of Aristotle that bear witness to his familiarity with the significance of the hand and its lines, and he is reputed to have discovered during his wanderings a book of great antiquity on an altar dedicated to Hermes, messenger of the gods. It was inscribed in letters of gold, written in Arabic, and dealt with the subject of palmistry. Legend has it that the book was dispatched to his pupil, Alexander the Great, with the injunction that he read it immediately. Some say the book was written by the philosopher himself.

Juvenal (AD 60–130), the Roman poet and satirist, speaks scathingly of the current fad for divining from the hands, while Plautus (254–184 BC) and Virgil (70–19 BC) also seem to have been well acquainted with the subject. The Jewish historian, Josephus, tells us that Julius Caesar himself was so well versed in the art of palmistry that it was 'impossible for any man whose palm he had seen to deceive him in any way'. Josephus goes on to relate an incident when an imposter claiming to be Alexander, son of Herod, was unmasked. Caesar had been unable to find the 'rajah loop', or mark of royalty in his hands which, to him, was proof positive that the man was a liar.

Chiromancy – which originally meant a way of revealing the future, the character and the psychological make-up of an individual from his hands – survived the era of the sceptics (*c*. 340 BC) and was on the syllabus of subjects studied by priests at the Roman College of Augurs.

The palmistic traditions of India and China are quite different from those of the West, but hand reading is known to have been practised for at least five thousand years in these countries and is thought to pre-date any written history. It is in common use today, particularly in the towns and villages of southern India, and books on the subject, written in ancient Tamil, are still read and understood.

One of the oldest such manuscripts is attributed to Valmika Maharishi, a legendary figure mentioned in the religious literature of four or five thousand years ago. . . . . It is written in exquisite poetry and comprises 567 stanzas, each eight-line stanza covering one marking or formation.[2]

The Indian palmist K. C. Sen has identified the earliest known documents on hand reading as the sacred Sanskrit scriptures, or '*slokas*', which had been hidden away from the vulgar gaze by members of the Brahmin castes.

Tradition has it that the art of divination in this form, known as the Anga Vidya, was passed on to mankind as a gift of the sea god, Samudra. It is also believed that, when Buddha was incarnated, he could be identified by the existence of certain marks on his feet and hands which were known only to the sages who had awaited his coming.

Chinese palmistry is thought by some to have been imported from India. Be that as it may, the Chinese version seems to owe nothing to Indian or Western methods now. An old lady who learnt her art in China as a girl read my hands, and I am still trying to discover how she was able to be so accurate when she was looking for quite different areas and signs from those I would have looked for.

The Romans probably introduced palmistry into Europe during the fourth century BC and it wasn't until the Middle Ages, after Rome fell, that hand reading – in fact all forms of divination – was condemned as the work of the devil, and forbidden by the Church.

It was during this period of its history that palmistry and palmists were tainted with the aura of notoriety that lingers still. Man's insatiable desire to know what tomorrow will bring made it a simple matter for charlatans and necromancers to move in. Irresponsible practitioners of such arts have always existed, and it's all too easy to part a gullible fool from his cash, telling him what he *wants* to know rather than what he should be made aware of.

The Dark Ages mark the point of palmistry's lowest ebb, too, with the fathers of the Church not above using people's superstitions to enslave them. It is ironic that many passages in the Bible seem to imply that the principles of hand reading were known and used in Old Testament days. The following are examples of this:

And he said, Wherefore doth my lord thus pursue after his servant? for what have I done? or what evil is in mine hand?

(I Samuel 26:18)

Length of days is in her right hand; and in her left hand riches and honour.

(Proverbs 3:16)

He sealeth up the hand of every man; that all men may know his work.

(Job 37:7)

The famous Irish seer Count Louis Hamon, or Cheiro, as he was better known, claimed that this last was purposely mistranslated by those responsible for the Authorized Version of the Bible. In his view the correct translation was omitted because 'it gave divine approval to palmistry'.[3] It should have read, 'And God placed signs and marks on the hands of all the sons of men, so that all men might know their works.' A rather subtle but vitally important difference.

References to hand reading are made in the holy books of many old-established religions, including the Jewish *Kabbalah*, while Buddhist missionaries were certainly responsible for scattering seeds of its knowledge far and wide. The Egyptian priesthood, the Brahmins and Hindus, and the Magi, or Persian priestly caste, were adept in all such mysteries of science and nature.

Astrology, palmistry and the like, though they developed thousands of years before the birth of Christianity, had always been kept hidden and secret. Jealously guarded from the uninitiated by these priestly castes, the knowledge was used to inspire awe, honour and respect for their gods.

A system of fortune-telling based on the fingerprint patterns, and interpreted in accordance with the principles inherent in the *I Ching*, or 'Book of Changes', is still widely used in China today. The patterns are correlated with the Yin and Yang or opposing polar forces:

The hand is divided into eight basic areas or palaces, each of which corresponds to the eight trigrams of the famous Chinese *I Ching*. . . . If one superimposes these palaces over the zones and mounts of the traditional European system, then very interesting relationships may be established.[4]

There are one or two societies which cover both Eastern and Western palmistic traditions, but it remains to be proved whether correlation and investigation of the varied disciplines will reveal a common thread linking all together.

On the whole, the Eastern approach is rooted firmly in the doctrine of fatalism – the belief that one's destiny is fixed and wholly immutable. It's not altogether surprising to find a corresponding belief that the lines and shape of the hand do not change either.

While this may well be true – for those who accept the premise – in the West it has been proven that the hands can, and frequently do, show quite dramatic changes, sometimes over a relatively short period of time. Examples of this will be given later.

Another correspondence that almost goes without saying, even if you have little more than a nodding acquaintance with the subject, is that between palmistry and astrology. Although no one has yet developed a valid system for integrating the two, the nomenclature and meanings attached to the mounts and fingers accord remarkably closely with those given to the planets in astrology.

Modern scientifically based hand analysis takes a firm stand and makes no claims to be able to forecast specific events. What it can and does do extremely well is to indicate the likely reaction of an individual in a particular set of circumstances, and determine what the effect of those circumstances will be on his delicate hormonal and psychological balance.

This seemingly dramatic shift from divination to pure character analysis started at the time of the Renaissance. The narrow outlook and active discouragement of independent and original thought that had been prevalent for so long gave way, slowly, to a climate of questioning and rationalism. All the old beliefs that had previously been taken at face value were now dusted down and looked at from a completely different angle.

It was, nevertheless, not until the late eighteenth century that the noble and ancient arts of astrology and palmistry started on the long road leading to recovery from the evil and unreasoning prejudice of these centuries of abuse and misuse.

By the early nineteenth century hand reading, popular as both a science and art form, had reached a new peak. It had once more gained champions who were both illustrious and reputable – Honoré de Balzac and the two Alexandre Dumases, father and son, amongst them. Napoleon had his hands read, and his name was given to a type of forefinger indicative of a power-seeking nature.

There is a certain amount of disagreement today about who was the father of modern palmistry. Claims to this title have been made for Captain Stanislas d'Arpentigny (1798–1865) and Adolph Desbarrolles (1801–86). What is certain is that, between them, these two laid the foundations of palmistry as we know it now.

D'Arpentigny is said to have made a completely fresh start, ignoring ancient chiromancy completely, giving 'his whole attention to the outward aspect – the physiognomy, so to speak – of the human hand', while Desbarrolles 'modified and improved' this system to the point where, according to the French émigré and founder of the National School of Palmistry in Chicago, the self-styled 'Comte de Saint-Germain', it forms 'the first and indispensable step towards a complete and logical knowledge of the hand'.[5]

D'Arpentigny researched, sifted and analysed all his information before concluding, after years of painstaking study, that all hands could be classified under one of six 'pure' headings: the Elementary, the Spatulate, the Square, the Conical, the Psychic, and the Philosophical (see page 27). Those hands whose characteristics were too indefinite to be fitted neatly into one of these categories were designated 'Mixed'. This concept was so novel that it stood all previous ideas about the subject on their heads; it was tantamount to a revolution. It is a system that has served us well for almost two hundred years, but its limitations are apparent to anyone who has to deal with hand type-casting. Unfortunately, all subsequent attempts to replace it with a more workable approach appear to have failed miserably. Doctors, psychologists, astrologer–palmists, dilettantes and occultists have all tried – to no avail. In Chapter 3, I shall introduce a method with which I have been working for a number of years, and which gives me the results I want without throwing out the baby with the bath water.

The upsurge of interest in all forms of divination that occurred towards the end of the last century led to the publication of hundreds of books, good, bad, but mostly indifferent, on the subject of palmistry alone. In spite of, or perhaps because of, this popularity, it is only comparatively recently that hand reading has been regarded at all seriously.

Years of prejudice have taken their toll, and 'the melody lingers on'. Unfortunately, many eminent and much publicized exponents of the art – such as Cheiro – gave the impression that it was possible to provide specific information on particular events, both past and future, from the hand alone. Cheiro's books imply that anyone can easily learn to read hands, and that the techniques he described were practical, capable of rational explanation, and sufficient to transform the reader into a master palmist.

The name of Cheiro is one that springs readily to mind whenever palmistry is mentioned. Christened William John Warner, and born in Ireland in 1866, he was a spectacular success in Europe and America. He read the palms of politicians and society doyens wherever he went, including those of Arthur James Balfour, Oscar Wilde, Edward VII (when still Prince of Wales), Leopold II of Belgium, Lord Kitchener, 'Mark Twain' and, reputedly, Rasputin. There is no doubt at all in my mind that Cheiro was a brilliant seer, but his work seems to have owed as much to his vivid imagination as to his remarkable psychic talents. It is worth remembering that, without the aid of clairvoyance, no one is able to forecast exact dates – and even the manner of dying, as Cheiro did – from the hand.

There are other media available for the use of the fortune-teller and his like – the Tarot, crystal ball, magic mirror, etc. Is it any wonder that hand analysis has been relegated to the fairground and the seaside palmist's parlour for so many years? A change of attitude and approach is long overdue.

The publication in America of the *Practice of Palmistry*, by Comte de Saint-Germain in 1897 can have done little for palmistry's flagging reputation. This was reprinted in 1974, vaunted as a practical textbook and encyclopaedia, and described by the publisher as 'undeniably the best in its field'. The poor comte seems to have spent much of his time searching palms for signs of insanity:

Insanity, Hereditary, Erotic – A star at the end of a branch of Line of Heart drooping into Mount of the Moon.

Insanity, Religious – The Sign of Saturn on the Mount of the Moon.

and there are entries on 'Hydrophobia, Danger of', 'Haemorrhage' or quite simply, 'Failure in Life'.[6]

Saint-Germain takes specific and isolated markings and reads dire threats of death, doom, gloom and destruction into almost every one. His obsession with such possibilities as insanity, murder, degradation and debauchery makes depressing reading, and nowhere is it pointed out that it is quite impossible to make any sort of judgement on the basis of one small sign! He was a great admirer of Desbarrolles, and eulogized him to the point where he pretended his introduction was by the 'Master'. This is later retracted in an 'Introduction to the Introduction', which lends an air of farce to the whole work.

A palmist making similar negative pronouncements nowadays would rightly be considered totally irresponsible. He would rapidly run out of clients, too! There is the risk that the ignorant or unscrupulous practitioner may – like some stage hypnotists – encourage the more credulous of his customers to fulfil the worst of his predictions. Suggestion can be a powerful tool – or weapon.

In this sort of climate it is hardly surprising to find the American William G. Benham, speaking in 1900 of the 'entire absence of any literature on the subject' of palmistry. He goes on:

No help was found from professionals, for nearly all proved to be ignorant, unlettered, and trying solely to gain money, without any effort in the direction of scientific investigation.[7]

It is rather ironic that it was a meeting with a gipsy fortune-teller in his youth that set Benham off on his voyage of discovery. He determined to approach the subject as though it had never before been studied, and his way was to 'take a mere tradition, and apply it to hundreds of hands, noting the result. . . . The investigation of a single indication often consumed a year, and in the end [was] found unreliable. . . .'

He devoted the remainder of his life single-mindedly to one aim – to 'make Palmistry not an amusement, nor a centre around which cranks might congregate, but a study worthy of the best efforts of the best minds'. His dedication was such that he studied medicine in order that he might become familiar with 'the entire anatomical construction of the body' and in particular the hand. Benham's greatest contribution to palmistry was to clear away the outdated dross and, strangely enough, in view of his stated opinion of its value, to confirm and clarify much of the ancient knowledge that had been passed down the centuries by the savants of old. It seems that later in Benham's life, his somewhat arrogant opinion that all that had gone before was inconsequential was modified to the degree that he did at least condescend to read some of the previously written works.

Benham's efforts were based on his certainty that there was a scientific basis underlying the whole concept of hand analysis. He was one of the first to prophesy that some of palmistry's greatest and most important applications would be in the areas of vocational and marriage guidance.

It is largely due to his influence that the climate of public opinion began to change – very slowly at first – and palmistry gradually began to interest more scientific and rational minds. In England, Noel Jaquin had an answer for those unable to see beyond the fortune-telling image:

The main object of this study of the hand is prevention – the prevention of the development of latent disease . . . and the prevention of the waste of years of effort and energy [spent] following a career for which the individual is unfitted.[8]

The palmistry of five hundred years ago bears little relation to hand analysis as it is practised today. It, like mankind itself, has evolved and grown. Over the years there have been many contradictory interpretations and reversals of doctrine. But, if we sift through and extract the ideas that have remained constant and unchanging, we will find a common thread that cannot be explained away.

2

Palmistry – a Personal View

When I come across a 'new' book on palmistry, or one I have not read before, I look for the answer to one important question. What basic premise is the author working from? Is he, for instance, an out-and-out, dyed-in-the-wool fatalist? Or does he believe that each of us has full and complete autonomy?

It is often difficult to judge whether the author has any strong views of his own, because the same old chestnuts keep turning up – rehashed and presented in a slightly different guise, it's true, but in essence the same. And why not – there are not many new ideas about, and palmistry is a perennially fascinating subject.

While acknowledging that the hand can and does change, often dramatically, many writers continue to talk glibly of Lady Luck, Fame and Fortune. This, I feel, has more to do with pandering to popular prejudice than revealing, in a practical, down-to-earth way, what modern hand analysis has to offer mankind.

I will now nail my own colours firmly to the mast and proclaim my heart-felt belief that fate and free will have equal parts to play in every human life . . . and I'm not fence-sitting when I say that!

I believe that we each have an allotted task – or tasks – to complete during our three score years and ten. And, although we have our obligations, and must be in the appointed place at the appropriate time, we can please ourselves which form of transport we use. But any one of a dozen paths will get us there, and in this we do have a free choice.

If there's an element of challenge in this, so much the better. Homo sapiens does not appreciate anything that comes too easily. He thrives on pitting his wits, his strength and his all against seemingly insuperable odds . . . and on the glow of satisfaction that results from overcoming them. Perversely, without that struggle, we are all inclined to feel somehow cheated and let down.

Many of my clients make the mistake of asking when they are going to be rich. They do not say, 'Would being wealthy make me happy?' They're only interested in getting the money and do not bother to think what will come next.

Understandably, I seldom meet people who are either satisfied or happy with their lives. With notable exceptions, all my clients have been searching for ways of escaping from their own particular maze; they are desperate for a grain of hope.

In the vast majority of cases, I am forced to point out that the answer is, quite literally, in their own hands, and it is entirely up to them to identify their dream . . . and then go on to visualize it in such detail that it becomes fact. But each must make the first move for himself. It is no good expecting the palmist or clairvoyant to do it for him.

The point of this book is – first and foremost – to show you that you can achieve nothing until you *know yourself*. Until you are able to look yourself realistically in the face and, perhaps for the first time in your entire life, acknowledge yourself warts and all, you can be neither realistic nor practical in approaching your problems.

Accept what you see in that mental mirror, setting aside the distorted image of yourself broadcast by mother, father, sister, brother, husband, wife or peers, and you will have taken the first positive step towards freedom. It is a fundamental tenet of human psychology that most of us are bound and limited by early conditioning, like a fly caught in a spider's web. We are unable to 'throw overboard the negative ballast' that burdens our minds, preventing 'positive realisation of [our] true dispositions'.[9] So many of us are terrified of doing this, envisaging our innermost desires in the light of the contents of Pandora's box, afraid that, if the box is opened, disaster will inevitably result. Except in the most extreme case, where repression has been total and absolute, this is highly improbable.

I do not believe in 'luck' either. We make our fortune with our own hands. Luck does not, like the good fairy, land on our shoulder out of the blue and proceed to grant our heart's desire. We have to work at it – and that means having a clear idea what we want to do first.

An elderly gentleman who shared my philosophy told me that someone had once remarked to him, 'Isn't your son lucky? Look at the way he's got on in the world!' His response was dry and to the point. 'Yes,' he said. 'The harder he works the luckier he gets.' This anecdote is well known to clients who complain about their pathetic and inadequate lives. Sadly, it seems to take a crisis for them to understand my point.

Humans seem to fall into two camps. Those of us who believe in self-determination and the fatalists whose credo tells them not to bother struggling – their lives are pre-ordained anyway, so what's the use? I am looking for as many converts to the first cause as I can get! I am not suggesting we cannot ask for a helping hand now and again. Or that we must travel a lonely road, fighting our battles without friends and allies. I am suggesting that we should look for assistance if we have temporarily lost the way, but never to expect it as our due to be carried.

If a client comes asking for advice, I'm more than willing to present the alternatives; to sort the wood from the trees. But it is not my place to decide which alternative is right. That can only be the client's decision.

I have the dubious advantage of having experienced both points of view – those of the palmist and the client – during my lifetime. Until the age of thirty-seven, I was a victim of my upbringing, as were my parents before me. I inherited a feeling of worthlessness and impotence in the face of adversity. Money was regarded not as a tool, or means to an end, but as something not for the likes of us. Several suicide attempts, broken relationships, and failed businesses left me feeling inept and incompetent – a listless vegetable, existing courtesy of anti-depressants and sleeping tablets. The lives that touched mine during that bleak period were not improved by the contact.

In 1970 came the final crisis. I sat down one day with some orange juice and a bottle of tablets. I could see no other way out of the mess I was in, and I wanted desperately to get back at the girl I was living with, and whom I blamed for my troubles. I had given up completely, and wanted no more to do with a world I felt to be totally hostile. I managed to get down about three hundred aspirins before my poor stomach rebelled.

It was not to be so easy, however. Five hours later I was dragged off, semi-conscious, to the hospital to undergo the indignity of stomach pumps and the understandable hostility of the staff, who resented such a waste of their valuable time and energies.

After almost two months of drug therapy and E CT treatment my mental attitude was unchanged. I was even plotting suicide again as soon as I could get out of hospital. The situation outside was no different. If anything, it was worse. The girl I felt to be responsible for my current state had proved she no longer needed me. While I had been away she had coped not only with her side of the situation, but mine too. She had made me almost totally redundant.

Up to this point, whenever I hit a low patch, I would stagger from one so-called help agency to another and all I found were well-meant platitudes or indifference.

When I needed help most, with my life at the cross-roads, I found what I needed. Not, as you might imagine, someone to care for me with love and understanding, but, quite simply, homeopathy. My homeopath did not give me advice on how to live my life, or come up with trite, unhelpful clichés or mind-dulling drugs. I returned a completed questionnaire to him, and in return he sent me a course of potassium phosphate.

As far as I was concerned at that time, it had to be a con trick. If sleeping tablets, tranquillizers and E CT had not helped, how could one powder a day do so? It took all of two weeks to convince me. For thirty-seven years I had suffered a potassium deficiency. This may have been due to faulty diet, malabsorption, an inherited tendency – or a combination of all three, but potassium is essential if the mind is to remain clear and uncluttered, and the brain used to full capacity.

My changed attitude was a miracle, it seemed to me. But all those fifteen powders did was to give my potassium-starved brain a gradually strengthening dose of this vital nutrient. Day by day, my mind grew sharper and the fog cleared until I started to make plans in an organized and constructive way.

No more impossible, impractical ideas, but alternatives that suited the situation I found myself in. I was, for the first time, able to think clearly, lucidly and energetically. The short course of treatment had enabled me to face life with courage and I knew that I would never sink back into that suicidal state of mind again.

Some months later, I discovered that a series of chains on the Head line of the hand reveals potassium deficiency. I took my own hand-prints and compared them with the illustration in Beryl Hutchinson's *Your Life in Your Hands*. Sure enough, there was a long chain on the left Head line, with a shorter series of islands on the right hand.

My confidence in modern medicine had been badly shaken. The allopathic approach invariably concentrates on treating symptoms rather than causes, and it seemed far more sensible to attack the problem at grass-roots level.

Though I had been dabbling in palmistry in a desultory and haphazard way for about ten years with little success (lack of concentration again), it was not until 1971 that I decided to learn as much as I possibly could, and perhaps go on to become a professional. Because I had been treating hand analysis as a game, I had ignored all the other signs in my hands that gave warning of impending nervous and physical breakdown. Had I taken notice, I could have averted the catastrophe.

I now know that, in the vast majority of cases, the signs are apparent well in advance and, once we know what to look for, the trouble can be avoided. If some of my present clients had been warned beforehand of a difficult or dangerous situation, they could have taken evasive action, instead of rushing blindly like lemmings towards disaster.

Even adversity can be turned to good account, as in my own case. It was my tutor who first pointed out that, had I not suffered these dehumanizing, demoralizing years, I would have been unable to understand and sympathize with – and therefore help – those undergoing similar traumas today. The other side of the coin is that, had I taken note of the message in my hand, I would not be doing the work I'm doing now!

It is important to note that it is not usually the problem itself that causes despair and desperation – but a negative reaction to it. It is possible after a time to accept and come to terms with the loss of a beloved husband or child, but I have known cases where the individual was unable to do this. A recent instance involved a client who first came to see me two and a half years after the death of her husband. She was an intelligent woman in her late forties, and her husband had made ample provision for her, but she was unable to bring herself to consider any sort of future without him. No one, she felt, would ever be able to fill the void he had left in her heart and her life.

No matter what I suggested, what remedies I recommended, she returned to the same theme over and over again. Why had God taken him from her? What was she to do? After a lifetime depending on him for every kind of support, how could she be expected to manage?

Brutal frankness had no effect. I told her she was wallowing in self-pity, and was too lazy to do anything for herself. Had she consulted a homeopath, or even taken some of the supplements I advised to counteract the deficiencies caused by alcohol and a poor diet, the downward slide could have been halted, but she went away convinced that I didn't understand at all.

So she systematically, and quite literally, set about drinking herself to death. She was found on Boxing Day, surrounded by empty bottles, having choked to death on her own vomit.

It is possible to lose one's job or a limb, to break one's spine, contract polio or an incurable disease, and still rise above it, to make the most of what is left, and even to use it to spur one on to greater heights. History is full of stories of those whose achievements were negligible till they were struck down. Only when faced with an interminable future of uselessness or immobility did they determine to prove they would not be beaten.

How many of us could cope without arms or legs, as an amazing number of Thalidomide-affected children have done? Nothing could better illustrate my case that it's not the disability that holds us back; it's our gut reaction to it that makes all the difference.

It is not faith in an all-powerful deity that enables us to move mountains, but faith in our own abilities. Once we are able to accept the fact that our mission is to get from point A to point B in this life, and that we will not be asked for more than we are able to give, we can transform and revitalize the tempo of our existence.

In my view, palmistry can put us on the right track by helping us to understand, acknowledge and accept both strengths and weaknesses, not only in ourselves but in our family, friends and fellows. The applications of modern hand analysis are many and varied, but we have not yet managed to do more than scratch the surface. There is so much still to be learnt from the human hand and the way it is constantly changing to meet the demands of contemporary life.

3

A New Method of Classification

Each palm reader has his own, often highly individual, way of working. One may prefer the clients to sit in front of him, hands illuminated by a bright, well-focused light. Another may have no physical contact at all, preferring to work from prints that have been sent to him. Yet another may organize things so that a pair of hands is presented through a small window, and the reading is given to an anonymous client. Gipsy palmists, working mainly through intuition, usually read only the left hand and, though most hand readers see the right hand in a right-handed subject as the major (or dominant) hand, some make no distinction at all.

Whatever our individual approach to the client, as scientific hand analysts we have one important common discipline. The miraculous and indisputable fact is that every hand is unique, never to be repeated. For this reason, there has to be a basic system of classification. Until a category has been specified, the reading cannot begin. The analyst will be like a rudderless ship – quite unable to orientate himself.

Because we are all different, obviously very few hands will slot smoothly into place, but any course of study has to provide a few 'pegs' on which to hang the elementary principles. No matter what system is being used, each archetype must be memorized and mentally associated with a particular set of qualities. A successful hand reader must have instant recall of these facts. During a reading there is no time for hesitation or leafing through reference books.

The value of such a system will soon become apparent when you are faced with a 'difficult' hand – one in which each feature seems to contradict every other, rather than confirming a pattern. Whenever this situation arises (and it happens to us all), I recall my tutor's advice and 'return to basics'. The shape of the hand is the corner-stone on which the reading is founded, so the sooner the archetypes are reduced to keywords and pictures, the better.

D'Arpentigny's 'System of Seven' was described in general terms in Chapter 1 (see page 16). This was the first successful attempt to relate specific personality traits to particular hand shapes. Prior to this, and especially during the decline of palmistry in the Middle Ages, each individual feature was looked at and interpreted in isola-tion. Seldom was any attempt made to synthesize and coordinate the various – and possibly conflicting – points into a composite and fully comprehensive analysis.

D'Arpentigny's descriptions of his seven human types tell me as much about his upper-class background as about his ability to analyse character. The Elementary, for instance:

... belongs to the lowest grade of human intelligence. ... Such a hand as this betokens a crass and sluggard intelligence, incapable of understanding anything but the physical and visible aspect of things, a mind governed by custom and habit, and not by inclination or originality. Such a character, inaccessible to reason from sheer want of originality of intellect to under-stand it, is sluggish, heavy and lazy as regards any occupation beyond its accustomed toil.[10]

However, a relatively short study of the Elementary reveals that it includes not one but two character types – one more evolved than the other, and neither as bestial as d'Arpentigny makes out.

The upper classes of the nineteenth century knew little of the lives led by their servants. They were careful not to offend their own sensibilities and made sure of remaining well cushioned and cocooned from the lower orders. In complete contrast, very few 'upper-class' people today lead such luxurious lives as their nineteenth-century ancestors. Furthermore, it would be almost impossible for one class to remain isolated from another. A modern worker is just as likely to be found holidaying in the Caribbean as his managing director.

Class barriers have been forcibly torn down, with mass unem-ployment no respecter of age, position or rank. Graduates can be found sweeping the streets, while bricklayers and blue-collar work-ers sit for their degrees at the Open University.

As a result of the integration of many different nationalities and cultures, the hands that I see now have little in common with those described and illustrated 150 years ago. Although the System of

Seven is widely used, even now, it seems rather unrealistic to divide the whole of humankind into a mere six categories. When it was devised, it was a great step forward for palmistry, but it is a system that seems to have outgrown its usefulness.

Several attempts have been made in recent times to bring in a more up-to-date method of classification. Muchery tried in the 1930s, as did Fred Gittings after him, to justify a link between astrology and palmistry. Muchery described eight classic hands, relating the characteristics of each to the qualities traditionally represented by Saturn, Venus, Mars, Mercury, Jupiter, the Sun, the Moon and the Earth.

In *The Hand and the Horoscope*, Gittings prunes back drastically until he is left with only four basic hands, representative of personalities motivated by earth, air, fire or water. He then proceeds to expand and elaborate on these till the permutations become almost unmanageable.

The fingers and mounts have borne the names of the planets for hundreds of years; and fifteenth-century treatises point back to the origins of this relationship in antiquity. My own limited knowledge of the subject of astrology is almost exclusively confined to the qualities traditionally associated with these heavenly bodies, and owes as much to mythology as to horoscopy. In any case, I am told that it is impossible to make any sort of character assessment without knowing either the relevant ascendant or the position in the houses of the horoscope of the various planets. Neither palmistry nor astrology is simple.

In palmistry, too, many features have to be taken into account, and a mass of often conflicting data must be reconciled before any opinion can be passed about the personality of the individual under discussion. But, you may ask, won't two people whose hands have a similar shape have a good deal in common? Indeed they will – in much the same way as a rough outline of character can be given from the astrological sun sign alone. Though such an outline would in no way be full or comprehensive, it would be accurate enough to give many a sceptic pause for thought.

One day, a successful means of linking palmistry and astrology will be found. I am not yet convinced that it has been. . . . A good deal of painstaking research will have to be done first in both areas.

Be that as it may, while no system can ever be 100 per cent satisfactory, there must be a starting point, or platform on which to build the reading. The method set out below is one that was developed for my own use and that of my students. My aim has been to take the best of the old and bring it up to date.

It takes a good deal of observation and practice before the student is able to identify a particular type of hand correctly. I find that the best way of doing this is to become familiar with hand shapes in outline only. The beginner would be well advised to start his own collection of prints and outlines as soon as he can. Correctly annotated, these will prove invaluable later. At this stage, it is only necessary to learn how to outline the hands. Directions for taking handprints will be given later in the book.

Hand outlining

The method for outlining is simplicity itself. All you require are a few sheets of A4 paper – not too thin – and the metal innards, or 'skeleton', of a ballpoint pen. A Paper Mate refill would be ideal.

Have your chosen subject place his right-hand palm down in the centre of your sheet of paper. It is important that he feels at ease and natural. A stiff, defensive pose will not do at all – unless that is typical of his normal attitude to his fellow men. It is a good idea for you to get into the habit of holding the wrist and shaking the hand until it is quite limp. Then ask him to put his hand on the paper. If the fingers still remain close together, you will know that this person is an introvert who only relaxes with friends. Wide-spread fingers mean a subject has to have personal freedom, and loves to meet new people; he is naturally outgoing and adventurous.

Hold the barrel of the pen absolutely upright and, maintaining a lightweight pressure against the skin, start to draw round the hand. Commence at the wrist, about an inch below the palm and mark carefully round the fingers and thumb, finishing an inch below the palm on the opposite side. Now ask your subject to place his right thumb flat on the paper, next to the main outline, and mark round it as before.

If you repeat the procedure again with the same hand and the dimensions are different, your technique is at fault. But do not be discouraged – this is almost inevitable at first. Practice is the only sure remedy. You must get into the habit of following the procedure through, in a systematic way, until, like the twelve character types discussed below, it becomes second nature. The acid test of your proficiency comes when you can hold up two outlines to a strong light. If the two can be matched together showing no apparent difference, you have passed.

An outline of the hand of the same individual taken a month or so later may not necessarily be quite the same shape, or have the same measurements as the earlier one. Dramatic changes can take place, even in such a short time. The fingers may have become broader, straighter, or the opposite, and the palm wider or thinner. Should the individual have made any drastic changes to his life-style, the hand type itself may be different. This is a phenomenon that will be dealt with at greater length in Chapter 6.

Let us take a look now at our twelve hand prototypes, and the characteristics that are most commonly associated with them. Before you can decide where the particular hand you are studying fits in this spectrum, you should note any variation from the norm, and take its implications into account.

—————— *1 The Primary hand* ——————

The Primary hand (see Figure 1) is distinguished by a short, broad, coarse-skinned palm and short stubby-looking fingers and thumb. The few lines that are in evidence will be short and deeply etched. The hand as a whole gives the impression of stiffness and clumsiness. The fingernails, though wide, will have little depth, and there is rarely, if ever, a moon. The Primary hand corresponds closely with the Elementary classification used in earlier systems.

PERSONAL CHARACTERISTICS

In its purest form, this is a hand that is often found in peasant communities. Its owner is able to withstand pain and discomfort with a stoical indifference, and will usually labour uncomplainingly in his master's vineyard or farmyard, and remain content with his lot.

At the other extreme, he can be a lazy-minded, uninspired plodder without the imagination to plan for more than the basic necessities of life. Because of this lack of imagination, he is unlikely to suffer from stress, nervous problems or temperamental ups and downs. The

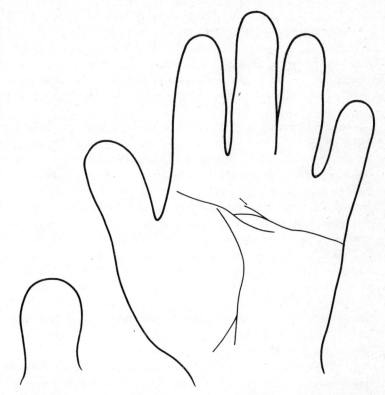

Figure 1 The Primary hand

short fingers imply that he is inclined to act first and think later, so there is little or no chance of a stressful situation building up. This impetuosity can be a problem should anyone dare to threaten or wrong either his family or his code of honour.

When roused, he can be violent, but with no malice aforethought. The short, stubby thumb often has a large, ungainly tip, signifying both impatience and a dearth of reasoning power. If the tip is any larger, it is likely that its owner gives vent to stormy displays of temper. Under certain circumstances he can be overcome by sheer, unthinking, murderous rage.

The Primary type prefers to maintain a certain distance between himself and his fellow man – all the more so when they are obviously more intelligent than he is. He is well suited to the nomadic life and can be found on building sites throughout the land working as unskilled casual labour. He is not concerned about finding a regular job with a pension, preferring to live each day as it comes.

His enormous appetite for the 'good things' of life can lead to drunken brawling or other anti-social behaviour. At the other extreme, he can be extraordinarily gentle and kind when it comes to children and animals. In fact, these are often the only creatures he will allow himself to trust.

The Primary makes an excellent soldier, provided no calls are made on his limited ability to reason. He is not afflicted by 'nerves' because he cannot visualize himself in a position of danger or suffering from pain. Wounds that would destroy a more sensitive man have no effect on him. Were he ordered to crawl across a minefield, he would do it without a second thought and – probably – come out the other side unscathed. A strong instinct for self-preservation, coupled with his innate lack of imagination, would see to that.

That same instinct for looking after number one means that he will also do as little as he can get away with in the way of work. If he has a boss who is weak or easy-going, he has no compunction about taking advantage of this, and he will revel in the belief that he is more than a match for his so-called betters. Though adopting a subservient mien, he has the utmost contempt for weakness and can only respect the law of the jungle, looking up to those who are harder or more ruthless than himself. Men of this type are the drones without which a dictatorship could not survive. The Primary can justify any act of brutality by saying that he was only acting under orders – and what is more he will be genuinely hurt and puzzled if he is considered in any way to blame. After all, there was no personal animosity, was there?

The best of the genre – both male and female – will be found working closely with nature, patiently and lovingly coaxing a living from the land and instinctively following natural rhythms. The worst will be represented amongst the thugs, bully-boys and killers on the fringes of society, who act not from personal motives of revenge or conviction . . . but merely because it is a quick and easy way to get into the big-time.

2 The Useful hand

This type of hand, like the Primary, is short and broad, but the skin is less coarse and thick (see Figure 2). The fingers are short, but more rounded at the tip, as is the thumb. The lines are longer, with a tendency to slope down towards the base of the hand, and there may be some peripheral lines in evidence. The nails are broad and short, and often bitten.

PERSONAL CHARACTERISTICS

To look at, the Useful hand bears a strong resemblance to the Primary. The major difference shows up when the hand is grasped, for the rough, hard feel of the Useful hand is only superficial. There is an underlying elasticity – even a softness – that sets it apart immediately and betokens a degree of sensitivity totally lacking in the Primary.

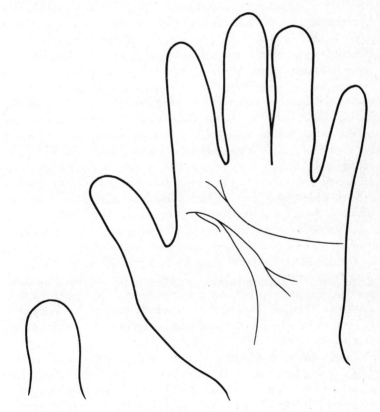

Figure 2 The Useful hand

Unlike the Primary, the Useful type does occasionally use his hands to make or clarify a point. He finds it almost impossible to express himself verbally and often prefers to translate his feelings via primitive, yet amazingly eloquent, paintings, sculptures or carvings.

If asked to describe a method of working, he succeeds best when allowed to demonstrate actual techniques, rather than by trying to talk about it. Though by nature taciturn and reserved, he can be encouraged to wax lyrical if you engage him on the subject of a pet passion or hate – especially if the fingertips veer towards the conical.

He is closely allied to the Primary in that he sees no sense in wasting time on protocol and proprieties. He hates undue pomp and ceremony and is frequently judged as uncouth and boorish. Crowds are anathema to him and he feels out of place in up-market areas like Mayfair or Kensington. The author Brendan Behan typified the Useful character. He had the social graces one would expect of a well-bred bull, and it would have been almost impossible to imagine him rendering a lucid and cohesive speech to contemporary and more conventional literary lions. But he could certainly write!

The Useful type has difficulties in communicating because he has a dual-sided nature, which makes him feel confusion and resentment – an inevitable result of not knowing which half to present to the world. If he maintains a rough and ready front, utterly without sophistication, he is frequently taken at face value and feels misunderstood. If he exposes his gentle, kindly, understanding and extremely soft underbelly he feels vulnerable and open to attack.

Such ambivalence and emotional insecurity can make victims of partners. Should a woman be warm-hearted and unselfish, her husband's moodiness and brutality may be enough to destroy both her and any chance of a fulfilling, long-term relationship.

The owner of the Useful hand is an emotionally motivated being with the power to reason – unlike the Primary. If he cannot unleash his dammed-up negativity on a nearby victim, his anger may turn inwards on himself. The resulting chemical changes in the body may in time bring about such debilitating, degenerative conditions as arthritis or cancer.

The Useful hand is equipped with the same short, quick-acting fingers and thumbs as the Primary, but the long, sloping Head and Heart lines mean that its owner is fully aware of the likely results of precipitate action. He is always conscious of the damage his uncontrolled rage would wreak, and – unless the provocation is intolerable – anger is still-born.

A safe method of releasing this tension is discharging the energies into daily work. If that involves hard labour, or sculpting, painting or carving, so much the better. Such need for catharsis often results in highly acclaimed and powerful works of art, expressing irresistible and primitive passions.

The twin forces represented by this hand are almost impossible to reconcile, and almost as difficult to understand. The Useful type cannot be happy or fulfilled if the two sides of his character are battling for dominance. His only hope is to develop fully one aspect or the other so that he can finally accept and comprehend his own complex nature.

The Useful type seems to delight in self-denigration, and prefers to be criticized rather than praised. He sees praise as an insult, for he does not believe that his work is in any way worthy of appreciation, and laurels are cast aside impatiently. He himself is intensely self-critical (note the ugly, short, bitten nails – Chapter 8) and sees nothing but flaws.

The world needs the kind of genius this hand represents. Without the Useful type, it would be a poorer and far less colourful place. More's the pity that our lives are made richer through his sufferings.

3 The Energetic hand

The first and most obvious difference between this and the other hands we have looked at is the almost triangular shape of the palm (see Figure 3). There is extra length in the fingers and thumbs, and the fingers tend to have spatulate tips. (That is they are broader at the fingertip than at the base.) There is a feeling of cushioned resistance when the palm is squeezed gently. Typically, the Life line will swing out confidently into the palm, and the mounts of Venus and Luna will be well developed. The nails are broad, widening at the top, and may also be bitten short.

PERSONAL CHARACTERISTICS

As the bottom third of the hand – the widest part in this example – represents the material world, we can assume that the Energetic individual places greater emphasis on the physical and tangible than he does on mental or spiritual matters. If the second phalanges of fingers and thumbs predominate, reasoning power will be strong,

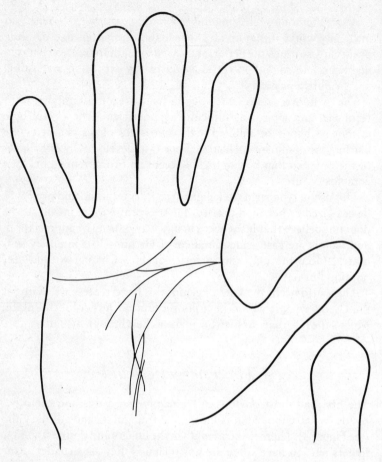

Figure 3 The Energetic hand

and there will be an ability to think in logical, constructive ways.

When the hands are hard, energies will be blocked and not properly utilized. When they are soft, energies will be dissipated. When they are springy, as they are here, expenditure of vitality can be controlled, but the normal Energetic type works on full power twenty-four hours a day. His high metabolic rate is often reflected in moistness of the hands. Unless he is able to make time for relaxation, and to ease the tremendous pace he sets himself, he may be on the way to health problems such as hyperadrenalism, adrenal exhaustion or other glandular malfunctions.

The Energetic hand as a whole gives the impression of reaching out eagerly to life, and it is almost impossible to slow down its outgoing, vital owner. He just is not happy unless he is doing something. If he can defuse his restlessness by means of a suitable sport, fine. If he cannot, it will have to be channelled elsewhere – and that usually means work requiring intense concentration and a good deal of physical effort.

The Energetic type is a pioneer who insists on breaking new ground. He will not knowingly follow in another's footsteps or cover ground that is already well mapped. If the second phalange on the Mercury finger (see page 153) is broad and long compared to the tip and base sections, an all-devouring curiosity about his environment can lead the Energetic type to one scientific breakthrough after another.

Like a healthy, intelligent child, he has to have all the answers, and right now. Tomorrow is too late. Having absorbed all the available background knowledge, he will go a step further and better it. Then he will start to look round for the next challenge. Any laurels that come his way will be regarded as pure incidentals, not at all important, and certainly not the aim of the game.

Astronauts, explorers, test pilots, speed aces and mountaineers are likely to have among them a predominance of Energetic hands. It is a tragedy when this vast store of power is left unharnessed. It can short-circuit and damage the human mechanism or generate an excess of criticism and self-criticism which often shows up in bitten nails.

The Energetic type's drive, determination and ambition can only be discharged through action. Testing his strength against the odds and the elements is the only way he gets real satisfaction.

The Energetic type makes an excellent and stimulating partner – provided his 'other half' makes no attempt to confine him to a nine-to-five routine – the equivalent of throwing a wild and noble beast into a cage for life. I have seen too many casualties suffering the effects of stress-induced ailments to doubt the truth of this statement. Such restrictions strain the relationship to breaking point.

For the Energetic type to be happy and reasonably content, a partner must be equally energetic – or prepared to put up with roaming. That way the zest for life that is their birthright will never be lost.

4 *The Dynamic hand*

This hand, like the Energetic, is triangular in shape, but in this case the narrowest point is at the wrist edge of the hand (see Figure 4). The palm will be springy and the skin pink, fine and glossy. The fingers will be heavily knuckled with a wide-spread stance on print and outline, and with a variety of fingertip shapes. The thumb will be set high on the hand and either spatulate or conic in form. Fingernails are usually deep pink, longish and rounded, while the lines are long, sloping and often finely etched and islanded.

PERSONAL CHARACTERISTICS

The upper third of this palm is top heavy and visibly out of balance. As this part represents the spiritual and emotional elements in our nature (see Chapter 5) and the remaining two-thirds the practical and material respectively, it should be no surprise to learn that, in the Dynamic personality, the spirit is strong, but the body is weak. His inherent belief that faith *can* move mountains keeps him plugging away when tougher mortals would admit defeat. The base of the hand also indicates the state of the constitution, and the Dynamic is as narrow here as any Intuitive or Egocentric hand, neither of which is remarkable for having great reserves of strength.

This type of hand is found more often in women than in men, but wherever it is found there will be little or no sex drive. For a Dynamic type, the first priority in any relationship is to have complete mental rapport, and she is more than happy for it to remain on a platonic level. Her partner must be well endowed with warmth and human understanding for she is an idealist – an unrealistic one perhaps, doomed to wander alone and lonely, fruitlessly seeking the impossible.

The excessive mental energy symbolized in the extra width at the top of the hand is usually directed into a full-time professional career. Provided her work doesn't tax her limited physical resources, but concentrates on ideas, the Dynamic can produce answers for every eventuality.

Whatever she sets out to do is done with the utmost speed and efficiency, for she is a genius when it comes to delegating. In fact, she often gains a bit of a reputation as a tyrant.

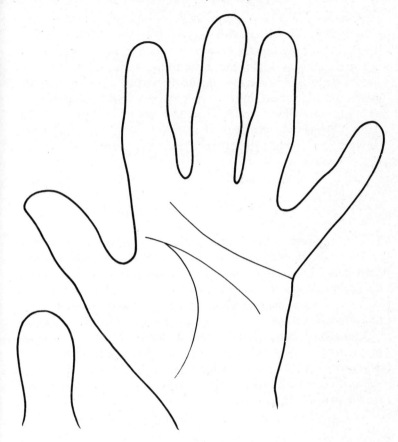

Figure 4 The Dynamic hand

With the Dynamic, work is found to be an end in itself rather than a means to an end and her ideas flow freely and abundantly. Material gain is unimportant, and the Dynamic is inclined to neglect her physical well-being in favour of the satisfaction to be gained from assuaging her mental restlessness. When the body rebels and breaks down, she is disgusted and resents its limitations, but break down it often does.

The strength of mind and will-power suggested by the size of the thumb means that it is difficult for the Dynamic to find a mate who can dominate and support her. Unless he can, she will despise him. If he does, she will begin to feel small and insecure and start a fight for

supremacy. Unless he is exceptionally strong, determined and dip-
lomatic, her achievements will soon put him in the shade and, when
the feelings of inadequacy become unbearable, he will opt out.

The Dynamic is not an easy hand to live with, and the owner of
such a hand is destined to remain the victim of frustration and
insecurity unless she is able to learn from her mistakes. She will never
be a conventional wife and mother, and only when she can come to
terms with this will she regain that essential yet precarious balance
between the spiritual, the practical and the material.

—————— 5 *The Practical hand* ——————

The first impression here is of a capable, sturdy, workmanlike hand
that is almost entirely angular. The square, inflexible palm is quite
deep at the Plain of Mars (see Figure 5), and surmounted by square-
tipped, heavy-looking fingers of medium length. The hand's resilience is springy to hard, with skin texture dry and rough. The skin
itself may be calloused, but it is basically a healthy pink colour.

A longish, dominant, square-tipped thumb is fairly typical, as are
square fingernails. Like the Primary, the Practical hand has a tendency to short lines placed high on the hand, though the Heart line
will be longer than on the Primary, reflecting greater integrity and
readiness to abide by society's rules.

PERSONAL CHARACTERISTICS

This is the hand of the down-to-earth, stolid and dependable artisan
and builder. He thinks with his hands rather than with his head, and
is a traditionalist through and through. Destroy the routine that his
whole life is founded on, and he will fall apart at the seams.

The Practical individual stands for loyalty and unquestioning
obedience to authority and the law. If it is in the rulebook, it must be
obeyed. He is happiest employed, or self-employed, in a trade requiring a high degree of manual skill – such as carpentry, plumbing, gas
fitting, electrical work or similar. Projects that need imagination are
not his forte.

He makes a strict, no-nonsense employer, and expects his men to
follow his own stringent rules. If they are loyal, he will back them to

the full, taking the blame in public for any mistakes they may have made. In private later, though, he will make sure they know where they have gone wrong.

The employee may not be able to understand his Practical boss, but he usually respects him. The Practical type rarely befriends an employee – in fact he has very few friends of any description – but when a man is in trouble there is no better ally than he.

At home, too, he runs a tight ship and is just as unyielding in his views on right and wrong as he is at work. He soon settles down in a comfortable rut with one week placidly following the routine of the

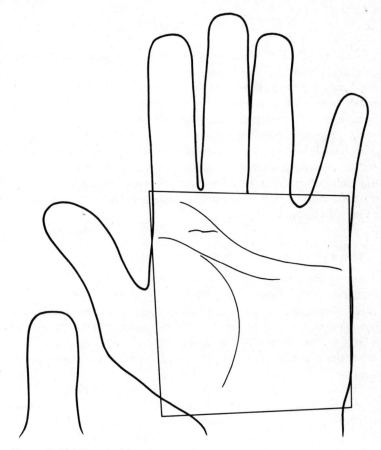

Figure 5 The Practical hand

previous one and, if the children dare to question his authority, they are very soon made to toe the line – or fly the nest.

Marriage to a woman with a Lively or Sensual hand is always a mistake, for both of these types will do her best to shake him out of what she considers to be apathy. Neither is likely to have much success, for the Practical type is truly an immovable object.

The only possible match for him is a Practical-handed woman who is able to understand and sympathize with his strong traditionalist views, and who will not be hurt by his inability to be romantic and demonstrative in his wooing.

—————— 6 *The Analytical hand* ——————

Like the Practical, the Analytical hand is also angular and short on curves (see Figure 6). The palm is oblong rather than square and the digits are longer than those we have previously looked at. The skin is smooth and pink (occasionally with a greyish tinge), the resilience springy, and the palm quite deep at its centre.

Fingertips are mixed, with conic predominating, and the fingers often heavily knuckled at the second joint, while the thumb is low-set and generally square-tipped. No one shape of fingernail is found more often than any other. The major lines are long and set high on the hand, and there is a tendency for superficial worry or stress lines to mar the palm.

PERSONAL CHARACTERISTICS

At first glance, you could be forgiven for thinking this is another Practical hand. Closer examination will reveal that the Analytical hand is more rectangular in shape, reflecting a greater capacity for independent and logical thinking. The extra length in the thumb and fingers reinforces this ability, and is usually found in the second, rather than the nail, phalange. This middle section represents reasoning power.

Though, like the Practical type, the Analytical is inclined to look on the rulebook as his Bible, he is more flexible and will listen to another point of view – perhaps even going so far as to compromise. If some of the fingers have conic tips, this is even more likely. Conic tips also endow their owner with a creative streak, lifting him (often

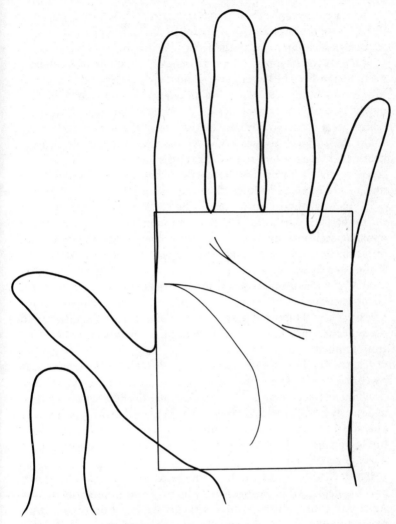

Figure 6 The Analytical hand

to his own surprise and discomfiture) out of his secure and comfortable rut.

His gift for cutting away the inessentials and getting to the heart of things is revealed by the rather heavy knuckles. These give the fingers an air of awkwardness but are the keynote of his personality.

There is usually a good angle at the back of the thumb, showing an acute sense of timing. This applies to anything from being punctual in the conventional sense, through musical ability and appreciation, to always seeming to be in the right place at the right time.

The Analytical type is, first and foremost, a planner and tactician, particularly when he has conic tips and long, sloping lines. He draws inspiration from Luna, and driving energy from Venus. Unfortunately, he often has to fight lack of confidence – shown in the fingers, which are a little too narrow for the size of the palm.

On the surface, he may seem self-assured and capable. Underneath, there is a seething mass of insecurity and doubt. As a result, he is constantly setting up fresh hurdles and challenges for himself, each one a little more demanding than the last.

In this way, almost without realizing it, he drags himself up out of the rut beloved of the Practical type and sooner or later gravitates to a managerial position of one sort or another. When the index and little fingers are both long and conic-tipped, this may involve selling. If they are square, engineering or construction are more likely.

Many hands of this type are found working in local or national government offices. The long, rectangular palm seems to encourage an excess of red tape, but it depends on the quality of the fingers and the other features in the hand whether the Analytical type will be truly fulfilled in this sort of work.

The routine-loving palm may be at odds with the demands made by conic fingers. The owner of such fingers must have change and excitement if he is to be happy. He must have the best of both worlds, and satisfy both Jekyll and Hyde. So he may plod away, year in, year out, at a safe, secure and steady job, but marry a lively, vivacious and fun-loving mate who will encourage him to fulfil the more adventurous side of his nature.

If he fails to recognize this need for excitement, and pushes it down into the depths of his unconscious, he may find himself one balmy April day running off to Paris with his secretary or anyone who seems to offer the opportunity to escape from the confines of a suddenly oppressive humdrum existence.

No matter that he returns some weeks later, contrite and apologetic, in response to the promptings of a troubled conscience. The need has been acknowledged, but only temporarily appeased, and will reappear with ever-increasing frequency unless the routine can be varied in some other way.

The owner of the Analytical hand will achieve the greatest

fulfilment by mentally reducing his personality to its component parts, quite dispassionately. Having recognized and acknowledged his own talents and requirements in this way, nothing in the world can hold him back.

—————— 7 *The Intellectual hand* ——————

This type of hand is distinguished by a long, angular, bony palm and heavily knuckled fingers (see Figure 7). The hand as a whole has a rugged, craggy appearance, and the sallow skin is tough, horny and unyielding. The depth of the palm is medium to thin, the length of the fingers medium to long, while the low-set thumb has a broad nail phalange which tapers to a fine tip. Fingernails are generally long and narrow. Nails and the long, sloping lines will also have a slightly jaundiced appearance.

PERSONAL CHARACTERISTICS

The Intellectual is, first and foremost, a loner. He does not mix with mere mortals, preferring the peace and quiet he finds in the realm of concepts and ideas. If you were looking for an example of the type, the most likely place would be a monastery, where he would be found living a life of strict contemplation.

He is withdrawn, inward-looking and other-worldly, and in no danger of succumbing to either the flesh or the devil. He is quite imperturbable and can, in a few, well-chosen, often cynical words, tell you exactly where he stands, and why.

Cheiro's description in his *Language of the Hand* of the 'Philosophic' is as true today as it was then. For the Philosophic, as for the Yogi, it is no real hardship to 'separate himself from all claims of relationship and kindred, and starve and kill the body, that the soul may live'.[11]

The Intellectual gives the impression of being an outside and impartial observer of the vagaries of life, and this, together with his egoistic approach to it, are good solid reasons for seldom, if ever, considering marriage or partnership. Even if he did, there would be a scarcity of takers!

Money and prestige, and the trappings of materialism, are of no

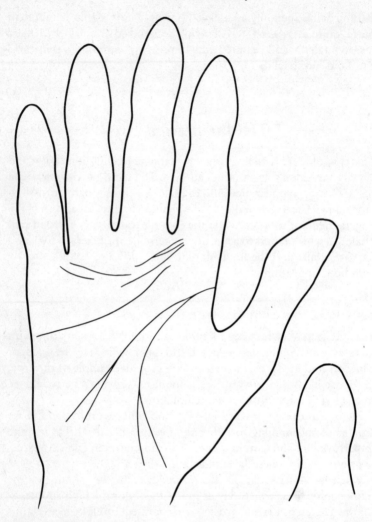

Figure 7 The Intellectual hand

interest to him. As Cheiro implies, the Philosophic/Intellectual is a student of humankind, and knows and understands the 'weaknesses' of his younger brothers and sisters. But, though he may have understanding of their foibles, he will never be a participant. He is in the world, but not of it, and truly an outsider – not as other men.

———— 8 The Sensual hand ————

This hand is noticeable for its soft, pudgy – in some cases almost bloated – appearance (see Figure 8). In sharp contrast to the acute angles seen in the previous hand types, the Sensual hand is full of soft, flowing curves and gently rounded mounts.

The skin is often moist to the touch, the resilience soft to flabby, and the colour light pink to white. The medium-thick palm is surmounted by short, conic-tipped fingers with full, often over-developed, third phalanges. All the digits are flexible, with the short,

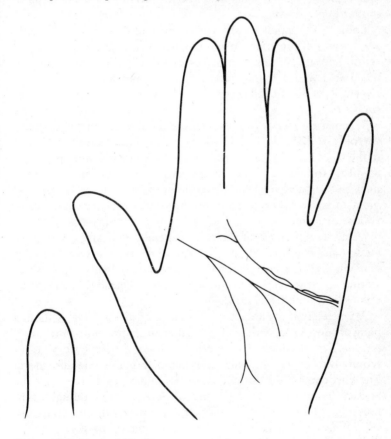

Figure 8 The Sensual hand

high-set thumb inclined to bend backwards at its conic tip, or from the second joint.

The nails are oval and light pink in colour, while the long, sloping, rather anaemic-looking lines may be islanded or badly formed.

PERSONAL CHARACTERISTICS

When hands are as doughy as these, and accompanied by fingers with softly padded third phalanges, you know you are in the presence of a languid, luxury-loving hedonist. Personal comfort is his first priority and the satisfaction of his physical needs is of paramount importance.

Look at the hands of any confirmed and dedicated gourmand. Most will fall into this category. Their owners are impulsive and self-indulgent, gorging themselves to full capacity on all sorts of unsuitable and fattening goodies, including curries, cakes and sweets. This may be reflected, particularly in later years, in a weight problem.

When a person is grossly overweight due to an under-active thyroid gland, the skin will be rough and dry rather than moist as it is in the truly Sensual hand. Whatever the root cause, other problems are likely to follow, such as thrombosis, weak heart, or diabetes. It may be a natural urge for the fleshpots rather than any chemical imbalance that is at fault, but the end results with regard to health will be the same.

Depth at the centre of the palm generally indicates a wealth of vitality and plenty to spare. The Sensual hand is the exception, for here, though the energy levels are constantly being replenished, vitality seems to seep away through the soft, flaccid skin leaving its owner listless and enervated.

A Sensual type of either sex will sit around all day long, without a pang of conscience, with work piled high in all directions. *Mañana* is too soon. If it's ideas you're after, that's a different story. Ideas require little energy – though carrying them out may require more! The fine, conic fingertips and the long, sloping Head lines give the Sensual hand access to the world of pure, creative thought. But, unless he can find a Practical partner to transform those dreams into reality, they will remain beautiful, useless pie-in-the-sky.

The Sensual female will look for a man she can depend on. He must be capable of bringing home enough 'bacon' to keep her in the delicious state of lassitude to which she has become accustomed – and in which her best ideas come to fruition. For this she usually requires a hard-working team of drones to do the rough and menial tasks around the house, and to keep an eye on the children.

The Sensual hand denotes, first and foremost, a dreamer, someone who is ambitious for position, worldly success and wealth but without the dedication or the industry to achieve them. Charismatic, impulsive, and generous to a fault (once their own needs have been satisfied), they live to love, and love to live.

Meet a Sensual type at a party, and you will be impressed by his ready appreciation and understanding of what you have to say. Later you may come to see that most of his knowledge is gleaned from a variety of sources, and is largely superficial. You may be impressed with his energy and drive when he expresses an idea in inspiring and inspired tones. Later, when you realize he hasn't the momentum to sustain that forward movement, you may learn to distil the essence of that idea and develop it profitably for yourself.

Emotionally, the Sensual type will also prove to be somewhat superficial, and mood follows mood with kaleidoscopic rapidity. To quote again from Cheiro's *Language of the Hand*:

Men and women possessing this class of hand respond quickly to sympathetic influences; they are emotional and rise to the greatest heights of rapture, or descend to the lowest depths of despair, over any trifle. . . . They are more easily influenced by colour, music, eloquence, tears, joy, or sorrow, than any other type.[12]

9 The Lively hand

Like the Sensual, the Lively hand is full of gentle curves with well-developed third phalanges on the fingers (see Figure 9). Here, though, the firmness of the palm ensures that the creative energies are not dissipated but flow evenly when required. The resilience of the hand is springy, rather than soft, and the skin texture fine and baby-smooth, coloured a healthy pink.

The palm is medium thick and the fingers taper gently to conic tips, as do the medium-set thumbs. Fingernails are a delicate almond shape and pink. Lines are long and sloping, pink and finely cut.

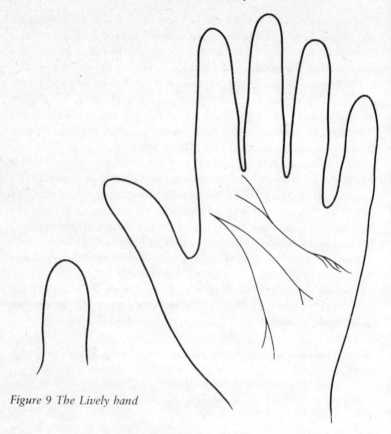

Figure 9 The Lively hand

PERSONAL CHARACTERISTICS

The elasticity of the palm reflects the bouncy personality of the Lively type. The conic fingers mean that the ideas will flow, while the strong thumb suggests that those ideas will be transformed into tangible realities with speedy facility.

The Lively-handed personality is emotionally motivated, and it is more often found in women than men. The owner of such a hand will prove shrewd – even cunning – but extremely likeable, in spite of being a manipulator of men, and mercurial of temperament. She is volatile and unpredictable, and thrives on variety and movement. Routine is anathema to her lively mind for it represents laziness to her. She will go to the other extreme and reduce order to chaos, rather than settle into a rut.

The Lively hand goes with expensive tastes in everything from furnishings to fashions to food, and over-indulgence at the fleshpots can transform her, if she is not careful, into a lazy Sensual type. She has no scruples about finding herself a rich husband and then supplementing her sexual and emotional income by doing a little moonlighting. As far as she is concerned, he is extremely lucky to have her as a wife at all.

And she may well be right! She is an excellent cook (though not so keen on the washing-up afterwards), has a marvellous eye for colour and style, is an animated raconteur, musician and/or artist, provided the Mercury finger (see page 153) does not let her down.

Do not expect this type of person to study or work hard at anything consistently. Unless it comes naturally, and is born of the emotions, it is not for her. In the same way, it is her charm and her silver tongue that can get her what she wants. If there is any suspicion that effort or exertion is required, forget it, for she certainly will.

Though it is the Practical hands who are left to oil and maintain the wheels of commerce and industry, you can be quite certain that the first firm pushes that set them in motion were given by Lively hands. Having supervised the project from the drawing board to independent life, there is no further interest for the Lively personality – it's bye-bye and on to the next challenge.

—————— 10 The Egocentric hand ——————

It is impossible to mistake this hand for any other type (see Figure 10). The long, narrow palm is icy cold, hard and resistant to pressure, while the skin is fine textured and pale. The palm lacks depth and substance, and the fingers are thin, bony and heavily knuckled at the second joint. The tips are more often pointed than conic, and the high-set thumb sits close to the hand, almost as though asking for protection.

The lines, like the hand itself, are pale pink to white and placed high up the palm. They are often islanded and usually poorly marked, with a mess of superficial worry lines marring the surface. The most distinctive mark of all is the form taken by the nails. They are pale, long and tough, and bear a marked resemblance to the talons of a bird of prey, particularly at the moment when it grasps its victim.

PERSONAL CHARACTERISTICS

Do not allow yourself to be taken in by owners of hands such as these. They are more than capable of looking out for themselves – their own interests are of primary importance at all times.

It is a type of hand that is found more often in women than in men, and a man with such a hand is very likely to be effeminate or to have marked homosexual tendencies. Whatever their sex, the owners of Egocentric hands all possess a finely tuned sixth sense. Unfortunately, it is a gift that is rarely used for the benefit of mankind as a

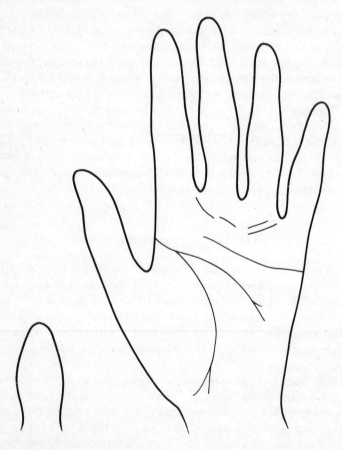

Figure 10 The Egocentric hand

whole; but seems to be another weapon in their personal survival kit, and is invaluable when it comes to sorting out the predators from the potential providers and sugar daddies.

Even a husband who is extremely rich cannot assuage the pangs of insecurity to which the Egocentric hand is heir, and the resultant stress takes its toll on the finely balanced nervous system. This shows in the palm in the form of innumerable superficial lines, known as worry lines. The same stress can cause nervous asthma, migraine and other such ailments, including mental breakdown.

This kind of woman is clever and will use every trick in the book, and a few of her own that aren't, to ensnare her man. She will work very hard at it, too, until she has caught him. Then, unless there seems to be some danger of his escaping, she will drop the mask and revert to cold indifference.

She rarely has children, for she has no wish to see her husband dividing his attention between her and their offspring – and that goes for his money as well. If she does make the mistake of becoming pregnant, she will make sure a nanny is appointed to keep the child out of her way.

Egocentric personalities are more deserving of pity than contempt. They are never happy for a moment, for fear that all they have fought for may be stolen from them. Unless they are able to turn their thinking upside down, and start to put others first, there is no hope for them.

11 The Intuitive hand

The immediate impression given by this hand is one of fragility (see Figure 11). It is long and slender, soft and almost insubstantial. The thin palm is usually clammy and luke-warm when touched, and the skin colour white, or blotchy pink and white. The fingers are thin and usually smooth, with fine, conic, almost pointed, tips; the thumb is weak and inadequate looking, and the fingernails are pale, narrow and easily broken. All the lines will be an anaemic white, with major lines poorly marked, broken and islanded, and a web of superficial lines obscuring much of the skin-ridge patterning.

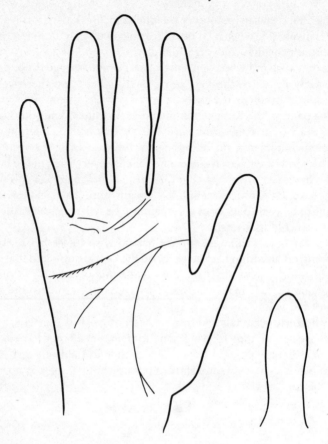

Figure 11 The Intuitive hand

PERSONAL CHARACTERISTICS

As the name suggests, this is a hand that goes with powerful intuition, particularly when the Head Line drops diagonally down the hand towards the Luna mount. Clairvoyance, the ability to predict future events, and frequent disturbing feelings about people, places and things are unwanted gifts, and most Intuitive types try unsuccessfully to keep this part of their nature well hidden. The unfortunate result is to increase rather than reduce their suffering. In spite of themselves, they are strongly attracted to the occult and the supernatural but they are gullible and easily taken in – mainly because they lack self-confidence and prefer to lean on someone who has enough for both of them.

It is a thin, fragile-looking hand and invariably associated with a romantic and highly impractical nature. This is a dreamer of beautiful dreams, with no understanding of worldly, practical matters at all. Like the Egocentric individual, the Intuitive's main preoccupation is to ensure material and financial security, but there is an equal need for love and understanding.

With this type there is an almost magnetic attraction towards broad-handed, generous, capable personalities who have the patience to withstand the traumas caused by insecurity and self-doubt. No matter how reassuring and supportive the partner, such traumas will always be a problem. The partner is set on a pedestal and idealized, but, being human, it is all too easy to fall from grace.

Intuitive types resemble small, defenceless creatures of the ocean, at the mercy of the waves and any predator that happens along. Their need is for protection, succour and encouragement. Almost invariably they are crushed and destroyed by the callous and unthinking cruelty of those who do not try to understand them. In the latter part of the nineteenth century, Heron Allen described the type in the following words:

They are guided only by their idealism, by impulse, by their instinct of right in the abstract, and by their natural love and attraction for the beautiful in all things, whether mundane or celestial. . . . They are incapable of strife or struggles for glory, but, if their instincts of the ideally just are aroused, they will devote themselves even to death in defence of what they consider to be ethically right.[13]

───────── *12 The Composite hand* ─────────

When a hand has few characteristics that obviously correspond to the types already described, the personality will be a more complex one. Before an attempt can be made to synthesize the indications, each and every feature must be considered on its own merits.

The example of the Composite hand shown in Figure 12 has an awkward and ungainly appearance: it has a Primary (though Practical-edged) thumb, a Sensual rounding of the outer, or percussion, edge of the hand, a capable, Practical palm and a strange mélange of fingers with peculiarly mixed shapes and nail types.

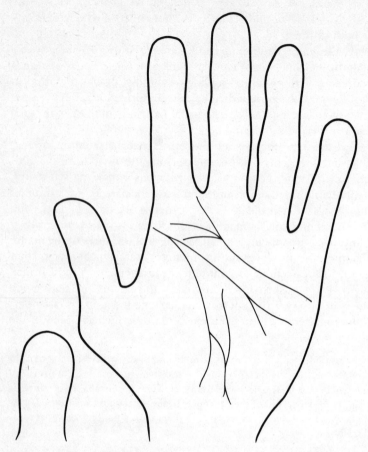

Figure 12 The Composite hand

With experience, you will be able to assess borderline cases on their individual merits, and quickly decide whether to assign them to a category that is relatively 'pure' or to the Composite sector. At this early stage, however, if there is any doubt at all, it is far better not to take short cuts. You should try to reach the correct destination safely and surely.

Composites are inclined to be versatile and adaptable – some would say two-faced or hypocritical, or even schizoid – but their mixed personality enables them to change the colour of their sympathy like a chameleon. Blanket judgements on them are just not possible. Whether this multiplicity of talents can be drawn together and woven into a strong and cohesive whole is reflected in the size and shape of the thumb, and the strength of the lines.

Far from being considered the rag-bag of the system, the Composite, or mixed, hand should be regarded as a test of the hand analyst's ability and his comprehension of his art.

4

The Whole Hand

*Texture, temperature, resilience, colour,
size, and other factors*

A character assessment starts the moment a client enters the room. The way he uses his hands – his gestures, or lack of them, the normal position of his fingers when at rest – and the texture and temperature of the hand when it is held provide the trained analyst with a wealth of information, even before he has looked at the palm and the lines. The handprint gives only the bare bones; additional information gleaned from other factors fleshes out this skeleton.

Data from initial impressions alone, with no reference to the lines of the hand, should give you plenty to talk about, and provides fascinating insight into the client's personality.

First note the resilience of the hands. Are they soft and yielding, springy and supple, hard and leathery? Are they hot, warm, cool or cold at normal room temperature? Is the skin texture fine and silky, or coarse and rough? The implications inherent in the basic hand shapes have already been discussed, but the depth of the various mounts must be noted, and their significance assessed with the help of the information given in Chapter 7.

As there is no way for the average individual to retain, much less recall later, half of this essential information, it will be necessary to note it down at the time of taking the handprints. It is a good plan to devise your own questionnaire, similar to the one shown on page 178. This also ensures that all the details will be available for comparing with a later check print of the same individual.

Skin texture

When you hold or shake hands with someone for the first time, you will unconsciously form an opinion of some sort about that person from the quality and feel of the hand. Texture, temperature and resilience become apparent.

Smooth, silky skin hints strongly at a fussy and fastidious nature. Everything must be just so, and the remotest hint of brashness or crudity is found offensive and immediately off-putting. This quality is common with the owner of the Egocentric type of hand, for whom nothing but the best is good enough. Here the refined texture shows devotion to self alone and the ability to be completely ruthless when such selfishness is opposed. Though the Egocentric hand gives an impression of fragility, it is in its apparent weakness that its greatest strength lies.

A fine-textured skin is also a feature of the Sensual type of hand, but here it shows a nature that is warm and outgoing, easily hurt and often taken advantage of. Self-indulgence goes with a belief that everyone is ready to encourage and attend one's every wish.

Rough or coarse skin invariably suggests a lack of refinement and a rather pragmatic approach to life. Those who possess it are rough and ready, the salt-of-the-earth, with a manner as straightforward as it is direct, and with little or no time for social niceties.

Coarse and leathery skin is usually found in the hands of the Primary, the Useful and the Practical individuals. A generous allowance of wine, women, and – if not song – good, wholesome food is enough to keep the first two happy and contented. The Practical is a little more austere; for him, enough is as good as a feast.

A skin that is naturally rough should not be confused with the results of under-activity of the thyroid (see Chapter 13). Although a deficiency of thyroxin can make us sluggish and depressed, and weaken our perceptions, it is a state that can be relieved by a change of diet, or in the extreme by medical treatment. When the characteristic vertical lines appear on the tip of the little finger, the thyroid gland should be checked.

Occasionally, one hand will differ from its mate in temperature, texture or some other detail. The implication here is that the individual may have had, or still be having, difficulty reconciling opposing facets in his nature. It may also imply that his parents were worlds apart temperamentally, with little or no common ground between them.

Temperature

Temperature generally gives a few clues to personality traits but in the majority of cases (where the temperature is 'normal') we must rely on the other features for information.

Obviously, before deciding whether a person's hands are cold, very cold, 'normal' or warmer than average, it is necessary to allow for the outside and inside temperature, and for the relative warmth of your own hands.

Having allowed sufficient time for your subject either to warm up or cool down, as the case may be, go ahead and make your assessment. If the hands are still cold, you can be sure that their owner — though avidly interested in every word you utter — will not give you the satisfaction of knowing when you hit a nail on the head.

The cool hand is always ready to take, but never has much to give, and such a hand is also likely to be thin and hard, as described under the Egocentric type in the last chapter. In this way one feature frequently confirms the indications given by another, and the more hands you are able to study, the sooner you will begin to look for certain features reinforcing each other.

The cold-handed type will not enter into any sort of contract or agreement — particularly employment or marriage — until he is absolutely sure that he is not going to lose out on the deal. Likely examples would be the male gigolo, the female gold-digger, or the wife who is only prepared to concede her husband his conjugal rights if he buys her the bauble she is currently coveting.

Hot hands are indicative of spontaneity, impulsiveness and generosity of spirit. Their possessors are swept along on the crest of the mood of the moment, flourishing in an atmosphere where they are wanted and needed. They have a surplus of energy, which tends to overflow into all kinds of charitable works and deeds, and it is most unusual to find them sitting around with nothing to do. In fact, for this type of character, to be still is to be ill!

Warm-handed people have a similar approach to life but are inclined to look before leaping, in stark contrast to their hot-handed brothers and sisters. They also respond to encouragement. Self-motivation is not sufficiently powerful to get things done.

If the hands are neither extremely hot nor unnaturally cold, they are 'normal', which indicates a more equable temperament. Look at the lines, the nails and the basic hand shape for additional information and deeper insight.

Resilience

This section covers the resilience of the palm in general terms and that of the Plain of Mars in some detail. The mounts are of primary importance and are dealt with fully in Chapter 7.

Once again, the initial handshake is informative in this context. Some hands may put you in mind of an amorphous, floppy jellyfish, while others have the firmness of granite. These extremes and the subtle gradations in between supply invaluable data, particularly regarding the individual's inner strength and determination.

The soft, flabby, almost insubstantial hand gives the impression that, given a hard squeeze, it would disintegrate altogether. In this kind of hand, the Venus and Luna mounts (see Figure 32, Chapter 7) are high and soft, with large, soft third phalanges on the fingers.

It is a hand that is common to Sensual types and, unless accompanied by a dominant, determined thumb, there will be a strong tendency to be lazy and unreliable. Poor workers, the possessors of such hands will do as little as they can get away with, bemoaning the while the unfairness of it all and begrudging their paupers' pay and disgusting conditions of employment.

It is not unknown for the Sensual-handed person to lose his job for constant lateness. He just cannot get up in the mornings. When he does turn up, you can be sure his work will not be too demanding. He is likely to have a cosy little niche somewhere, and he is quite happy to be able to while away the hours dreaming and vegetating. Not that it stops him complaining about being passed over again when it comes to promotion. He may even genuinely feel slighted!

In like manner, the Sensual housewife will loll around all day, seemingly unaware of the dishes piled in the sink, and the dust and cobwebs that are proliferating. Her husband can only succeed in getting her to do her share if he is not afraid of arguments and angry scenes, with his wife in the starring role of martyr.

Many successful people have large, full-mounted hands, but with one obvious difference. Their palms will prove to be springy rather than flabby. Ideas, far from remaining beautiful, impractical dreams, will be eminently workable and acted on immediately and, furthermore, will be implemented at a tremendous rate.

It is almost as though the resilient, elastic palm is able to store and reserve energies for later use, while the soft hand is permeable and allows the energy to dissipate needlessly.

When the hands feel hard, the personality may also prove to be inflexible and unbending. Their owner will be quite self-contained, with no apparent need for the company or companionship of others. Should he marry, his wife will be sure to find that domestic and business worlds are two different and separate kettles of fish. He is the appointed breadwinner, and she the housekeeper, and as such she will be expected to keep her nose right out of what he invariably considers to be *his* affairs.

The hard-handed individual is an energetic worker – dogged and determined, but above all conservative. He will not be found in the vanguard of any rebellion . . . but, later, once it has become respectable, he and his ilk will often form the backbone of a movement.

Get on the wrong side of him and he will be an indomitable, unflinching enemy. On the other hand, though he does not make friends easily, once you have gained admission to the inner sanctum of his heart, it is for life, and you will know you can always count on him for support.

It is a common fallacy that hard hands are gained through doing hard – that is, manual – labour, and soft ones are the prerogative of the white-collar employee. This is not necessarily so, though it may be true in general. The tough, uncompromising executive or negotiator may have nothing more strenuous to do with his hands than occasionally exercise an index finger, or play an irregular round of golf, yet his palms may have the grain and stamp of well-seasoned leather.

These qualities are commonly found in Primary hands, where there is an underlying hardness, and Useful ones, where the superficial roughness is deceptive, as we have already noted. Although many of these people, more particularly in the former category, are employed in farming, bricklaying or suchlike, it is not the chosen occupation that causes the hand to become hard and unyielding – it is the nature behind them.

I have many examples on file of men who spend the major part of their working day on rugged, manual labour; carpenters, welders, bricklayers, builders and decorators among them. Many are remarkable for their soft, smooth, uncalloused hands, which indicate a degree of sensitivity and refinement that is missing in the hard palm.

RESILIENCE AND DEPTH OF THE PLAIN OF MARS

The part of the hand known as the Plain of Mars (see Figure 32), Chapter 7) is another useful indicator of the availability of energy resources. A thin, hard Plain implies a selfish, self-centred individual. It tells us, in effect, that he does not have much to offer and what little there is will be reserved for himself. Insidious feelings of insecurity are his worst enemy. So much so that, even when he hits a profitable lode, it is never enough. He worries constantly that his luck is about to run out.

When the Plain of Mars is thin and soft, the mean, avaricious nature will be harder to detect, and its owner may hunger for emotional, rather than material, sustenance. Whichever it is, the end result never varies – he will still drain your own resources.

If this area of the hand is deep, well padded and firm, the individual will have vitality to spare. He or she will prove to be loving and giving, though never to the point of foolishness. You will not be able to pull the wool over this one's eyes, so be warned!

Deepness in this part of the palm shows a materialistic nature. If it is also soft and flabby, any resources will be frittered away on self-indulgence. In complete contrast to the firm-handed type, such people prefer their worldly goods to be handed to them on a plate (preferably a solid gold one), thus avoiding the necessity to work for a living.

Colour

Character and health are strongly linked – to a far greater extent than most of us realize – and the colour of the hands, and the palm in particular, give valuable clues to both. In his brilliant book *Man, The Unknown*, Alexis Carrel tells us:

Envy, hate, fear, when these sentiments are habitual, are capable of starting organic changes and genuine disease. Moral suffering profoundly disturbs health. Businessmen who do not know how to fight worry die young. Emotions affect the dilation or the contraction of the small arteries through the vaso-muscular nerves. They are, therefore, accompanied by changes in blood circulation. . . . Pleasure causes the skin of the face to flush. Fear turns it white.[14]

Pale, white hands are a well-known symptom of anaemia – prevalent today as a result of our over-consumption of refined and chemically adulterated foods. Shortage of red blood cells may be caused by any one of a number of mineral deficiencies. As these cells carry oxygen throughout the body, a lack of them can lead to fatigue, irritability, depression, lassitude and an inability to concentrate.

This lack of vitality may cause the subject to seem unfriendly and austere. He will be far from gregarious and sensuality will not be his vice. Quite the reverse; he may give the impression of being in the world, but not a part of it, and given over to mystical imaginings.

A yellow tinge to the skin, provided it is not the remains of a fading suntan, may point to a liver dysfunction, and the yellow-handed individual often has a jaundiced view of the world, together with a bilious constitution. The subsequent pollution of the system may once again cause irritability and depression, while a poisoned mind naturally leads to a negative, gloomy way of looking at things. Vitality will again be lacking.

Look closely at the palms of those who seem to carry the weight of the world's problems on their scrawny, inadequate shoulders, year in, year out. It's a safe bet that there will be a sallow tinge to the skin.

Hands that are consistently blue or mauve, in spite of variations in the weather and temperature, indicate that oxygen is not being properly exchanged in the body, and that blood circulation is poor. Like anaemia, this could be caused by any number of weak links in the system. The cause should be isolated and therapeutic treatment started at the earliest opportunity.

If the base of the nail is also tinged with blue there may be some form of heart disease developing, and the subject should be advised to have a thorough medical check-up. But take care if you suggest this not to alarm him. Your reputation as a budding hand analyst is not going to be enhanced if you have to call an ambulance to carry away the hapless victim of a careless and unwarranted diagnosis.

This may be a good place to emphasize that anyone who puts himself in a position where he is giving advice and guidance takes on a tremendous responsibility. When a palmist becomes proficient in the art, people will consult him for all manner of reasons, with motives ranging from the merely curious to the tragic. Unless technical knowledge is tempered with sympathy and human understanding, his clients may leave more demoralized than when they arrived.

Redness of both hands and lines usually accompanies hotness, the implications of which have already been noted. There will be an abundance of energy in the subject and, provided it can be used for positive ends, there should be no problem. If a surplus of energy has been allowed to build up, take care. It is equivalent to sitting on a pile of unstable gelignite, with frustration, belligerence and aggression a direct result.

It is best for the type with naturally ruddy hands to focus his inborn ebullience and intensity on an occupation challenging enough, both mentally and physically, to absorb it all. Otherwise the residue may be transmuted into murder or mayhem.

Once again, it is important to remember that the colour of the hands and lines can also have a physiological significance. Unwarranted redness may result from an inability (caused by disease or inadequate nutrition) to metabolize iron in the normal way and, instead of being eliminated, any excess is held in the tissues.

When the redness is only confined to one part of the hand – the Jupiter mount, for example – the good or bad traits represented by that mount will be exaggerated. See Chapter 7 for more specific information on this. Sensitives, healers and spiritual mediums find that, when they are working, the base of the hands, particularly the mounts of Venus and Luna, become suffused with pinkness and a warmth that can be quite uncomfortable.

Rosy-pink hands are the prerogative of those who are healthy and normal in every respect. Observe the skin of a tiny baby. His heart is doing its work well, the blood is neither too rich, nor too thin, and is circulating freely. An adult whose hands are a similar colour will generate a feeling of optimism rather than pessimism, and he will have a loving and generous spirit.

If your doctor is not concerned by symptoms which include skin that has become abnormally sallow, pale or flushed, and dismisses you with a tonic or prescription for anti-depressants, it might be worth while considering one of the many 'alternative' systems of medicine. Herbalism, homeopathy, naturopathy and acupuncture are all based on principles that have been known and used for centuries. Almost all of these therapies concentrate on building up the body's resistance to disease.

Allopathic medicine focuses on eliminating the symptoms of disease, frequently missing the basic cause entirely. Which puts me in mind of the five blind men asked to describe an elephant. Each one is positioned at a different place, and each describes a different part of the elephant's anatomy. One feels an ear, another the trunk, another the foot, yet another its tail, and the last one its vast flank. When they paint their word-pictures, all the men are right – but not one of them is in full possession of all the relevant facts.

The allopath treats the body or the mind, and seldom concerns himself with his patient's spiritual well-being. Traditional medicine seems to have retained an awareness that a man's good health is dependant on achieving and maintaining a balance between all three, which is why it often works when all else fails.

COLOUR AND THE NAILS

The digits and fingernails, and the significance of their colour and shape are discussed at length in Chapter 8. The nails will usually reflect the colour of the rest of the hand, and reinforce the message given there.

— Breadth, length and depth of the hands —

Though breadth and depth vary considerably between one hand and another, length seems to follow a predictable pattern. Size and shape of an individual's hands can change measurably over a period of time – length hardly at all.

Researchers have measured hundreds of pairs of hands, correlating the results with figures on weight and size. The subsequent assessment suggests the possibility of forecasting any person's height to within a couple of centimetres given only the size of his hands, and vice versa.

My own observations have produced similar results which are set out in the following table. Each hand is measured from the tip of the Saturn finger to the base of the palm where the first bracelet (or rascette) is found. The average length is then related to the subject's height and sex. My own findings are based on assessment of the hands of 130 males and 130 females.

HAND LENGTH/HEIGHT CORRELATIONS

	5 feet to 5 feet 1 inch	5 feet 2 inches to 5 feet 3 inches	5 feet 4 inches to 5 feet 5 inches
Male	18 centimetres	18.50 centimetres	19 centimetres
Female	17 centimetres	17.50 centimetres	18 centimetres

	5 feet 6 inches to 5 feet 7 inches	5 feet 8 inches to 5 feet 9 inches	5 feet 10 inches to 5 feet 11 inches
Male	19.50 centimetres	20 centimetres	20.50 centimetres
Female	18.50 centimetres	19 centimetres	19.50 centimetres

	6 feet to 6 feet 1 inch	6 feet 2 inches to 6 feet 3 inches
Male	21 centimetres	21.50 centimetres
Female	20 centimetres	20.50 centimetres

The well-balanced hand is neither too broad for its length, nor too long in relation to its depth. Though the proportion of finger size to palm size may vary, the overall length will not exceed, or be less than, the above mean by more than 5 per cent.

Hands that are broad and deep imply a vast armoury of wide-ranging talents. Whether or not these will ever be developed depends on the individual. If the hands are also soft, or soft and flabby, his talents are fated to remain quiescent until he is thrown forcibly on to his own resources. His normal rate of progress is slow and steady, and the longer his fingers the more ponderous his approach to life. Should the occasion demand it, however, he *can* move with amazing rapidity.

Broad, deep hands – when accompanied by fingers that are long and proportionately broad – go with an approach that is strictly no-nonsense. Their owner could never be accused of being a romantic, and he will fight to ensure that the material needs of his family are met.

A long, broad hand is eminently suited to work requiring precision and close attention to detail. Contrary to popular belief, people with large hands are capable of far greater dexterity than those with small hands.

Observe the hands of craftsmen such as watchmakers, menders and the like. One of the most prolific tailors I ever knew had amazing banana-like fingers, yet, when he sat at his bench, he worked with such speed and deftness that those fingers scarcely seemed to touch the cloth.

If the hand is short and broad, like those of the Primary and Useful types discussed in the previous chapter, the approach will be completely different. Its owner will also be quick, but at the expense of detail. Minutiae irk him and, provided the whole is in good order, he is more than ready to turn a blind eye to any superficial blemishes.

Small hands see life depicted on a large canvas, and the smaller the hand the greater the horizons. The Lively hand is small and softly rounded. Its owner can project a brilliant and inspiring image of what he wants – but he makes sure of handing over the painting of the picture to someone else!

Small-handed people are past masters at directing from the sidelines. They will only be found where the action is – never in the planning or logistics department – demanding, 'Can it be done? Well, why haven't you done it, then!'

Short fingers go with speed, but rarely with accuracy. They co-opt long, broad hands to do the donkey work and tie up any loose ends. Long-fingered types may reach the same conclusion as their short-fingered colleagues, if not quite as quickly, but you will not find them speaking up till the facts have been checked and double-checked, and they are 100 per cent sure of themselves.

The owner of a short, narrow hand should always be handled with care; all the more so if it is also hard and cool to the touch. He will be instantly aware of the opportunities inherent in every situation, and ready to turn them to good account . . . as long as the account is in his name. Anything or anybody unable or unwilling to further his ends will be swept unceremoniously aside, or completely ignored.

Such a person is best employed in work that makes full use of his gift for criticism, such as newspaper reporting, or reviewing books, plays or films. He would make a good satirical cartoonist, and would probably be renowned, and even feared, for his asperity and waspish humour.

There is a single-mindedness here that goes with this type of hand which, though it may not be emulated, is often envied. In the market place or a store, the owners of short, narrow hands will not be distracted from their purpose. They will head directly for the appropriate stall or counter, take in the entire display at a glance, select and buy – or reject if the item is not up to their standards – and be off. No lingering, last-minute decisions or impulse buys for this type!

Long hands mark out the philosophical character. He will be known more for his heavy and tedious deliberations than for any actual 'doings', and the longer the fingers the more exaggerated the tendency.

A deep, well-padded hand shows great reserves of energy and a contagious enthusiasm for living life to the full that is almost an insurance against mental or physical breakdown. It is generally found in Primary, Useful and Energetic types, but seldom in the Egocentric or the Intuitive hand (see Chapter 3).

If the hand you are examining is shorter or longer than the averages given in the table on page 67, check the width too. If it is broad as well as long, its owner will prove to be capable and generous, with plenty of time for the problems of others. If it is long and narrow, selfishness will be the most obvious quality. Extra length makes for pedantry and restraint. The shorter the hand, the more impetuous and impatient the nature.

Keep the large-handed individual happy by telling him exactly what you see, and where. If you can make him see that the mechanics of hand analysis are based on sound logic, he is more likely to heed any advice you are able to give.

Small-handed people get irritable if you waste their valuable time with mere technical detail. They want your conclusions straight from the shoulder, without preamble, and will not thank you for keeping them any longer than necessary. Just give them the facts, and let them go.

Hair

No particular note need be taken of hair growing on the back of the hands, unless it is obviously inappropriate. Fine skin, for example, combined with coarse, thick hair, or coarse skin combined with fine hair are a little out of the ordinary and may be an indication of glandular or hormonal imbalance. Beryl Hutchinson suggests that:

[if] coarse, stiff hair grows out of fine textured skin, there may be a warning of conflicting inheritances to be questioned on the palm. Soft hair growing out of coarse skin may be on the genetic path towards a hairless condition. [15]

The clues to personality that are gained in this way are invaluable when you come to decide on the particular approach that will be right in any instance. If you misinterpret the signs, at best you risk alienating your client, and at worst a bout of hysterics or a punch on the nose.

5

Interpreting Right and Left Hands

Another bone of contention among palmists is the degree of importance to be attached to each hand, and the actual significance of right and left. It is an area in which controversy is rife and misconceptions flourish. Most modern hand readers agree that it is essential to take both hands into account, though some gipsy fortune-tellers persist in following the tradition handed down to them and concentrate on the left palm exclusively, simply because it is nearest the heart or 'supreme organ'.

Cheiro rightly condemns this as one of 'the many superstitions which degraded the science in the Middle Ages'.[16] Unfortunately, he also encourages us to believe that the left hand invariably shows what we are born with, and the right what we have become. Many of my contemporaries continue to follow Cheiro, but I feel that a partial truth has been grossly over-simplified.

If the above assumption were correct, there would be no change in a man's left hand from birth to death, with lines only gradually making their appearance in the right hand as he developed and matured. As anyone who has marvelled at the intricate and delicate tracery of lines on the hands of a new-born baby will tell you, this just isn't so.

Another important point is that we are not all right-handed. A recent survey shows a rise in the incidence of left-handedness – which now, at a conservative estimate, stands at 12 per cent of the British population. The taboo against being 'different' is stronger in conformist states, while a society dedicated to the promotion of individual freedom and development boasts a greater proportion of 'southpaws'. For this reason, it would seem to be more appropriate to get into the habit of using the term 'objective', or 'major', when speaking of the dominant hand, and 'subjective', or 'minor', when referring to the hand that takes the subordinate role.

It can be embarrassing to give a reading based on the assumption that the individual is right-handed, and then find that he is not. If the hands are very dissimilar, your client may not recognize himself at all, with the result that palmistry in general, and your reputation in particular, will suffer a setback. This is not likely to do much for your confidence, either, so get accustomed to asking your clients at the outset if they are right- or left-handed.

If there is any doubt at all, the objective hand will usually be the one with the greatest muscular development, and the thumbnail is normally squarer at the tip. The lines themselves are often clearer, too. Both hands are subject to change throughout the client's life, with the major, or objective, hand reacting more rapidly.

Trying to read one hand without reference to the other is like a surveyor assessing the soundness of a house without checking on the foundations. The subjective hand indicates the nature of the sub-structure, and the objective hand that of the superstructure: the hand analyst looks to the former for clues to inherited characteristics, latent talents, and health trends; and to the latter for the development of individuality which has been influenced by upbringing, early training or environment.

When the right hand in a right-handed person is obviously stronger, firmer, deeper, more capable – than its partner, the individual will find it comparatively easy to outgrow the limitations imposed by conditioning and live an independent life. If, however, the left hand is the more powerful in an individual who is definitely right-handed, you will find that he probably showed great promise as a youngster either as an athlete or scholar – or both – only to fade away into mediocrity on approaching his thirties.

When faced with such cases, I am forced to provide a verbal 'kick in the pants'. The potential is there, waiting to be developed, but lack of confidence or laziness is holding the client back. It is my job to show him how he can best use those hidden talents.

The potential shown in the left hand may be for good or ill, but in either case we all have free will and can act on or ignore any warnings indicated there. An inherited tendency towards obesity or heart disease, for instance, could be taken as a timely reminder to watch our diet and give our body all it needs to maintain a state of health. Instead, many of us are inclined to sit back and wait, fatalistically, for 'the inevitable'.

Forewarned is forearmed, and even if the signs appear in both hands all is not lost. Preventative medicine relies on such early warnings and will usually eliminate the problem before any overt symptoms come to light. The danger lies in ignoring the signals, and not seeking the appropriate treatment in good time.

The major hand can also be regarded as the 'active' hand. It indicates what our probable course of action will be if there is sufficient time to think about a problem. Traditionally, this is the hand of reason and shows how we will cope when the conscious mind is in charge. In a crisis, do we lose our head or tackle the problem step by step, logically and methodically?

The minor, or 'subjective' hand represents the quality of our response when there just is not time to stop and think. Would our instinct lead us spontaneously to endanger our own life to save a child who had stepped into the path of an oncoming bus or lorry? Or would we remain standing there, paralysed by the enormity of the decision to be made?

Recent physiological and psychological studies into right- and left-handedness and brain functions have been coming up with conclusions which bear out what palmists have been saying for centuries.

The right half of the brain controls the left side of the body, and the left half controls the right side. So, in the right-handed individual, the motor impulses controlling his fork originate in the right hemisphere, and those controlling the knife in the left.

The two halves of the brain are physically almost symmetrical, and the hemispheres that make up the cerebral cortex are joined by the corpus callosum, estimated to contain approximately two hundred million nerve fibres. As the hands are the most complex and flexible organs in the entire human body, they take the lion's share. Indeed, it has been said that, if the nerve endings in the hands were spaced at the same intervals as in the rest of the body, we would have hands the size of beach umbrellas!

In spite of their physical symmetry, each half of the brain has been proved to have a different function (see Figure 13). Research concludes that:

the left brain [is] logical, verbal, with mathematical and general scientific abilities. . . . The left brain is often referred to as the dominant hemisphere, and the right as the minor hemisphere. The right hemisphere, however, seems to be superior in spatial awareness, non-verbal communication, awareness of the body's orientation in space, and musical ability.[17]

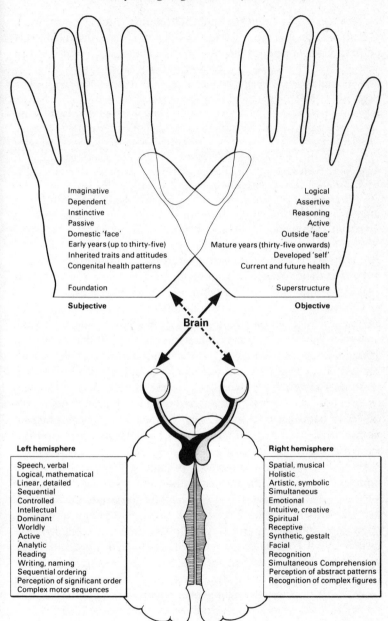

Figure 13 *The effect of the brain on the hands*

Palmists and physiologists alike have fallen into the same trap: classifying one function as major and the other as minor is not very constructive, since both have equal importance:

Why should the right hemisphere or brain (or left hand) have been considered the minor of the two? One explanation for this must lie in the importance which we attach to speech. Both hemispheres have highly specialised abilities, and it can be argued that both are equally important. One reason why the left brain was considered dominant is because it is the verbal hemisphere – it can talk! The right brain (left hand) has difficulty expressing itself verbally, and therefore cannot articulate its abilities. The left hemisphere seems to have more control over the bodily function on both the left and right sides than does the right hemisphere. Many researchers argue that it is more appropriate, however, to regard both hemispheres as dominant as they both have essential roles.[18]

In view of the above comments, which back up my own feelings regarding the relevance of each hand, I prefer to use the keywords 'objective' and 'subjective' when referring to the hands.

The following handprints graphically illustrate the extent of the similarities between the findings of physiologists and those of hand analysts. The physiologist says that the right brain (left hand) has strong associations with the emotional and intuitive faculties, with the left brain (right hand) controlling communicative ability and reasoning power. The palmist looks to the subjective hand for clues to subconscious motivation or creative imagination, and to the objective hand when he is assessing the degree of logical, practical ability. Many of the traditional palmistic beliefs are being borne out by actual clinical evidence, thereby confounding the sceptics.

Even if you have no knowledge of palmistry at all, it is easy to appreciate that the right and left handprints reproduced below are very different (see pages 76–77). They are the prints of an unsuspecting gentleman who 'volunteered' to let me use him to demonstrate the uses to which practical palmistry can be put. I had given a lecture to his colleagues after they had attended a gruelling sales conference. I think they had anticipated a 'fun' evening, but amusement soon gave way to amazement as I pointed out to each of them some little characteristic, weakness or talent that was apparent from the shape of the hands or position of the fingers.

My subject later admitted that he certainly would not have volunteered had he been aware how accurate scientific palmistry could be.

I started by pointing out the features in his hand that kept him on top in his particular field. His right hand is a textbook example of an intelligent salesman who has the ability to make the complexities of his product intelligible to the uninitiated (see Prints 1 and 2).

So far so good. When I began to describe the person represented by the left or 'home' hand, he started to look embarrassed and disconcerted. It was obvious from the hand that, at home, it was his wife who wore the pants. Amidst ribald comments from his fellow salesmen I described a far meeker, milder individual than most of them had ever seen.

I also pointed out that he had overcome a tremendous handicap – crippling feelings of inadequacy and inferiority – only by sheer bloody-minded determination (see the strength of the thumb in both hands). He agreed that this had dogged his progress during his early years. He had not got into his stride as a salesman till his mid-thirties, and was only now, at forty-three, coming into his own.

Let's look again at the idea that the left hand represents the character we are born with, while the right reveals what we have done with our talents. There is a point in life when we transfer from one hand to the other – but at what age do we stop 'being' the left, and start 'living' the right?

My own researches have led me to believe that the point of transition is usually in or about the thirty-fifth year. The vast majority of the hands I read show evidence of some upheaval or crisis at that age, and my clients frequently confirm the details of some tragedy or disaster precipitating a break with the past.

Strangely enough, what often seemed at the time to be a terrible misfortune later proved a blessing in disguise. Comments along the lines of, 'It was like being born again. At the time, I was heartbroken, but my life has changed so much I feel a new person!' are common.

In *The Theory of Metaphysical Influence*, Noel Jaquin postulates his belief that, up to the age of thirty-five, we are paying the price of the misdemeanours committed in a previous lifetime. After that age, in his view, we are free to enjoy ourselves, having made due recompense.

This will only ring true if you go along with the doctrine of reincarnation, and has no meaning if you do not. Nevertheless, thirty-five comes halfway through our average allotted time span of three score and ten years. By the early thirties, most of us have

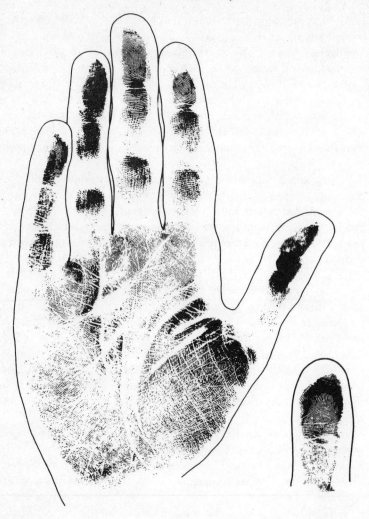

Print 1

thrown off the restraints imposed by any early conditioning and come to terms with our individual needs and abilities.

The law of synchronicity, formulated by Jung, operates here. Having personally noted the frequency with which the magic age of thirty-five came up in the hands I was reading, not only did I stumble on corroboration in Jaquin's book, I also met a young man recently

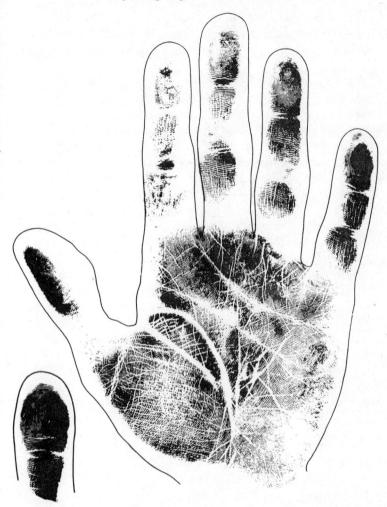

Print 2

returned from India who mentioned the same age as having great significance. Like many others of his generation, he had been reasonably successful in a secure, if uninspiring, job. He gradually came to feel that it was important to discover the meaning behind his existence, and against all advice, threw up everything to travel East.

In southern India, he met his guru – who happened to be a highly esteemed and respected palmist. He spent a year learning to read hands and had just returned when I saw him. We agreed that, as he had very little money, he would read my hands in return for my own services.

When I had given him my appreciation of his hands he began to read mine. He seemed to concentrate solely on the left hand while describing my early years, and his assessment of my childhood and youth was accurate regarding both timing and events.

When we reached the age of thirty-five, he turned to the right hand, and rarely consulted the left. I was intrigued, and quite deliberately questioned him again about my youth. Sure enough, back he went to the left hand before answering.

When he had finished, I asked him to explain his method of working, which was so different from, yet just as exact as, my own. After a good deal of deliberation, and having sworn me to the strictest secrecy, he told me how the system worked.

On several occasions, I tried using his method, only to find that, for me, it didn't work. Obviously, he had been forbidden to pass on a vital piece of the jigsaw, and to discover it I too would have had to make the pilgrimage to India.

Had this meeting been an isolated incident, I would have thought no more of it. Coming as it did so close on the heels of similar information, I was forced to sit up and take notice. Empirical observation since that time has led me to believe that the point of transition from one hand to another is thirty-five years of age in 85 per cent or more of my clients.

A typical example was an Austrian woman who came to see me in London. For her, the death of her husband four years earlier had marked the end of her own life. They had lived only for each other, and they had had no children. To use her own words, 'the world might just as well have stopped turning', when her husband died.

When her sister in Canada had invited her to stay for a while, she had reluctantly agreed – more to avoid hurt feelings than anything else. Shortly before she was due to return to Austria, she was offered a marvellous job working in the same store as her sister. Surprisingly, she accepted. At the time of our meeting, she was in London on company business, and as radiant and fulfilled as anyone could hope to be. The case is interesting because she had been widowed at the age of thirty-five.

Another example was a man whose marital problems almost

destroyed him. He tried to end his life at the age of thirty-five, but was unsuccessful. The marriage finally disintegrated, and it took him seven years to get back on his feet again. This seven-year 'recovery period' also seems to be a recurring factor, with the age of forty-two significant as a time for making a fresh start.

This is not to suggest that a crisis at or about the age of thirty-five is inevitable! It isn't. If all parents and guardians were themselves mature and far-sighted enough not to project their own limiting, subjective experiences and desires on to their young charges, it wouldn't happen at all! Unfortunately, we are nearly all guilty of the same 'error', and 'the sins of the fathers' will therefore continue to be visited on their children until we are able to accept ourselves as we really are.

A cursory investigation into the lives of many eminent and illustrious figures throughout history reveals that few of them achieved anything of note before the age of forty – Churchill, Henry Ford, Andrew Carnegie, Mahatma Gandhi, for example. Only the name of Alexander the Great springs readily to mind as one who attained greatness before the age of thirty-five – he died at the age of thirty-three. It is interesting to speculate which of his hands was the stronger.

6

Interpreting Gesture

Conversation has a tendency to discourage overt displays of emotion. It is not 'the done thing' to verbalize extremes of anger, irritation or grief. Even the expression of ecstasy or euphoria out of the proper context may be frowned on. Our early conditioning soon teaches us how far we can safely go.

Psychologists are in the process of rediscovering the value of an art whose significance has been appreciated by palmists for many years – the art of gesture. Used astutely, 'non-verbal communication' can, and does, lay bare our innermost feelings, no matter how well we think they are hidden.

The hand is the servant of the brain, and shows not only general capabilities, but also the true state of our emotions at any time. Should a man tell you he has nothing to hide, whilst keeping his hands firmly hidden in his pockets, it is safest not to believe him!

The following drawings are taken from a book first published in 1900, and the poses and gestures illustrated here have exactly the same meanings today as they did eighty years ago, even though the characters naturally have an old-fashioned air about them.[19]

Who has never experienced the sort of situation that provokes an involuntary clenching of the fists? This action may be the only outward sign of frustration and impotence. Though we may successfully hide our feelings, even from ourselves, tremendous inner tension cannot fail to be revealed in our hands and body.

When the hand analyst interprets gesture, he is aware of the importance of making a distinction between the hand that is relaxed and the hand which is 'talking'. Contrary to popular expectation, the position of the digits in the relaxed hand varies from one person to another. To those who know how to read the signs, the position of the hands tells more about character than any face-to-face evaluation can ever do.

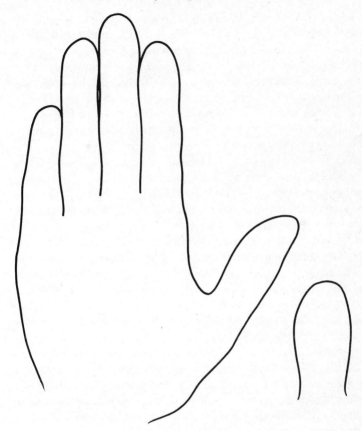

Figure. 14

To a greater or lesser degree we all tend to hide behind a mask, and the extent to which we are able to relate to the world outside is shown in the relative stiffness and flexibility of the hands, and the particular way the fingers and thumbs are held.

One of the first clues I get to any client's personality is the 'pose and carriage' of the hands, as Benham puts it, and their ability to reveal the *'unconscious gleam* of the *real inner self'*. This impression will be confirmed or modified by the subsequent handprints, and if, as in Figure 14, the fingers are still held closely together, you can be sure the individual is not by nature an outgoing, extrovert person.

The outline reproduced in Figure 14 is that of a well-known radio disc-jockey and celebrity who is rarely, if ever, seen on television or featured in the newspapers. Before meeting him, I had imagined a fairly free and easy kind of man, relaxed and comfortable in any circumstances. When a second attempt to take his handprints still resulted in tightly closed fingers, I knew I had been mistaken.

This is the sort of hand I would expect to find on a fearful, timid mouse of a man – certainly not on one who has dedicated a large part of his life to communicating with the public. When the fingers are habitually held in this way – almost like a bulwark against invasion – a good deal of underlying stress is present.

Anyone possessing such hands is usually 'strung up', even within the security of his own four walls, and this particular celebrity is constantly fighting a battle against stage fright and lack of confidence. Only the strength of will shown in the size of his thumbs preserves him from being defeated by his shyness and insecurity.

The angle at which the thumbs are held makes it obvious that he is not unfriendly – provided others are prepared to make the first approach, he can respond without fear of a rebuff. The closeness of the fingers dictates the need for a small group of close friends, on whom he can rely implicitly.

Unfortunately, this same need leads to possessiveness and jealousy in all his relationships, especially with women and, because he tries to chain women to him, he loses them. Few of his confidants are aware of the real reasons behind his desire to monopolize them.

Figure 15 shows the hand position adopted by an individual with rather more anti-social tendencies. He is an actor, but a disturbed and lost young man whose natural inclination would be to shun mankind altogether. Like most of us, he is forced to earn a living, and acting has offered him the advantage of occasionally escaping from himself into the characters he portrays.

These fingers pull away from one another, symbolizing their owner's compulsive hatred of restriction. Contact with each other, or with people in general, is obnoxious to such fingers. Their owner is more comfortable when he knows he is on the outside of society looking in, and actively pursues the state of solitude. He delights in being alone, far from humanity, and often flees to the wilds, carrying only a sleeping bag and the most basic of survival kits.

His home, when he does return to it, is built not for entertaining visitors, but to keep the world out. For him, it is a castle and inviolable, and he is more than happy to turn the key, preserving the sanctity of his retreat.

These two examples represent extremes of a very wide spectrum. In most cases, the characteristics are not quite so exaggerated, but a glance at the position of the two middle fingers of any hand will suffice to suggest a tendency in one direction or the other.

When Saturn and Apollo (see pages 145 and 149) stand close together, even though the other fingers do not, you have an individual who, for preference, works within a small and dedicated group. The hands of nurses, teachers, social workers, civil servants

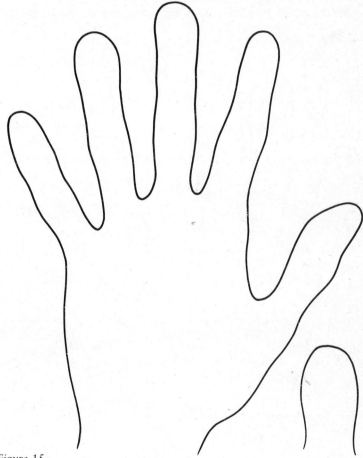

Figure 15

and the like – provided they are fulfilled by what they do – usually have these features. The ability to identify with the aims of a large organization is important, too. Without this, there would be no sense of comfort or security – feelings which are essential to this type of person.

Open middle fingers are to be found in the hands of long-distance lorry-drivers (and runners!), gamekeepers, gardeners and lighthouse keepers. Anyone, in fact, who prefers to work alone and answer to no one in particular. They are usually outdoor folk, for they hate to be imprisoned by bricks and mortar, and they insist on being free to 'do their own thing' in their own way.

Wide spacing between any of the fingers implies a need for per-

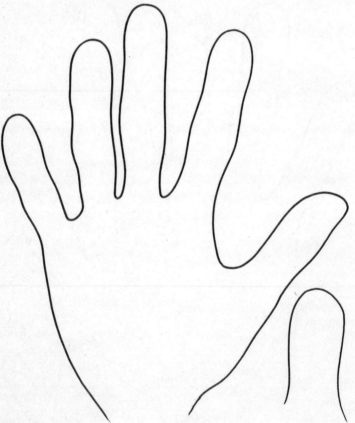

Figure 16

sonal freedom in the areas represented by those fingers. A gap between the first and second digit, for example, indicates a free-thinking non-conformist with no time at all for enforced orthodoxy. Widely spaced Mercury and Apollo fingers suggest, above all, a need for freedom of action. Figure 16, an outline of the late Bing Crosby's hand, is a good example of this type.

When the little finger leans away from its fellows as it does here, there is an almost pathological fear of being confined either physically or mentally. Bing certainly wasn't a loner – see how the two middle fingers stand closely together – but he found it difficult, if not impossible, to acknowledge his need for people. Though the love songs he made famous were crooned the world over, he was never able to commit himself by uttering those three little words. His second wife, Kathryn, is on record as making some rather bitter comments about this failure.

It is possible for such individuals to love their families dearly yet still fight emotional chains. They shrink from the thought of a 'permanent' relationship, and commitment of any kind is anathema to them.

Because the position of the fingers is linked to fixed or semi-permanent mental attitudes, it is unlikely to change much and, if another outline is taken a week, a month or even a year from the first, it will be almost identical. When it is not, the subject was probably ill-at-ease when the original outline was taken.

Gesture, though just as revealing, expresses only the mood or emotion of the moment. In ballet, mime and drama it is an integral part of an art form with stylized and explicit meanings. In everyday life, it takes a little more effort to translate the meanings of unconscious gesture and 'body language' into easily understood terms, but it is a study that can be infinitely rewarding.

In general, it is the outgoing, gregarious type who uses his hands freely to illustrate a point. Be careful not to confuse him with the nervy, neurotic individual whose movements are quick, jerky and staccato. I made this mistake on a trip to Spain in my sixteen-year-old motor caravan. I had been having trouble with my engine and was delighted to see a fellow Commer owner. I hoped he would prove to be a better mechanic than I was, and approached him eagerly.

My simple inquiry set off a veritable tirade of invective directed against motor engineers of every size, shape and creed – in particular the Spanish and Irish varieties. He too had been having problems, on which he proceeded to elaborate, arms flailing like windmills and fingers jabbing the air for emphasis.

It seemed that I was better equipped to assist him than he was me, and I duly made a minor, but vital, adjustment to his carburettor. In return, I acquired a set of handprints for my collection and proved a point into the bargain. His long, thin, heavily knuckled fingers and inward-leaning thumb were enough to confirm that he was every bit as inadequate, highly strung and emotionally unbalanced as his frenzied gesticulating had implied.

It is wrong to imagine that only the Latin races use their hands to elaborate or clarify a point. Some people, notably those from northern climes, are less flamboyant and more restrained than the Latins. This makes observation and analysis that much more difficult, but we do use gesture extensively as a means of communication – albeit less obviously, which is quite in keeping with the British reputation for insularity and introversion.

When the hands are clasped behind the back, or thrust into pockets, the individual is, as Benham says, not yet ready to 'show his hand'. If the arms are folded across the chest, and the hands hidden, the individual is defending himself against what he feels is an unwarranted verbal attack or intrusion.

If at rest the left hand lies, palm down, over the right, the subject is receptive and aware of what is going on around him. If the right covers the left, however, he is waiting for an opportunity to interrupt the conversation, or actively to disagree with what is being said.

If the hand covers the mouth, the individual is unsure how to proceed next, and is reserving judgement. When the chin rests on a closed fist, there is an air of quizzical and rapt concentration.

It is impossible to mistake the meaning of a wagging forefinger whatever country you're in! It is communicating its owner's wish to impose his will on another, and is the universal sign of assertion and domination.

Thumbs that habitually, or occasionally, hide in the palm of the hand imply trepidation, a desire to abdicate some responsibility or pass the onus for making an important decision on to someone else. Just as a dog shows its fear by running away with its tail between its legs, a man's thumbs will automatically disappear, often into a clenched fist, if he is frightened.

Any serious student will be able to add to and considerably expand on the above list, and a working knowledge of this lesser-known branch of palmistry will prove to be invaluable. Let's take a look at Benham's diagrams and comments.

Nine times out of ten the subject of Figure 17 has been put in a situation where he feels ill-at-ease, out of his depth and acutely self-conscious. By pushing his hands into his trouser pockets, he hopes to hide this with a deceptively casual air. The tenth time he may be trying to conceal, as Benham puts it, 'a dark side to his character' which he knows would make him unpopular. Keeping the hands out of sight is an unconscious expression of this.

Figures 18 and 19 are not as clear as they could be, but the hands in Figure 18 are alert and purposeful, the arms comfortably held by the sides. This man's hands are only partially open, implying an individual who is self-sufficient, impartial and honest, with the ability to see both points of view in an argument.

In Figure 19 the hands are held in a 'limp and lifeless manner' and give the impression that their owner has abandoned hope, has little or no mind of his own, and is consequently ready to 'be lazily directed by some other mind stronger in purpose than itself'.

The subject of Figure 20 approaches with a determined and purposeful air. The closed fists suggest that he has an idea fixed in his mind and he has no intention of changing it for anyone's benefit. The

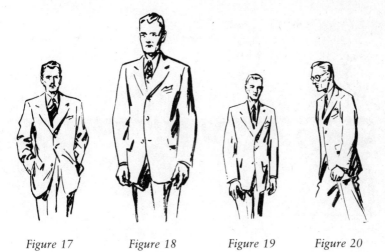

Figure 17 *Figure 18* *Figure 19* *Figure 20*

degree of tension shows 'the *quantity* of determination as well as the *quality*', and any assessment must be based on whether this is a temporary response to immediate stress, or whether this particular individual meets all comers as though they were spoiling for a fight.

The subject of Figure 21 adopts a pose that we, today, would consider rather affected and self-conscious. Benham equates it with an awareness of 'the beautiful and tasteful things of life' and sees it mostly in 'people of refined society'.

Figure 22 shows a similar pose, but in a man. Benham rather scornfully describes the 'mincing gait' and the 'smelling bottle held listlessly in the fingers, and either whirled or swayed gently as he walks'. I would judge this person to be fussy, pernickety, and hyper-critical – and certainly difficult to live with.

Figure 23 depicts an individual with fidgety, restless hands and mannerisms. Again, this may be only a passing phase brought about by an emotional disturbance, or it may represent a permanent personal characteristic. It could also be caused by a purely physical ailment of nervous origin, or a simple mineral imbalance.

When I see the latter features in a client, I immediately check the prints for signs of magnesium deficiency (see Chapter 14). When such a deficiency exists, a simple dietary adjustment or a course of biochemic tissue salts can work wonders.

Figure 24 illustrates a type I have, fortunately, never come across,

Figure 21   Figure 22   Figure 23   Figure 24

Figure 25   Figure 26   Figure 27   Figure 28

with his hands held 'in front of the body, or slightly at the side, waving them about as though trying to keep from touching anything'. The nearest approximation I can think of is Tommy Cooper in the middle of his comedy routine – and who is qualified to assess the meanings behind those gestures!

Figure 25 illustrates what would appear to be another fidget, similar to the one shown in Figure 23.

Figure 26 illustrates the type of woman who is calm and self-contained, ready to come more than halfway to meeting you. According to Benham this is 'a most eloquent indicator of repose and evenness of temper, one which will present an unruffled front to all exciting circumstances and events'.

Figure 27 depicts a steam-roller of a man, who will obviously brook no opposition. He approaches full of intensity and purpose, with clenched fists and slightly raised shoulders. It is almost as though he is expecting trouble at any moment and is constantly prepared for it. Benham sees him as no more than a 'bruiser and fighter' and not to be antagonized. I find that this is an attitude frequently adopted to conceal feelings of inferiority, and goes with the Primary personality described in Chapter 3, especially when such a personality is out of his depth.

Figure 28 shows an ingratiating, obsequious individual rubbing his hands together insincerely in the classical manner of the hypocrite. Benham says, 'You cannot depend on him at all,' and I would be inclined to agree with him wholeheartedly.

Figure 29   Figure 30   Figure 31

Figure 29 shows a person – and I cannot better Benham's description here – 'full of self-importance, impressed with his own dignity [who] will quickly resent anything like an attempt at familiarity, or anything tending to show that you do not fully agree with him in his estimate of himself'. He moves regally and seems to expect all eyes to be on him. The only way to stay on good terms with such a man is to pretend to agree with everything he says and does.

The subject of Figure 30 has hands which hang uncomfortably by his sides as though they do not really belong there. This great lump of a man has no imagination and no time for mere flights of fancy. If something is not tangible, then, for him, it does not exist. His prime interest and preoccupation is to amass a good store of worldly goods – as Benham puts it, it's 'no use trying to lift him out of his trough of materialism. It can't be done'.

The man who walks along with hands clasped behind his back is regarded by Benham as timid, well-meaning and suspicious. I personally find this trait (see Figure 31) linked with a feeling of apprehension concerning a particular situation. The gesture is common in those who are naturally of a retiring nature or who suffer from shyness.

A useful exercise, and one that demonstrates the major part played by gesture in communication, is to turn down the volume control on your television set. You will find after a little practice that you are quite capable of following the plot of most plays just by observing the gestures made.

7

The Mounts

Nine specific areas in the hand are traditionally named after the planets (see Figure 32). Palmistry's early links with astrology are shown in both the names and associations that have been given to these areas. For centuries they have been termed mounts – regardless of whether they are developed, over-developed or under-developed – and this is something of a misnomer which can be confusing to the novice.

The degree of development of each mount indicates the extent to which the trait represented by that mount has been developed or is capable of development. Each finger shares the name of the mount at its base: the index, or Jupiter, finger is associated with the ability to lead or dominate; the middle, or Saturn, finger with sobriety and stability; the ring, or Apollo (Sun), finger with creative abilities and material prosperity; and the 'little', or Mercury, finger with sexuality and the power to express ideas.

Directly beneath the mount of Mercury, within the area bounded by the Heart and Head lines (provided the Head line is high) can be found the mount of Upper Mars. If the Head line sinks down on to the mount of Luna, the lower boundary can only be found by drawing an imaginary line across from the point at which the thumb joins the palm. Development here indicates that we can harness the energy of the god of war and translate it into inner strength, fortitude and perseverance.

The whole of the centre of the palm is, in one form or another, dedicated to the Martian deity. The Plain of Mars, which represents the quality of our physical resources, may be thick or thin in its own right, but care must be taken when looking at this area. If the mounts that encompass it are large, it may seem deceptively undersized, and vice versa. The mount of Lower Mars is located above the mount of Venus, on the thumb side of the hand. A well-developed mount here

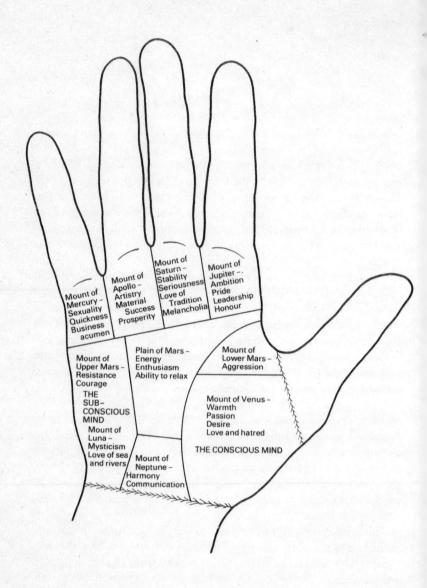

Mount of Mercury – Sexuality Quickness Business acumen

Mount of Apollo – Artistry Material Success Prosperity

Mount of Saturn – Stability Seriousness Love of Tradition Melancholia

Mount of Jupiter – Ambition Pride Leadership Honour

Mount of Upper Mars – Resistance Courage

THE SUB-CONSCIOUS MIND

Mount of Luna – Mysticism Love of sea and rivers

Plain of Mars – Energy Enthusiasm Ability to relax

Mount of Neptune – Harmony Communication

Mount of Lower Mars – Aggression

Mount of Venus – Warmth Passion Desire Love and hatred

THE CONSCIOUS MIND

Figure 32

shows a forceful personality, with a tendency to react to stress with aggression rather than discussion – especially if there is a short thumb.

The mount of Venus is commonly known as the ball of the thumb and is confined within the area of the Life line. The width and depth of this mount indicate our capacity to generate the emotions of love, hate, warmth, sympathy. When the mount is lacking in depth and substance, the individual lacks vitality, and physical resources are low. What little energy is available tends to be jealously guarded. The welfare of others is a secondary consideration.

The mount of Luna is situated below the mount of Upper Mars, opposite Venus on the percussion edge of the hand. Development of this mount means a fertile imagination, a magnetic attraction towards water in all its many shapes and forms – and frequent hunches that are often winners.

The conscious mind is represented in the hand by the Venus mount, and the unconscious by Luna. The mount of Neptune acts as a bridge between the two, and is strongest in those who are able to reconcile without conflict the material and the spiritual in daily life. Gifted psychics, salesmen, teachers – anyone in fact who uses intuition as an aid to communication – come into this category.

Some palmists see the mounts as important indicators of character in their own right; some disregard them completely. I find them a valuable source of back-up information, confirming other factors in the hand. Benham, in his *Laws of Scientific Hand Reading*, goes so far as to base his entire system of character classification on the mounts alone. In his extremely popular *Palmistry for All*, Cheiro relegates them to a few pages near the end of the book, where he treats them in a rather far-fetched and unlikely fashion that is loosely based on astrology and birth dates.

In physiological terms, the mounts are protective coverings for the nerve fibres and blood vessels that run through the palm and up the sides of the fingers. The location of the median and ulna nerves is shown in Chapter 10; the divisions of the palm and the arterial and vascular systems are shown in Figure 33.[20]

How then do the mounts relate to an individual's temperament and character? Let us envisage the palm as a tract of fertile and potentially productive land. On every side of a lush meadow (the Plain of Mars) rise grass-covered hills (the mounts). In such a place irrigation will not be a problem. Moisture falling on the surrounding

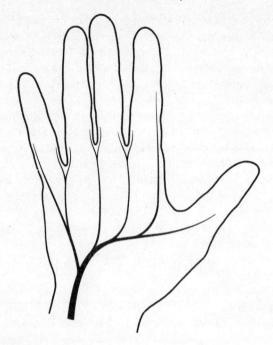

Figure 33

uplands meanders fruitfully down into the valley to sustain the growing crops. Everything here is fresh, vibrant and healthy. Now picture another piece of land. A flat, arid, windswept plain exposed, without the protection of the hills, to the elements. The parched soil stretches in every direction as far as the eye can see. Here the topsoil is almost non-existent and barely supports a few stunted trees and lichens. There is no water, and therefore no inhabitants.

In the first instance it is clear that crops will be abundant, and in the second they will be meagre and scrawny at best. The fertile area may well have sufficient produce not only for the local inhabitants, but also to give away or sell. In the barren lands, the people know only of the survival of the fittest, and it's every man for himself.

In the human hand, the same laws apply. When the mounts are full, there will be good reserves of energy. The Plain of Mars will be deep, showing a good basic constitution, and there will be sympathy and compassion.

The thinly covered, fleshless hand of the Egocentric individual exemplifies the other extreme. We can understand the apparent selfishness of the type a little better when we realize that, even when the quality of life improves, he is still haunted by fears that the next drought will soon diminish any stores he has managed to accumulate. To him, jungle law is the only workable one.

Look again at the map of the mounts shown in Figure 32. Each of the hills surrounding the plain is planted with a different 'crop', and a wide variety of produce can be grown there. Take away any of the hills and the irrigation effect is also diminished. The mount of Saturn is the only one that is better if it is under-developed. Development here means that the subject is inclined to pessimism and depressions. Storm clouds gather and break over this hill.

How then to judge whether a mount is high, low or even deficient? Figure 34 shows a relaxed hand. The little raised sacs of flesh that can be seen when the hand is in this position are the developed mounts. These seldom appear directly underneath the fingers; they are usually slightly to one side or the other, where they can best fulfil their function of protecting the nerves and arteries. They may be large, relatively flat, or concave, forming an indentation in the palm. The greatest and most obvious variation is seen in the mounts of Venus and Luna, which take up a good two-fifths of the palm. It is not necessary to flex the hand at all to see these.

When the finger mounts are well developed, Venus and/or Neptune and Luna are invariably of similar proportions. Seldom, if ever,

Figure 34

is a strong mount of Jupiter, for example, not found on an equally strongly developed hand.

In the size, shape and quality of the mount you will find important clues to modify or support the personality assessment you have already begun. The texture and resilience of the Venus and Luna mounts are particularly telling. Softness here marks out the dreamer and sensualist who accomplishes very little if he does not have a strong thumb, or unless he is working purely to provide the luxuries he craves. Hardness means that he tends to pin down the wings of imagination – he is a practical pragmatist rather than a vain visionary.

Traditional palmistry relied heavily on the minor marks and signs on the palm. Many palmists today still swear by them and the seaside fortune-teller would be lost without them. I myself am sure that the marks have meaning, but I am not at all certain that the meanings that have been applied for centuries are relevant in this day and age.

In readings where I have used these ancient interpretations the response has been ambivalent, with some clients meeting my pronouncement with a blank stare, some agreeing, and some contradicting it outright. I would therefore not advise making any judgement based on the minor marks alone, but suggest doing this only when it is backed by confirmation from another feature in the hand.

Figure 35 shows the typical formations; conclusions should only be drawn from these if the pattern is made up of definite and separate lines and not merely a chance crossing of two or more major or minor lines. It is all too easy to confuse the broken lines that make up the Girdle of Venus (see Chapter 13) with a small grille. Care must be taken, for each of these formations has a very different meaning. When the traditional meaning has been replaced by a more up-to-date version, both are included in the following analysis. We will start by discussing the minor marks on the mounts and then outline how the mounts themselves should be interpreted.

Figure 35

The mount of Jupiter

Jupiter stands for ambition and achievement and a cross on this mount traditionally heralds a fortunate and loving marriage.

A square used to be regarded as a sign of protection from personal loss and failure, but a more modern interpretation sees it as the sign of a born teacher. For this reason, it has become known as the Teacher's Square and, when it goes with a pointed or fine conic tip on the finger of Jupiter, there is usually no argument about the significance. The subject often teaches or demonstrates for his living, or has an undeveloped talent for doing so.

A triangle on Jupiter is a strong indication of organizational talent. When it is accompanied by a strong Jupiter finger on one or both hands, this may mean mere bossiness!

A star was said to foretell a brilliantly successful future, following an unexpected rise to fame and fortune.

A circle was thought to be extremely propitious in this position. I have never seen one, and am therefore unable to comment. By its very nature, a circle in the hand, anywhere, is rare, and is never perfectly round. It is made up of a series of small, sharply curved and fragmented lines that look almost like dots.

A grille is said to suggest a desire for power and prestige of almost megalomanic proportions.

The mount of Saturn

A cross here was thought to be the 'mark of the scaffold', indicating a violent or sudden end to the life. Fortunately, I have not encountered this sign as I would not know quite what to say if I did!

Saturn represents stability, and stability for most of us is irretrievably bound up with earning our daily bread. A square on this mount is therefore thought to signify a sort of 'guardian angel' watching over us and preserving us from harm at work.

A triangle on the Saturn mount means that an individual is inclined to serious thoughts about man's place in the universe, or about God or the esoteric. It suggests a questioning, probing mentality that is ceaselessly active.

A star on Saturn has a similar meaning to a cross. It was always said to warn of a tragic end for the unfortunate person in whose hand it appeared. It is now thought to predict a hard lesson which will nevertheless be of benefit to whoever undergoes it.

A circle is again extremely rare in this position. The Comte de Saint-Germain, usually so verbose on such signs, merely says, 'A favorable omen, specified by other indications.'[21]

A grille tends to exaggerate the sombre Saturnian qualities in much the same way as development or over-development of the mount does. Three or more rising lines on this mount, without the crossing line, are said to indicate a Jack-of-all-trades and master of none. Other signs in the hand will have to be consulted before making judgement for, though in many cases the subject achieves little and has too many fingers in too many pies, in many others he cannot be fulfilled without a multiplicity of interests.

The mount of Apollo

A cross that straddles a Sun line (see Chapter 12) suggests financial devastation. When the Sun line continues strongly after the cross, there will be no permanent damage – the setback will be a temporary one. If there is no Sun line, the cross on the Apollo mount indicates more than the average amount of difficulty in achieving material success and prosperity. This is, however, a jinx that can be beaten; if it is beaten, the cross will fade away.

A square is said to protect the owner from such misfortunes as the above and, if both cross and square are found on the mount, the bad effects of the former will be cancelled out by the power of the latter.

A triangle is said to predict fame and fortune as a direct result of working in the public eye in any field, such as sport, politics or entertainment.

A star on Apollo is also thought to presage good fortune, with the difference that it must be earned. There will be few 'lucky' breaks for this individual. If he gets to the top of the ladder of success, you can be sure he fought every step of the way.

A grille on the mount of Apollo goes with an exhibitionist streak, together with an excess of vanity and conceit.

Three small upright lines in this position are thought to indicate that the subject has an insurance against impoverishment! On the very brink of penury, fate relents and refills the coffers. An encouraging sign to have!

The mount of Mercury

Mercury stands for communication of all kinds, and for personal expression. A cross on the Mercury mount was thought to be a warning that the subject was the victim of dishonesty, deceit and dirty work. I see it as an indication that the power of self-expression and the individual's capacity to understand his fellows are limited. This gives him a tendency to react to real or imagined slights in a petty, vindictive and immature way.

A square is said to protect its owner from the fiendish machinations of his enemies – and from the effects of nervous stresses and strains.

A triangle on the Mercury mount is a useful feature, no matter what one's calling in life may be. The minimum effort will reap the maximum reward.

A star presages phenomenal success when it appears in the hand of one engaged in any of the Mercurial occupations which include all branches of medicine, science or communications.

A grille on Mercury should be interpreted according to the size and quality of the mount. It means that traits, whether good or bad, are extreme. Over-development of the mount, for example, is likely to lead to over-activity of both brain and tongue, while under-development could mean an individual is taciturn and incommunicative.

Unless there are three or more upright lines and three crossing lines, the formation is not a grille, and the meaning quite different, (see Chapter 13).

The mount of Luna

A cross on Luna is supposed to be a sign of a vivid and powerful imagination. My own findings suggest that this is substantially true, but that the imaginative gifts are often misapplied. Instead of being focused on creative pursuits, the mind dwells on purely negative possibilities.

A square on this mount protects its owner from misfortune on or by water. The Comte de Saint-Germain sees it as giving 'protection against the bad markings or exaggerated development of the mount'.[22]

A triangle implies latent or developed ability in such areas as clairvoyance, psychometry or other 'secret' arts. At the very least I would expect to find a strongly developed interest in the occult.

A star suggests a nautical bent, but it can also suggest danger at sea. Should the star be enclosed within a square, however, the danger is not likely to be fatal.

I have never observed a circle on the Luna mount but some palmists see it as a warning of death by drowning.

A grille on Luna has a similar meaning to the Luna cross, with intensified negativity. The individual with this mark never fails to look on the black side of life, and he is therefore rarely disappointed!

The mount of Venus

A cross on the Venus mount has been the subject of various and conflicting interpretations. Some see it as a life-saving 'St Andrew's Cross' and others as an indication that the subject will never be happy in love. As this mount is frequently covered with the marks of stress and emotional disturbance (see Chapter 11), it is extremely difficult to pick out any minor marks.

A square is thought to protect its owner from being hurt by those he cares for.

A triangle attracts and intensifies love and devotion towards the subject in whose hand it appears, and gives him charismatic appeal.

Depending on its position on the mount, a star on Venus, if we follow Saint-Germain, augurs any one of half a dozen things – all of them ending in disaster. I have never yet observed a true and fully formed star on the Venus mount, and so have no personal opinion regarding its meaning.

A circle may be found high up the mount near its boundary with Lower Mars. This feature suggests the development of cataracts, provided the circle is small and clearly formed. Half a circle implies that one eye only would be affected.

A grille on Venus is quite common, with numerous horizontal lines being crossed by as many as ten vertical ones. The effect of this is to intensify the effect of the 'worry' lines (see Chapter 11).

The mount of Neptune

Minor marks and signs are rare in this small area. I have never seen any. The lines that are found are the Fate line, and the Life line, which occasionally terminates in the Neptune mount. These are dealt with in Chapters 11 and 12. The meanings behind the lesser signs that may be found here will still be important, regardless of the dimensions of the mount.

Now we come to the task of interpreting the mounts themselves. Mounts relate to the basic structure of the hand much as a battery relates to a car. When the mount is low or deficient, dynamism is low or virtually non-existent. When it is high or over-developed, energy levels are high, and may even be stored – though, if the mount is also flabby, staying power will be limited and power dissipated on immediate rather than long-term ventures.

Full development of all the mounts, coupled with resilience, points to an individual whose infectious enthusiasm knows no bounds and bowls the opposition over before they know what has hit them. It is not often that I find clients with this combination. When I do, they are invariably forceful go-getters at the top of their professional tree.

Ideally, each mount should be elastic and resilient to the touch, so that the inner tension is in healthy relation to the outer. This is an indication that the flow of available energies will not be blocked or dissipated or given over to self-indulgence. The individual is, instead, self-sufficient and philanthropic – plagued neither with the insecurity that goes with undeveloped mounts, nor with the apathy that goes with flabby ones.

Hardness of any of the mounts, of whatever size, means that the life force is artificially sealed up. Man is by nature a social being and, without the free interplay of energies that comes through social intercourse and fraternization, loses his capacity to enjoy life. The artificial barrier indicated by this hardness is translated into callousness and inflexibility in the character.

Softness means that the subject has exaggerated qualities of sensuality and weakness; he is easily led and lazy, particularly when the softness is extreme.

The mount of Jupiter

Normal development of the Jupiter mount and a setting slightly towards the Saturn finger suggest a well-developed sense of justice, ambition and high moral standards. Its owner believes in his own worth and takes a reasonable amount of pride in his own achievements, being at the same time fully aware of any shortcomings in his nature.

The higher the mount, the greater the individual's conception of his own importance and, if an over-developed mount is accompanied by a strong, long Jupiter finger, pride becomes arrogance, generosity extravagance, and enterprise ruthless self-aggrandizement.

When the Jupiter mount is flat, the finger that surmounts it is generally short, and the shorter it is, the greater the feeling of being at the mercy of the fates. This subject is more inclined to follow than lead and to think along negative rather than positive lines. He is an obsessive worrier, and the slightest change of routine is likely to upset his equilibrium.

The mount of Saturn

The mount of Saturn is the exception to two rules. The other three finger mounts are normally situated between the digits, rather than directly beneath them, and it is best if they are medium to well developed. Saturn should be no more than a slight bulge, immediately under the finger.

The larger the mount, the more Saturnine the nature. Like the flat or deficient Jupiter type, this man admits defeat before he has even viewed the opposition. He is a real Scrooge and his cheerless, penny-pinching ways are more than enough to squash the cheeriest optimist; and it's hardly a surprise to discover that large Saturn mounts predispose their owners to a rather solitary, misanthropic life-style. This over-development goes with melancholia, suicidal tendencies and, often, an unhealthy interest in black magic. It has the effect of tying its owner to earth and materialism. It would be hard for any spark of faith, hope or charity to break through such gross insensitivity to the world outside.

The supreme optimist – otherwise known as the blithe Fool, in the

Tarot – can be identified both by his air of nonchalance in the face of disaster, and by a Saturn mount that is concave, rather than convex, and surrounded by mounts that are well or even over-developed.

The optimum size for this mount is slightly under-developed, but allowance must be made for the fact that large mounts on either side may make it appear more depressed than it actually is. The character will then be well balanced between caution and carelessness, with light-hearted optimism rather than recklessness taking precedence.

The mount of Apollo

Cheiro referred to this mount as the mount of the Sun, and its normal development means that the subject will have a sunny disposition. He has a sense of humour and can raise a laugh from the most unlikely situation. All other things being equal, he is inclined to be warm, generous and unfailingly optimistic.

The larger this mount, the greater the feeling that fortune cannot fail to smile on the subject and his interests. And, such is the power of positive thinking, it seldom does!

Over-development results in overwhelming, overbearing egocentricity. The subject is out of tune with the feelings of others and sees himself as the sun round which the planets revolve. The good taste that accompanies normal development is coarsened to the stage where only a garish, showy style is appreciated. For this type, the seeds of his downfall lie in his supreme susceptibility to flattery.

When Apollo is deficient and accompanied by thin, inadequate-looking fingers there is little room for vanity, false or otherwise. The extroverted, extravagant manner of the developed type gives way to a cold brusqueness and frugal consideration of essentials only. Food, clothing and surroundings will do as they are, provided they serve their purpose, and the simpler the better. What use are frills, fripperies, and folderols? Nothing but a waste of time and money!

The mount of Mercury

Normal development of the Mercury mount, together with a sturdy, well-formed little finger, means that, even if tongue-tied and dumb, the owner can get his message across to the rest of the world. Helen Keller should have had good development in this area.

People who have normal Mercury mounts cannot bear to be restricted, either in mind or body. Any totalitarian regime, dedicated to limiting freedom of movement or speech, is anathema to them, and it goes without saying that they are pledged to the fight against bureaucracy. They prefer to wear casual rather than 'conventional' clothes, and enjoy recreations that flex mental as well as physical muscles, such as tennis or fencing. For the less energetic there is always chess and bridge, backgammon and go.

The larger the mount, the greater the build-up of nervous energies. The devil is especially fond of the idle hands of this type – they are guaranteed to do his work well! The bigger the work load, whatever side of the law, the better, for the Mercury mentality thrives on challenge.

When the mount is under-developed or deficient, its owner will prove to have none of the 'gift of the gab' that distinguishes his talented brother. His sluggish mentality is often more apparent than real, however, and it is his terror of making a mistake or becoming a laughing stock that holds him back.

He is self-conscious and wholly gullible, and afraid to use the sixth sense that reaps such valuable rewards for those whose mounts are a little more strongly developed than his own.

———————— *The mount of Upper Mars* ————————

The locations of the Mars mounts and of the Plain of Mars are shown in Figure 32. Upper Mars lies immediately below the mount of Mercury and it is rather more difficult to identify than the finger mounts. If the rest of the palm is thin, a small bulge here may seem sturdier than it really is.

Normal development of this mount will combine a well-rounded firmness at the percussion edge with a deep, resourceful palm. Looked at from the side, the Luna mount tapers gently upwards, through Upper Mars, to narrow at the base of the Mercury finger.

A mount like this gives its owner the sort of stubbornness and fortitude in the face of inhuman treatment that was dubbed 'dumb insolence' in prisoner-of-war camps. Women whose upbringing allows them no option but to remain with a brutal drunkard of a husband may develop them. This sort of mount seems to indicate that the Martian energies are transformed into passive resistance, rather than used for actively fighting back.

Deficiency in the area of Upper Mars implies an equivalent deficiency in moral fibre. This type of person cannot bear the thought of pain or discomfort, particularly his own, and he will do almost anything to avoid it. Self-preservation will always take precedence over everything and, when it comes to the crunch, loyalty is expendable.

The Plain of Mars

I see this area as a reservoir for the energies that flow, like rivers, down from the surrounding hills. When it is well padded and firm, physical strength and endurance abound. A major aim of many people is to become and remain financially independent, and a subject with a Plain of Mars of this type has the resources to do just that. He is equable in temperament, loyal, friendly and generous – but only to a small and select circle of intimates and family members. Casual acquaintances often make the mistake of taking him at face value, only to find that he is no soft touch, and quite as canny as any Scot.

When the Plain is deep, flabby and soft, the subject is lazy and sensual. He will work for luxuries but, for him, a gold-plated carrot is essential. When it comes to providing necessities, he uses excuses such as not feeling well, or puts it off till next week.

A thin Plain of Mars denotes a lack of physical stamina and down-to-earth, practical common sense. It usually accompanies thin, fragile-looking hands with low or deficient mounts which, depending on whether they are hard or soft, mean that the subject is in the Egocentric or Intuitive category (see Chapter 3).

The thin palm goes with an other-worldly air. The owner is 'in the world, but not of it' and responds more to feelings and impressions than to the solid, tangible manifestations of Mother Earth. His intuition is generally sound when it applies to others. When he tries to use it for his own benefit he is afraid to trust to the still, small voice within and is plagued by insecurity and indecisiveness.

The mount of Lower Mars

In contrast to Upper Mars, this mount is identified with action. Average development means that the subject has a fight, rather than flight, reaction to attack, whether verbal or physical. Adrenalin flows readily into his veins, and courage, determination and aggression make him a natural sportsman.

Over-development of the Lower Mars mount goes with an argumentative, needlessly hostile type, whose answer to any dispute is to roll up his sleeves. If he can discharge some of his surplus aggression through boxing or other martial arts, so much the better for everyone!

A deficiency in this area points to an individual who is meek and mild mannered, and more than ready to let others tell him what he should do. In a quarrel, do not expect him to stand his ground. He will soon give way to anyone who can shout louder than he can.

The mount of Luna

Normal development of Luna shows a gradual widening and deepening towards the palm, with a slight curving outwards at the bottom of the mount. As in astrology, Luna stands for imagination, intuitive faculties and man's subconscious motivation, and the size of this mount represents the degree of sensitivity of the subject. If it is of average dimensions he is neither callous nor overly sentimental and mawkish. He will give sympathy readily, along with a helping hand when it is absolutely necessary, but more especially when those in distress have first attempted to help themselves. He is resourceful, imaginative and self-motivating, with a gift for knowing his limitations that is worth its weight in gold.

Over-large Venus and Luna mounts are generally found together. This combination results in a trusting, over-generous nature. Someone with such a nature invariably gives others the benefit of the doubt instead of heeding his instincts, and he is often disappointed.

With large, flabby mounts all the good intentions in the world are destined to come to naught. And people with full, hard Luna mounts only involve themselves in charitable works when there is something in it for them.

Full Luna types, whether soft, firm or flabby, seem to be magnetically attracted to water. They may swim, sail or join the Navy and, whenever they feel the need to relax or recharge their mental, physical or emotional batteries, they head – not for the hills – but for water.

When Luna is flat or deficient there will be little or no time for dreaming or creativity. Those with this type of mount view anyone who is 'different' and fails to conform, with grave misgivings. The owner of such a palm would find it impossible to understand Keats's philosophy that 'a thing of beauty is a joy for ever'. The wonder of a delicate and ephemeral sunset, a rainbow or the dawn chorus does not penetrate his phlegmatic constitution. Nor do the moods and ever-varying ambience of the sea excite and stir him as they do his full-mounted friends.

The mount of Neptune

Neptune, the second most remote planet in our solar system, was not discovered until 1846. It was named after the Roman god of the sea and symbolizes, in both astrology and palmistry, the bridge between man's conscious and unconscious mind, and his ability to tune in to the collective and omniscient group unconscious. The developed mount allows us to reconcile what we know with what we feel.

Until comparatively recently, the importance of this part of the hand was ignored. Though acknowledged it was a no-man's-land that had never been explored. In all maps of the hand produced before the middle of the twentieth century (see Figure 36) it is an area that was shown but not named.[23,24]

Beryl Hutchinson describes it as follows:

This mount does not have true boundaries. It is just a filling up in the centre of the palm next to the wrist as opposed to the hand with a distinct hollow between Venus and Luna. The effect when present is strong. The Life Force seems to flow so freely through the owner that a magnetism is given out. Such formation is found on the hands of doctors, nurses and less orthodox healers; all who make people feel better when they enter a room. No public speaker can get across the footlights without this bar across the base of the hand, but when it is very pronounced a speaker can give pleasure by reciting the A B C.[25]

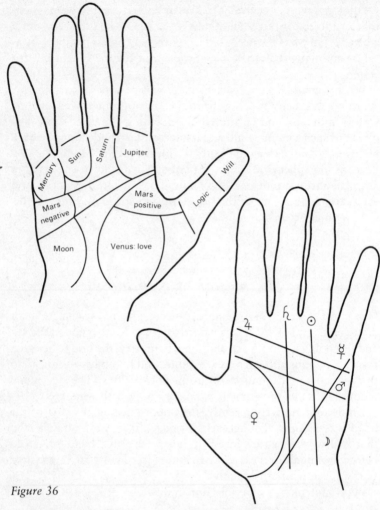

Figure 36

In my experience, a well-formed Neptune allows its owner to see himself and his motives clearly and to understand and empathize with the feelings of others. He is in tune with the world.

A wide and empty divide between the two base mounts indicates the reverse, and the subject will be a misunderstood and unhappy man. He has no idea why he seems to antagonize others, constantly putting their backs up, until his seeming insensitivity is spelled out to him plainly and unequivocally.

―――――――――― *The mount of Venus* ――――――――――

Good development of the Venus mount is traditionally associated with a strong and durable constitution. Beryl Hutchinson gives a masterly exposition of the physiological reasons behind this belief, and continues:

Blood is synonymous with Life. Two arteries, healthy, powerful and pro-tected by walls of healthy fascial padding, will take up appreciably more room than a poor blood supply system, with incomplete superficial arches and a poor bore to its main deep radial stream. In illness, the possessor of a generous, healthy circulatory system has a better chance of recovery; and in health, a fuller enjoyment of life.[26]

A normal mount is high, broad-based and circumscribed by a Life line that swings strongly and confidently out towards the middle of the palm. When the Life line clings bashfully to the thumb, thereby reducing the width of the mount, its owner can be expected to have a blinkered viewpoint and look at life with a closed mind.

A firm, springy Venus shows a corresponding resilience of charac-ter and suggests hidden reserves of energy. This type of mount goes with a forceful and dynamic personality – one who has the capacity to play as hard as he works.

When Venus is full but flabby and yielding, the energies are not available when needed. There is a gradual and constant power loss, with vitality being dissipated in indolence and sensuality. The type can also be extremely generous and sympathetic . . . provided no physical effort is called for! He makes an ideal counsellor and father confessor! Over-development of the mount, whether firm or flabby, means that all characteristics, positive and negative, are exaggerated. When discussing someone with a full Venus mount, you will usually find yourself describing their exploits in superlatives. Whatever they do is always larger than life, and never dull or boring.

A flat or under-developed Venus is usually confined by a Life line that is not quite as strong as it should be, and which clings to the thumb side of the hand, rather than swinging confidently out into the palm. Its owner will exhibit all the classic symptoms of insecurity and general physical debility, and the little strength he has will be dedicated to self-preservation.

If the hands are also hard, with thin fingers and narrow palms, the subject has a cruel and ruthless streak, and a nature that is intolerant and unfeeling. This type would always insist on his 'pound of flesh', whether he needed it or not.

8

The Thumbs, Fingers and Nails

Thumbs

More often than not we take the thumb for granted – until, that is, it is injured or we lose it. Then we are forced to realize that we are as helpless without it as we would be without an eye or an ear.

In the East, palmists learn as much from this one digit as the Western hand analyst does from labouring over the entire hand. The thumb is frequently the basis of the whole character assessment.

Anthropologists acknowledge that man's superiority over the animal kingdom is the direct result of the thumb's adaptation. Had it not been for the unique manner of the thumb's development in man, humanity as we know it would not have evolved, and that colossal jump from holding and throwing stones to manufacturing interstellar spacecraft could never have been made.

The lower primates were left behind when we began to use the hand as a tool in its own right and as a means of fashioning ever more complex implements and utensils. The smaller and therefore the more ape-like the thumb, the less its owner feels he is in command of his own destiny. He will often be seen to shrug his shoulders, confessing that he is 'at the mercy of the fates'. Try as he may, he cannot reverse or cancel out his fatalistic streak.

The Primary and the Useful types of hand (see Chapter 3) exemplify the limitations of the short thumb, which must be measured from its tip to its point of attachment with the palm (see Figure 37). It is a point which varies tremendously from person to person, for some thumbs are high-set and others are set low on the edge of the palm.

People with short thumbs have a great advantage over their longer-thumbed brethren, for they work purely on instinct. A long-

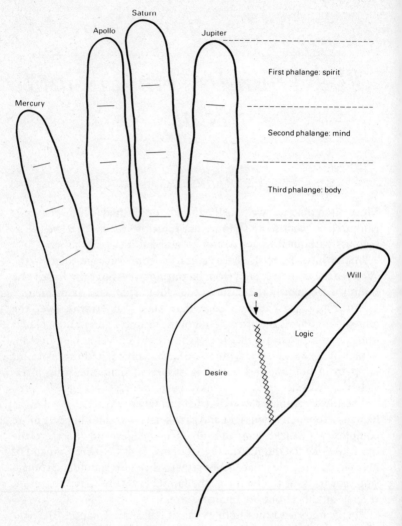

Figure 37 The fingers and their sphere of influence

thumbed person may achieve identical results in the end, but via a more circuitous route. While he is labouring long and hard over the implications of his proposed investment, trying to decide if the proposition is worth while, the short-thumbed person will have made the investment and be sitting back waiting for it to pay off.

Each of the five digits is firmly rooted in the mount below, but only the thumb incorporates its entire third phalange in a mount – Venus. Each finger is composed of three sections or phalanges. In the thumb, Venus stands for the intensity of the individual's desires and aspirations. The middle phalange reveals the extent of his capacity for thinking in logical and sequential terms, while the thumb-tip reveals the strength of his determination and resolve. I use the keywords 'I want' (ball of the thumb), 'I can' (middle phalange), and 'I will' (thumb-tip) when reading the thumb.

Without the strength of will shown by a good, strong thumb-tip, abilities lying dormant in the rest of the hand will not reach fruition. If Venus too is weak, dreams and desires prove unrealistic and impracticable. If it is full and firm, they will be feasible and readily accomplished.

A short thumb-tip denotes a deficiency of will-power; the subject is like a car whose engine is in excellent condition, but whose starter motor is faulty. Without it, the car will not move an inch. The owner of such a thumb-tip can solve the world's problems in a single afternoon, but he's all talk and can't follow through with action.

The shape and relative size of the thumb-tip are more than enough meat for the hand analyst to digest and use to decide if his client is stubborn, dogmatic, persistent or weak, irresolute or easily led – how, in fact, he uses his will-power to achieve his objectives.

A well-cushioned thumb-tip (see Figure 38) suggests plentiful reserves of nervous energy. Its owner is likely to have a reputation for ready sympathy and a tranquil, pleasant personality. He is self-possessed and unflappable.

A flattened tip (see Figure 39) denotes an individual who tends to live 'on his nerves'. He works energetically, even frantically, but in short bursts, rather than smoothly and methodically. When his efforts have reached their peak, he will be useless ... unless he can take a short 'cat-nap'. Then he will wake as fresh as a daisy, and ready for the next challenge.

Figure 38   *Figure 39*

A long, broad thumb-tip is usually accompanied by executive ability in its owner – the ability to control and command men. The more these qualities are exaggerated, the greater the power to do this (see Figure 40a).

While someone with the opposite – the long, slim tip (see Figure 40b) – is quite happy to direct operations from the bridge, the broad-tip person is side by side with his workforce, and loses not one whit of authority through rolling his sleeves up and joining them.

A broad thumb-tip, with its greatest width immediately above the joint, indicates an obstinate, bloody-minded type for whom it is automatic to resist pressure. Try to impose your will on him and he will immediately dig in his heels. Even if he later discovers it was for his own good, he will cut off his nose to spite his face, being too proud – or too stupid – to back down (see Figure 41a).

When the greatest width of the thumb is at the joint rather than above it, giving it a somewhat knotted appearance, the density acts as a block. Logic is powerless to leaven self-will. The effect is the same as that of the example shown in Figure 41b but more so. Reason cuts no ice with this individual once his mind is made up, so perhaps the best way of dealing with him is to argue strenuously *against* what you believe, because he is more than likely to oppose you.

Either of these stubborn types of tip may be reinforced by a ledge at the back of the thumb (see Figure 42). Outside influences stand little chance of scaling such ramparts and, should you wish to win over the possessor of a thumb like this, you must convince him that your plan was his, and how clever he was to think of it!

The broad nail phalange with its pointed tip (see Figure 43) bears more than a passing resemblance to an arrow head and, just as the

Figure 40a   *Figure 40b*   *Figure 41a*   *Figure 41b*   *Figure 42*

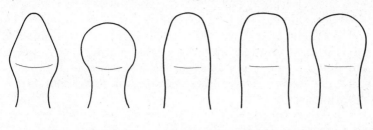

Figure 43   Figure 44   Figure 45   Figure 46   Figure 47

well-aimed arrow flies straight to its target, so does the owner of such a thumb make directly for his objectives. He is persistent and undeviating in his efforts and keeps right on until he has accomplished exactly what he set out to do.

A coarse, heavy-looking thumb-tip (see Figure 44) goes with a nature in which the qualities of tact and diplomacy are conspicuous only by their absence. It is short, signifying a lack of self-control, and squat. An extreme of this formation is traditionally known as the 'murderer's thumb'.

The longer the tip, the greater the ability to control one's own desires for the benefit of the community. Good taste and discrimination accompany the conic tip (see Figure 45). Unlike the 'arrow head' thumb, the conic is all too easily deflected. The attention can be concentrated for short bursts but then wavers and welcomes something 'new' and different.

Square-tipped thumbs (see Figure 46) are common on the hands of the Practical type of individual described in Chapter 3. They represent a reliable, commonsense approach to life, and the objective (or major) hand is generally more squarely tipped than the subjective (or minor) hand. This subject believes implicitly that whatever he does is right, though he, unlike the stubborn individual, is open to reason.

The spatulate thumb-tip (see the Energetic hand, Chapter 3) is usually found with spatulate fingers. Provided someone can fire its owner with enthusiasm for a particular idea, he will adapt and improve on it, until it is hardly recognizable as the same one. In fact, he is likely to take over the idea lock, stock and barrel – and completely forget he did not initiate the whole thing in the first place! (see Figure 47).

When any formation is observed in one hand only, the interpretation must be modified accordingly. If it appears in the subjective hand alone, it may refer to an inherited tendency that has been repressed or is still undeveloped. In the objective hand, it indicates that the subject has a life-style that is dramatically different from that of his forbears.

If the second phalange of the thumb has a 'waisted' appearance, gradually narrowing from the tip, its owner may have been accredited with a false reputation for tact and thoughtfulness. Diplomacy in this case is based purely on fear. He is scared that putting his own point of view will antagonize others – which amounts to a cowardly form of self-preservation, rather than to any real concern for their feelings. Because he is continually bending over backwards to avoid ruffling any feathers, he accomplishes little.

When the second phalange is broad and deep, the opposite is true, and the subject will possess a forthright and blunt manner. He says what he means, and he means what he says! Should anyone take exception to this, he is sincerely amazed, though he prefers to hear an honest opinion, even if it is not in the least bit complimentary. Such a trait is present in the capable, practical personality for whom diplomacy is synonymous with evasiveness at best, and out-and-out dishonesty at worst.

The third phalange, or Venus mount, should be treated as described in Chapter 7.

The position of the thumb is referred to briefly in Chapter 6. In general terms, the angle at which the thumb is held in relation to palm and fingers represents the degree to which an individual is inhibited. In a baby, or a young child overly dependent on an adult, the thumbs will be tucked in close to the palm, or even, in times of distress, inside the palm. In a more confident, naturally adventurous youngster or adult the angle of opening may exceed ninety degrees. Most of us carry our thumbs, with a little less blind faith, at an angle of around forty-five to sixty degrees.

The thumb's flexibility corresponds to its owner's ability to change and to evolve, to learn from his experiences and to adapt his life-style accordingly. A stiff, unbending thumb betokens a rigid, inflexible outlook. It occurs in the type of person who relies on his routine to survive as the snail relies on its shell. It is natural for him to conform to rule – any rule – and he is uncomfortable and lost if circumstances force him back on his own resources. To his credit,

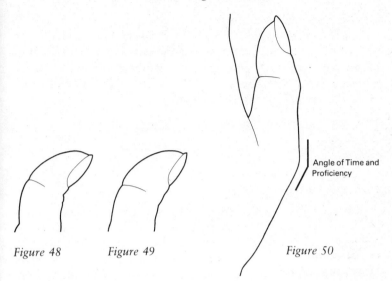

Angle of Time and
Proficiency

Figure 48   *Figure 49*   *Figure 50*

though, he is persistent and single-minded, and still plugs away long
after the majority has given up.

Flexibility is rather more difficult to categorize, for the thumb may
bend backwards from either joint, and the first joint itself has two
variations (see Figures 48 and 49). In Figure 48, the nail phalange is
extremely supple, and its owner is puzzling to an equal degree.
Pliancy here means that he will spend freely one day and be a
parsimonious scrooge the next – depending on his particular priority
at that moment.

Nothing can be taken for granted with this type and routine, or
anything resembling it, is anathema to him. He responds best to
situations where priorities change by the moment, with kaleidoscopic intensity.

Frequently, a thumb gives the appearance of suppleness, but closer
investigation reveals that the joint is stiff. Only the tip itself bends
back (see Figure 49). In such cases, the subject can remain true to an
idea, plan or ideal without bending like a reed in the wind, as does his
more flexible-thumbed friend. He is adaptable, versatile and capable
but prefers to finish one job before going on to the next. It is often a
sign of great manual dexterity, in which case it is always accompanied by an acute 'angle of time'.

The 'angle of time' or 'proficiency' is located at the point where the
second, or middle, phalange joins the palm (see Figure 50). If he has

this, an individual has no need of watch or clock. He has an in-built sense of timing that applies both to work and play. He will never be late for an appointment or miss an anniversary, and has an almost uncanny way of being 'in the right place at the right time'. Musicians, craftsmen, and those who work to any sort of rhythm, in the factory or on the shop floor, usually have it.

Fingers

GENERAL SPHERES OF INFLUENCE

In this section we will consider fingers in general. Their specific attributes will be fully discussed later. While the thumb is the barometer of both our desires and our chances of fulfilling them, the fingers show how we, as individuals, feel about the world around us. In daily life, we use our fingers to probe and investigate our environment, making a continual and automatic assessment of its compatibility or hostility, apropos our needs.

In a similar way, the dimensions of the fingers tell the palmist how we feel about other people, our family, our workmates – about anything in fact that is likely to affect our sense of well-being. The fingers show the effects of personalizing our environment – domestic and external – and whether we see it as 'good' or 'bad' for us.

FINGER SETTINGS

The way the fingers 'sit' on the palm is significant, and our first task is to decide into which of four basic settings the hand we are assessing falls. Take an outline, and rule a line, or lines, across the top of the palm.

Figure 51 is a good example of the most commonly found setting. Note that the first two fingers are almost level while the third drops slightly, leaving the fourth, or little finger sitting much lower than the others. A Mercury finger that crouches low on the subconscious side of the hand, as this does, implies a diffident approach to life. Such a setting restricts the ability to communicate, especially if displays of affection are called for.

I recall my mother saying about her friendless state, 'I keep myself to myself.' This is an apt way of describing the effect of a low-set

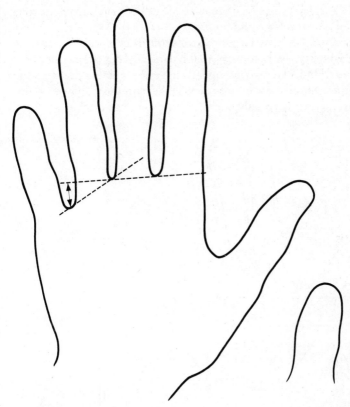

Figure 51

Mercury finger. The individual afflicted in this way is frequently described as being tongue-tied, which can only increase his suffering. How many tortured writers and poets took to the pen as a last resort, finding themselves quite unable to voice their protestations of love? When this setting is found in the hand of a client who also reveals a latent talent for writing, or any other creative work, I strongly advise developing and using it.

When the fingers are set squarely on the palm, as in Figure 52, self-confidence may border on arrogance. Their owner has no hang-ups about himself or his abilities. He cannot envisage defeat, and therefore is seldom defeated! In the hand of a super-salesman with strong Mercury and Jupiter fingers, the opposition and the prospective customer do not stand a chance. This type is unlikely to be found consulting a hand analyst, for he does not consult anyone, least of all for advice and guidance.

The setting shown in Figure 53 takes the form of a gentle arch, and those who possess it are very well balanced. They are neither arrogant nor diffident, and consequently have no trouble communicating with their fellow men. In spite of a lack of extremism, however, they are usually ready to fight for what they believe is right.

Figure 52

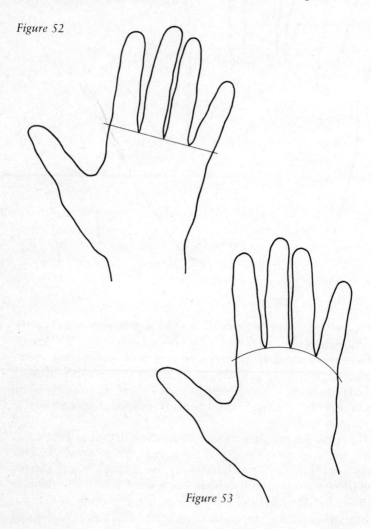

Figure 53

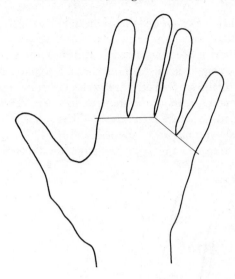

Figure 54

When Jupiter and Mercury are low-set (see Figure 54) problems are manifold. As Jupiter represents the ego and is located on the conscious area of the hand (see Chapter 9), this setting indicates a relative lack of self-esteem. The subject tends to feel that he is not the captain of his own ship, and that events just happen, as they did to Alice in Wonderland. If the low-set Jupiter in the subjective hand is counterbalanced by a higher one in the objective hand, this state of affairs should improve at about the age of thirty-five. Another possible interpretation of this feature is that lack of confidence is more apparent at home than it is outside. When a low-set Jupiter is found in the objective hand only, these meanings should be reversed. Another factor that must be taken into account is the comparative lengths of the fingers. Jupiter is often quite lengthy when set against the Apollo, or ring, finger – the setting can be deceptive and cause it to appear shorter than it really is.

RELATIVE FINGER LENGTHS

When deciding if the fingers are normal, long or short, it is first necessary to measure the Saturn finger, which should be seven-eighths as long as the palm.

When you have taken your print or outline, draw a line across the base of the hand (see Figure 55). Use a ruler to divide the palm into eight equal parts between this base line and the bottom of the Saturn finger. An easy way to do this without a ruler is to halve the distance, then halve it again, and again until you have your eight sections. Each represents ten years of the subject's life (see Chapter 12).

Now measure the Saturn finger. It should be equal, or nearly so, to seven of the above measures. Any less and the finger is short; any more and it is long. The three other fingers should then be compared with the Saturn finger.

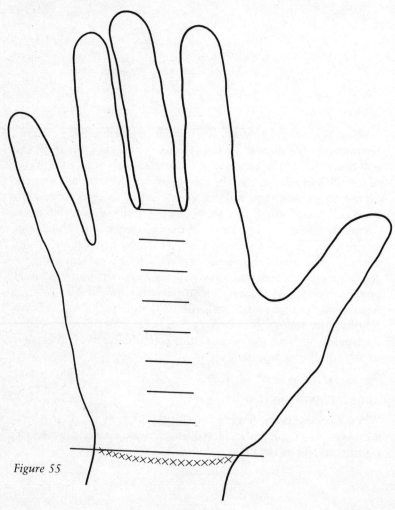

Figure 55

Long-fingered subjects

When all or most of the fingers are long, especially if they are also heavily knuckled, the subject is inclined more to deliberation than to impulsiveness. Do not expect a professor of mathematics or applied logic to possess short – or even average-length – fingers. It is essential for this type to have ample time for consideration, and to weigh up and ruminate on all the pros and cons before they can even think of tackling a problem.

Short-fingered subjects

When a job needs doing badly and you want to cut corners, seek out a short-fingered person. Red tape does not worry this type one little bit and they will ignore every last yard of it! Short fingers work on an intuitional level and, consequently, do what they 'feel' is right rather than following instructions from a manual or textbook.

Such people are wonderful organizers, but tend to skim through everything so quickly that the finer details are missed out. They are gifted with the ability to see the whole, instead of breaking it down into its component parts. They get on well, provided there are plenty of long-fingered employees or co-workers ready to follow them around and pick up the reins so casually tossed aside.

Mr Short and Mr Long at work

Invite Mr Short and Mr Long to provide comparative estimates for, say, decorating the house. Mr Long will come well equipped, with slide-rule, calculator, notebook and pen at the ready. Mr Short will breeze in like a breath of fresh air. Within minutes, while Mr Long is busily measuring, scribbling and pondering, Mr Short has raced through the house, sizing up the quantities of paint and paper needed without making a single measurement, phoned the best (and cheapest) man for the job and got him to agree to a ridiculously low figure and an impossible completion date.

He will then proceed to tell you how lucky you were to have found him, quote the price his competitor, Mr Long, would have charged, and give you his 'very reasonable' estimate, supremely confident that he has no opposition.

Mr Long, during this time, is still walking round with tape and slide-rule at the ready. He will not even hazard a guess at the cost or probable completion date, preferring to return to the office and cost up every last detail.

If you accept Mr Short's estimate, you would be well advised to check that the man who is actually going to do the job has long fingers – preferably with square, workmanlike tips. If you don't, it's more than likely that Mr Short has forgotten a 'few small details' and that the job will take far longer and be vastly more expensive than originally quoted.

BREADTH OF FINGERS

Broad-fingered people are never lacking in confidence, and can prove a little overpowering at times! They are resourceful, charitable and open-minded, and always prepared to live and let live without prejudice or rancour.

Narrow fingers, whatever their length, indicate that their owner has a critical, nit-picking approach to his fellow man. He has little self-confidence, and is often subject to nervous twitches or stuttering and stammering over his words. Because he suffers the pangs of insecurity, no matter how wealthy himself, a narrow-fingered man is invariably jealous of the resources of others.

STRAIGHT AND BENT FINGERS

The dictionary definition for the words 'straight' and 'bent' or 'crooked', although obviously not written with hand analysis in view, could be applied directly to a character interpretation which is based on the shape of the fingers.

Fingers that stand straight and proud are an indication that the subject is honest according to his lights. Honesty, according to conventional and legal standards, is not necessarily the same thing, and other features in the hand must be checked before making a definitive statement about morality.

A bent finger always indicates a somewhat twisted – even perverted – way of looking at the facet of life represented by that particular finger. Figure 56 shows the outline of the hand of a congenital and pathological liar, who cannot help but twist the truth even when there is no reason to lie. Like Billy Liar, he needs no excuse, preferring to live out his days in a world of fantasy, where the borders between real and unreal are blurred and fuzzy. With help, it may be possible to overcome this distressing (especially for others)

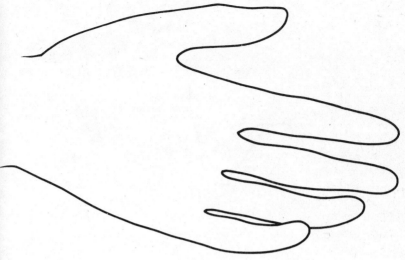

Figure 56

characteristic. The fingers would then start to straighten, reflecting a new-found stability.

It is important to note, at this stage, however, that the above relates to a bent finger rather than one that curves gently inwards. In the latter case, especially when the skin texture is soft, the occasional white lie is told, but only to spare the feelings of others, and not for selfish reasons.

SMOOTH AND KNOTTY FINGERS

Smooth, straight-sided fingers indicate the attitude of their owner to new concepts and ideas. Recently acquired ideas are soon exchanged for more avant-garde ones, and inspiration could be described as flowing freely – unimpeded by knotty barriers – up and down the fingers (see Figure 57).

This bland, easy-going character is rarely troubled by worries, unlike the possessor of knotted fingers, who tends to assess and analyse incoming data and fact, *ad infinitum* without arriving at a firm decision (see Figure 58).

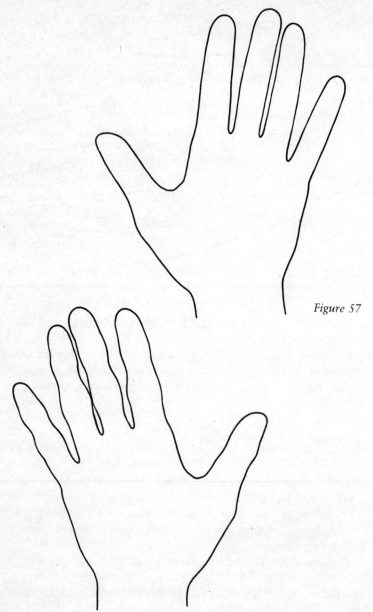

Figure 57

Figure 58

The joint between first and second phalange is known as the Knot of Philosophy. Any knot impedes the free flow of ideas, and can be seen as a point where incoming information is assessed for soundness and validity. Thinkers and philosophers, who dwell at length on life's higher meanings, will be found to possess strongly knotted joints in this position. Dürer's sketch known as *Praying Hands* is a good example.

The joint between second and third phalanges has been called the Knot of Order. It represents a barrier placed between the 'mental' and the 'physical' phalanges (see Chapter 9) and implies difficulties for the subject when it comes to manifesting creative thought on the physical plane. In my experience, it is found in the hands of the worrier, the man or woman who becomes fretful and anxious at delay, and who will build mountains where only molehills were before. Figure 51 is also a good example of this phenomenon. The actual handprint of a famous comedian shows innumerable worry lines crossing the Venus mount and, in fact, the Knot of Order is seldom found without these.

FLEXIBILITY

Flexible fingers go with a flexible mind. Suppleness of the first joint predisposes the subject to accept and act on the promptings of his intuition, while a pliable second joint suggests flexibility of a more down-to-earth nature. Fingers that bend easily from the knuckle mean a tolerant, easy-going attitude towards home and family (see Figure 59).

In extreme cases, where the fingers almost have the flexibility of india-rubber, the individual is full of nervous energy which is all too often expressed in a torrential flow of verbiage. You will find such a

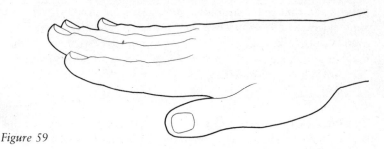

Figure 59

character at every party, telling his own history, and that of all his acquaintances, to anyone who will listen. If there is any gossip to be broadcast, whisper it in his ear – it will be all over the town within an hour, but the deed will be done quite innocently, with no malice aforethought.

'DROPLETS'

Tiny bulges on the fingertip, at the centre of the first phalange, show marked sensitivity in both the tactile and the emotional sense (see Figure 60). When tested, the subject is able to differentiate easily between a variety of similar textures, even colours, when blind-folded. He 'knows' too, on entering a room full of strangers for the first time, whether the atmosphere is friendly or hostile, happy or sad.

FINGERTIP SHAPES

It would be logical to expect the majority of hands to conform, in most respects, with the prototypes described in Chapter 3, with square fingertips accompanying Practical and Analytical palms, and spatulate tips complementing Dynamic and Energetic palms.

Happily, such conformity is as rare as the possibility of meeting the man who epitomizes the national average and possesses 2.5 children and half a dog, and is a non-practising Presbyterian. Just as well for, without variety, palmistry would prove to be a very boring occupation, with each feature inevitably confirming every other, and characteristics being exaggerated out of all proportion.

A square palm coupled with square fingertips indicates a heavy, ponderous nature, bereft of imagination or drive, with a stolid, overly disciplined attitude to life. Conic tips surmounting a similar palm mean that the dependable qualities of the Practical type are supplemented and enhanced by a more flexible, receptive, sometimes even impulsive, streak. If he were unhappy with current conditions, such an individual would have no compunction about throwing the rulebook away and initiating changes.

Pointed tips

Benham sees 'the vital life current entering the body through the tips of the fingers'.[27] He then goes on to explain how, in his view, psychic

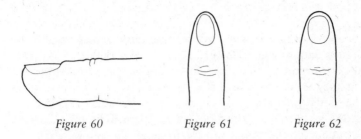

Figure 60   Figure 61   Figure 62

energies flow direct and unimpeded into the mind of the subject who possesses 'pointed' fingertips.

Both the idealist and the impractical dreamer have pointed tips (see Figure 61). They find the harsh reality of life almost unbearable, and are insecure and afraid of shadows. The unhappy visionary and the seer brooding over sombre portents for the future come into this category. They abhor coarseness and can survive only in an atmosphere of harmony. There is a low threshold of boredom but, once the need for change comes into opposition with an equally deep need for security, there is stress and internal conflict.

Pointed tips frequently go with a sharp tongue, which is at its cruellest when there is a danger of the subject's privacy being invaded or that all-important security threatened. In affairs of the heart, he can be a demanding lover – stifling in his possessiveness – but, let the lover give in and submit to chains being placed round her neck, and desire soon turns to contempt. Strength and determination draw him as a moth to the flame.

When pointed fingers top a broad palm and have a strong determined thumb to help them on their way, the subject may find fulfilment in an artistic career.

Conic tips
What the conic-tipped finger cannot do immediately is not worth doing. Though sometimes found on masculine hands, it is more common on feminine, intuitive ones (see Figure 62).

There is no time to bother with planning and thinking things through – to think is to act when conic tips predominate. The subject will make a move because it 'feels' right but, let that critical moment pass, and it's too late. Occasionally, she will make a mistake and run headlong into trouble but, quite unabashed, and with as little method, she will promptly set about extricating herself from the mire.

People with conic tips appreciate beautiful surroundings and often use their exquisite good taste to build up remarkable collections of antique furniture, *objets d'art*, fine china or porcelain. At the same time, they are fully aware of the investment value of their treasures.

Self-indulgence is a weakness of such people and, when the fingers themselves have thick third phalanges, there could be a danger of over-doing the chocolates and cream cakes. Though weight may be put on at an alarming rate, it will disappear just as quickly once the desire to lose it is ignited.

They have an impeccable good taste where dress is concerned and, though there is a tendency to keep up with the Joneses, the luxurious home can be an absolute shambles. In an ideal world, there would be a servant or two following in the wake of those busy and impatient conic fingertips, collecting and disposing of the cascading litter. As things are, when the place becomes uninhabitable, such people move on and start afresh!

Though this type cannot stick at boring, routine jobs herself, she is an adept at manipulating others so that they will do them for her. She surrounds herself with square- and spatulate-tipped co-workers and employees, thus saving her own nose from the grindstone. With a crew of methodical squares to back her, there is no risk that her brilliant schemes will go to waste.

Square tips

Squareness represents order, stability and conformity, and those with square-tipped fingers make marvellous workers, provided someone has already mapped out a series of guidelines for them. They are fine as long as the rulebook is close at hand (see Figure 63). These are the cautious realists, who keep the wheels of commerce turning at a steady, predictable rate. A good example is the bank manager who won't lend a penny till he has seen all the plans, together with a complete breakdown of the next seven years' trading prospects. To gain his cooperation, respect his attitudes and methods. They are after all usually based on sound common sense. The best way to antagonize and alienate his sympathies is to try to force him into a rush decision – he won't budge until he is good and ready.

The square-tipped subject fights innovation and change by the

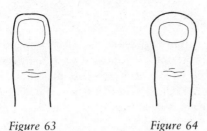

Figure 63   Figure 64

most effective possible means – he makes no allowance for it. He does not hold with 'new-fangled' ideas, quite forgetting that ten years ago he felt the same way about what is probably his present method of working! If he can be induced to change, however, he will be as constant a supporter of the new scheme as he was of the old, but only after it has proved its worth.

Spatulate tips

In Benham's view the 'vital life force' is somewhat diffused by the spatulate-shaped fingertip (see Figure 64). He sees the energies flowing round the tip in a circular motion, as though seeking out each and every nook and cranny. The life force then continues its journey down the hand and into the body, losing much of its spirituality en route. The spatulate-tipped person puts no trust in intuition and goes by what is tangible and visible, living wholly in the world of the physical.

Spatulate tips are the trademark of the individual who welcomes change for its own sake. He works best when carried along on a tide of enthusiasm, but can also command the sort of dogged determination more commonly found with the square tip. Once the task is complete, however, he will be impatient for pastures new.

He can prove to be a moody type, especially if his 'brilliant' schemes are sat upon by an over-cautious superior who lacks his own supreme confidence. On the whole, he prefers to be self-employed. Examples of the spatulate fingertip can be found wherever challenging opportunities abound – perhaps sailing the seven seas singlehanded, or digging in some God-forsaken spot, seeking El Dorado. These are the explorers and the pioneers – the fearless, irresistible giants dedicated to conquering the few remaining wildernesses. Today, they are pushing back the boundaries of space and the underwater worlds, and extending the limits of the human body.

THE FINGERTIP PATTERNS

Much can be learnt from the skin-ridge patterning, or furrows, at the tips of fingers and thumbs, about both personality and health. These patterns show up most clearly in a handprint but can frequently be identified with the naked eye. If it is not convenient to take handprints (see Chapter 10), a magnifying glass will prove invaluable.

The loop

The first and most commonly found pattern of all is the ulnar loop (see Figure 65). This shape means adaptability and versatility in the face of unexpected change; its owner fits in quite naturally with altered circumstances. He is not confined by a narrow viewpoint, but has wide-ranging horizons and liberal ideas. However, too many of these, unless backed by a strong thumb, could indicate a tendency to inconsistency, instability and vacillation.

The radial loop, which comes in from the thumb side of the hand, rather than the percussion, is unusual. It may be found on the thumb, or on the index finger, and is even rarer on the other three. While people with an ulnar loop seem to take impressions from the outside world and absorb them into self, those with a radial loop tend to have a more extrovert nature. Such a subject tries hard to impress himself on the world, rather than being open to external influences, and risks being accused of braggadocio and self-aggrandizement.

The composite loop

This is a variation on the previous pattern, and takes the form of an 'S' (see Figure 66), being a combination of two loops lying in different directions. There are two cores and two apices, giving the impression of a maze with exits at opposite sides; the dilemma suggested by this pattern has to be faced by its owner. There are two paths to take

Figure 65   Figure 66   Figure 67

and each looks as enticing as the other; he weighs up the problem for hours, sometimes days, at a time, becoming more and more confused and uncertain which alternative is best and most profitable. This is a pattern that is most often found on the thumb or the index finger of the subjective hand, and confusion will be worse if the thumb is double-jointed. The two features can kill effective action altogether. Hand analysts, clairvoyants and fortune-tellers see more than their fair share of these indecisive individuals, who expect to have their minds made up for them. Even with the benefit of good, impartial advice they still won't be sure who to trust or what to do!

The whorl

The whorl may be found on any finger, or the thumb, but I have encountered it most often on one or both Apollo fingers (see Figure 67). When found on the thumb, it indicates a strong tendency towards stubbornness and dogmatism for its own sake. No power on earth can make the owner of this pattern change his mind once it is made up. If time proves him wrong, he still will not back down, unless the other thumb happens to display an ulnar loop, in which case the combination of flexibility and determination should mean that success is assured in more than one field of endeavour.

When a whorl appears on one or both fingers of Apollo, it is probable that a fine sense of discrimination will be applied to the task of providing congenial, aesthetically pleasing surroundings for the subject. He has fixed ideas about what he does and does not like in the way of food, dress and interior decoration. Fashions and modes mean nothing to him. I have seen such a pattern in the hands of maîtres d'hôtel, café proprietors, 'school-dinner ladies', clothes designers and models but, even if the subject does not actually work in any of these fields, he will have a definite talent in these directions.

Wherever it is found, the whorl is the mark of the nonconformist; it individualizes everything that comes under the dominion of the finger or fingers on which it features. People with such a pattern strenuously resist being pressurized by others and will not have ideas or standards foisted on them, but they are equally determined not to force their own views on others.

A whorl is not normally found on the Mercury finger unless it is part of a complete 'set'. When it is, contrary to expectation, communication may be difficult. The subject's way of thinking has become so distinctive and specialized that he does not expect to be understood, let alone sympathized with.

I came across an example of this with a client who seemed silent, withdrawn and taciturn – until some grave injustice forced him to speak out. Otherwise he was quiet, seemingly lost in a giant grotto of echoing concepts and ideals. He could only relate to something that was a cause célèbre.

Noel Jaquin makes an interesting point about the whorl type when he describes him as possessing 'a healthy regard for convention, law and order' in the vast majority of cases. He goes on:

But they are conventional just as long as it suits them to be so; the moment convention tends to interfere with personal desire or ambition, then from that moment they quietly disregard its restrictions.[28]

The arch

The arch pattern is found infrequently. When it is, it is seldom found alone, but appears on two or even three of the ten digits (see Figure 68). Chances are that these will be the index finger and the thumb. Third- and fourth-finger arches are so rare that amongst my huge collection of prints I have only one example. I see this pattern as a bridge built to cross the gap between its owner and the rest of the world.

People who possess it have an overwhelming urge to provide security, in the first instance for the near family, and in the second for the community at large. Dedication and loyalty are their watchwords, and there is often a feeling that their path was 'chosen' for them.

Once they have given their word, no matter what personal sacrifices are called for, they will see the commission through. They are great managers but, more often than not, volunteer for a task either because no one else wants the job, or because, if they didn't, others, weaker and less able, would suffer. They certainly do not see themselves as saints! Indeed, frustration and deeply hidden resentment bubble away under a calm and competent exterior in more than a few instances; this is only revealed by a network of fine lines covering the palms. Tied to commitments and obligations almost in spite of themselves, they find it impossible to express doubts and uncertainties. When I, as a palmist, am able to identify and bring into the open this very real problem, the subject almost invariably expresses a feeling of relief that someone actually understands without their having to say a word.

Figure 68   *Figure 69*   *Figure 70*

In such cases, I recommend some form of artistic self-expression as a means of discharging some of the negativity and repressed anger before it can have a long-term effect on mind or body.

The tented arch

Of all the fingerprint patterns, this is the least common (see Figure 69). When it is found, it is likely to be on the index finger and, according to Beryl Hutchinson, 'Four examples among the ten digits are a high count.'[29] In my own experience, this is almost incredibly high! I see the tented arch as representing a degree of emotional sensitivity that verges on instability. Its owner is at the mercy of his all-absorbing response to music, to art, to emotion, sound and colour in all their multiplicity of guises. Listening to the *1812 Overture*, he can swing between pathos and exaltation in an instant, and can just as easily be swept along by the intensity of someone with a 'cause'. Other signs will reveal for how long he is likely to support it.

Because of the extreme sensitivity to stimuli in this case, it is advisable for the subject to look upon the home as a retreat to be maintained in as harmonious a condition as possible. Then his undoubted versatility and adaptability can be used to their best advantage at work, rather than being artificially stimulated twenty-four hours a day, possibly resulting in a complete mental and physical breakdown.

Quiet, peaceful surroundings are also recommended for another very good reason. The owner of a tented arch has particularly acute hearing and cannot tolerate anything like the normally acceptable decibel level.

The peacock's eye

Finally, we come to a pattern which I find on one finger only in 10 per cent of my clients, and on the fingers in about 5 per cent. I had one example of a subject who had three on his right hand, but without a magnifying glass they were indistinguishable from low-lying arches.

This feature bears a certain resemblance to the eye in a peacock's tail display (see Figure 70), which is how it came to acquire its name. When found on the Apollo finger, it seems to guarantee protection from accidental death. Beryl Hutchinson quotes Indian tradition which says that a third-finger peacock's eye promises 'protection in physical danger', though I personally have not found it to preserve its owner from pain and injury – just from mortality. When questioned, my clients agree, with amazement, that yes, they have indeed had some of the most hair-raising near misses: other people were killed outright, while they escaped with cuts and bruises or at most a broken leg!

When found on any of the other fingers, the peacock's eye indicates a high degree of penetrating perception. I feel that this is a pattern that needs further investigation, however, in order to reveal its true significance.

Noel Jaquin, writing in 1950, was one of the first to realize that the skin-ridge patterns applied as much to the physiological as to the psychological make-up of the individual. The following table shows his findings relating to the 'Psychological and Diagnostic Significance of Finger Prints'.[30]

Type of fingerprint	Psychological significance	Predisposition
Loop type	Great mental and emotional elasticity. Adaptable and versatile. Emotionally responsive.	Nerve trouble, digestive weakness, and faulty heart conditions.
Tented-arch type	Sensitive and emotional. Artistic and idealistic. High degree of elasticity on the emotional plane. Impulsive tendency.	'Highly strung' nervous system. Nerve disorders.
Arched type	Secretive in self-defence. Repressive emotional element. Suspicious.	Digestive weakness, ulcerations, and all faulty blood conditions. Marked tendency to infections and malignant conditions.

Type of fingerprint	Psychological significance	Predisposition
Whorl type	Independent and very individualistic. Secretive by reason of disregard of others. Degree of elasticity is self-determined.	Nervous digestive action. Heart disease or faulty heart action. Nerve troubles.
Composite type	Practical and possessing a material mind. Repressive, critical, and resentful. Lack of elasticity.	Fatty conditions. General toxic conditions. Mental troubles. Malignant conditions.

Without the backing of government, grants, laboratory equipment, or any of the paraphernalia available to scientists covering the same ground today, Jaquin's conclusions were effectively the same as those of modern science.

THE FINGERNAILS

First impressions count and, after the face, hands and nails provide many clues to character. With or without a knowledge of palmistry, we take a good deal of notice of the state of the fingernails. If they are shaped, manicured and well cared for, we assume a degree of refinement and 'breeding', while dirty, unkempt hands and nails suggest a manual or farm-worker – or even an itinerant.

The hand analyst is able to go one step ahead. He can see in the nails further indications of vitality and temperament. Should they be 'discoloured or badly shaped, there is some suggestion of an erratic or imbalanced personality, and/or metabolism'.[31]

Palmistic and generally accepted ideals vary somewhat when it comes to fingernails. Beryl Hutchinson describes the perfect nail as having 'parallel sides' and she continues:

The length from cuticle to quick . . . should measure half the total length of the nail phalange. . . . The moons should be milky in colour, clearly defined and about one-fifth of the length of the nail.[32]

In her opinion, the nail should follow the shape of the finger.

To the hand analyst the graceful, alabaster palm and fingers topped by pale, slender, delicately shaped nails an inch or so long, so beloved by artists and advertising agencies, suggest nothing but a cold, selfish disposition and a delicate constitution!

Long nails indicate emotionalism and hypersensitivity, and a person prone to 'nervous' debility. The subject is highminded and impractical, setting ridiculously impossible standards for his mate. When, inevitably, she topples from the pedestal, he will leave without a backward glance to continue his search for perfection (see Figure 71).

Long, narrow, tough nails go with the 'Egocentric' hand described in Chapter 3 and epitomize the predatory nature of the type (see Figure 72). It is possible to pity her (for it is usually a woman) for her insecurity, but not for her selfishness.

Short-nailed people (see Figure 73) are critical and hard-to-please, but their high standards apply as much to themselves as to anyone. Unfortunately, the shorter the nail, the greater the tension, and the shorter the fuse on the subject's temper! The best way to get on with this type is not to take his nagging too seriously. Try to see it as the only means he has of releasing pressure, other than taking it out on the missus on a Friday night. These nails are often bitten down to the quick – yet another manifestation of extreme nervousness.

When the nail is short and small, and dwarfed by the fingertip (see Figure 74), its owner is in his own view 'economy-minded'. Anyone else wouldn't think twice about saying 'cheese-paring' or downright parsimonious! Such a nail generally accompanies a squarish hand, with square-tipped fingers. Life for the owner of such a hand must be regulated and disciplined to a degree that others would find stultifying, and there is seldom room for anyone else in it.

Nails as broad as they are deep (see Figure 75) are the exact opposite of this. A man or woman with this type of fingernail is

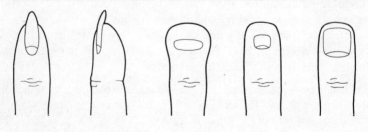

Figure 71   Figure 72   Figure 73   Figure 74   Figure 75

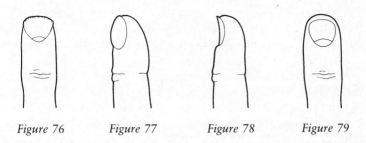

Figure 76   Figure 77   Figure 78   Figure 79

upright and honest, energetic and resourceful – an invaluable friend to have around in times of trouble or distress.

The nail that resembles a cockleshell (see Figure 76) is not a healthy sign. A nail can take on this shape after severe shock, nervous illness or other debilitating experience. Burning the candle at both ends over a long period has the same effect. For someone with cockleshell nails, it is important to remember that, if such problems have not yet manifested themselves, they are highly likely to do so – unless the subject heeds the warning signs and takes preventative measures.

My recommendations include the addition of plenty of fresh fruit, pure fruit juices, fresh vegetables and unsalted nuts to the diet. A more concentrated source of potassium – which is required to counteract the effects of stress – is the New Era tissue salt, Kali. Phos. in homeopathic potency.

If the nails seem rounded and at all bulbous there is, for one reason or another, a shortage of oxygen reaching the brain (see Figure 77). This could be due to lung or bronchial trouble, or to excessive smoking. Any kind of infection effectively increases the need for oxygen and, in such cases, a short course of Vitamin E can help.

A nail that is dish-shaped goes with an ashen pallor, a lack of vim and vigour, and a completely negative approach to life (see Figure 78). Nail abnormalities of any sort are a certain indication of dietary inadequacies, as any book on the nutritional sciences will assert. The dish-shaped nail seems to occur when the diet has been poor over a prolonged period. When it is improved, the nails quickly recover.

The same applies to nails that have become ridged vertically due to mineral deficiency. Timidity and nervousness of temperament may be an associated problem. Horizontal ridges result from past ill-health, stress, or sudden shock at the time the nail was emerging from the nail bed. As the normal time it takes for a nail to grow fully is between six and nine months, a ridge across the nail and approximately halfway up indicates a disturbance occurring between three and four and a half months ago.

Colour of the nail is another important pointer to disposition and health. Nails that are normally, and not just occasionally, white suggest that some form of anaemia is present. Yellowness of the nail is an indication of bile in the system, showing that the liver is not doing its proper job. The subject may also take a 'jaundiced' view of life and his fellow men. Nails with a blue tinge, especially at the base, are found with a weak heart, poor blood circulation, or poorly oxygenated blood. Redness of the nail usually goes with hotness and redness of hands and face – and, nine times in ten, a fiery temper! In this case there may be an over-sufficiency of iron in the system owing to its not being processed properly.

Fingernails that split, break off, are extremely thin, or fail to grow, indicate a lack of protein or Vitamin A, and in the past the rate of nail growth has been used as a measure of protein adequacy.[33]

As far as character and health are concerned, the best nails of all are broadish, round-based, with a good 'moon', and no ridges (see Figure 79). A medium pink tone showing through, unblemished by white spots, should be the subject's aim, for:

the personality changes that can occur when you or your partner are run down or unwell can place a terrible strain on the strongest of relationships.[34]

INDIVIDUAL FINGERS AND THEIR SPHERE OF INFLUENCE

In an integrated, fulfilled personality, palm and fingers are found to be perfectly balanced. A plant or a tree must be firmly rooted in fertile, healthy soil before it can grow tall and strong. The soil – or palm – must be capable of supporting growing shoots and fruit – or sustaining the demands made by the fingers.

The shape of each finger, its size and length, and the size of each phalange add a little more to the profile you are building up. It is a process that may seem slow and long-winded at first, but it is only by assessing a feature and weighing and balancing its significance against that of all the others that an accurate picture emerges.

In many cases, you will find all your preconceived ideas going by the board! It is absolutely essential to keep an open mind about your chosen subject until you have checked – even double checked – every last snippet of data. Hand analysis is a bit like baking a cake. Tasting the ingredients one by one will give you no idea how it will taste when it comes out of the oven!

THE PHALANGES

Each finger is divided into three sections, called phalanges (see Figure 80). In the average hand, the base (or third) phalange is the longest of the three, with first and second roughly equal to one another. When this formula does not fit the finger you happen to be studying, there will be more or less emphasis on that area, depending on whether it is longer or shorter than average.

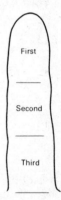

Figure 80

The first phalange, or tip, relates to the emotional and spiritual life of the subject; the second, or middle, section to his ability to apply his mind to mundane, yet essential matters; and the third to the extent of his physical appetites.

Each phalange must be checked and measured against its fellows. The Saturn finger is normally the longest, with the phalanges long in proportion. Jupiter and Apollo fingers and phalanges are roughly equal, with Mercury the shortest finger of all.

THE NAMING OF INDIVIDUAL FINGERS

The names traditionally given to the fingers are in keeping with palmistry's early links with astrology and are highly significant. Each finger is said to have dominion over a particular area in the subject's life, and must be considered separately, then in relation to each other and the rest of the hand. In this way, we can build up an objective and useful picture of ourselves and our subjects.

THE JUPITER FINGER

The index, or Jupiter, finger (see Figure 81), shows how we see ourselves in relation to the world at large. It is located on the radial

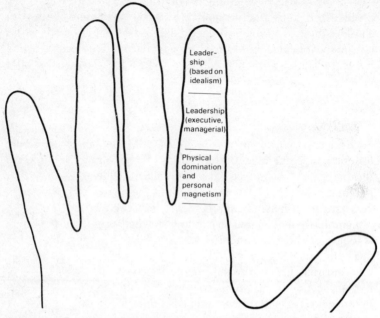

Leader-
ship
(based on
idealism)

Leadership
(executive,
managerial)

Physical
domination
and
personal
magnetism

Figure 81 The Jupiter finger

side of the hand (see Chapter 9) and physically reflects the needs we
are able consciously to acknowledge. It stands, in short, for 'Me,
Myself, and I'.

If the first finger is short compared with second and third, the
subject's prevailing sensation is one of being at the mercy of the
environment, instead of in control of it. If it is very much shorter,
there is often a feeling of total inadequacy together with a king-sized
inferiority complex.

In order to assess the comparative lengths of the fingers, we must
first decide whether Saturn is short or long (see Figure 55). Ideally,
the tip of Jupiter should be no shorter than the middle of the first
phalange of the Saturn finger and level with the tip of the Apollo
finger.

The subjective hand reveals the 'at home' self, and a short Jupiter
here implies that family and domestic commitments are primary
considerations. Its owner's early years are likely to have been marred
by more than the average degree of self-doubt and shyness. Jupiter is
frequently seen to lean inwards towards Saturn, showing an

increased awareness of domestic obligations and a readiness to accept them. When this movement is a positive bending sideways the subject may be afraid to face 'the world outside', resorting to a life of voluntary exile, or exhibiting a tendency towards agoraphobia.

When the 'objective' Jupiter compensates by being longer, introversion is replaced by a more outgoing personality from the mid-thirties onwards. Once away from the domestic front represented by the left or subjective hand the right takes over, perhaps even veering to the opposite extreme in business and social life, and attempting to dominate those with whom it comes into contact.

Jupiter is the finger of domination or assertion. Watch anyone stressing a point, or a parent admonishing a child. The index finger will be pointed, or wagged, and there is no doubting its meaning! A short finger is less likely to be used in this way, for a weak Jupiter is far less demonstrative and assertive. Self-consciousness often makes its owner hide his hands in his pockets – anything rather than draw attention to himself.

Long Jupiters often accompany narrow hands. An unworldly, insecure personality goes with a slim, inadequate Intuitive hand, and a desire to dominate loved ones and circumstances that is bred purely of fear of *not* being in control.

A broad, capable hand has no such fears and there is not the same need for a long first finger to help it through. Here Jupiter is often level with, or slightly shorter than, Apollo, and there is no lack of authority. If you find long Jupiters *and* broad hands, know that you are in the presence of a proud leader of men!

People with long Jupiters do not automatically welcome responsibility but often find it is their destiny to take command. It is the ambition, independence, even greed, that is found elsewhere in the hand that determines their willingness to shoulder the load.

Many of my female clients possess this feature, and confess to being thoroughly disillusioned with marriage. There seems to be a latter-day 'Newton's Law' whereby short-Jupitered men gravitate towards long-Jupitered women, quite instinctively. They know that they can depend on these women to make the more important and far-reaching decisions. Naturally enough, there comes a time when the woman yearns to meet a man who is able, and willing, to relieve her of some – if not all – of this onerous burden, and to support her for a while.

When the reverse is the case, there is usually less friction, with the woman secure in the knowledge that she can depend on a strong, decisive mate.

The first phalange represents the spiritual and emotional side of man. When long and well formed, there is a strong faith in God or a transcendental omnipotent power. It is a feature found in the hands of religious leaders and army generals – anyone, in fact, who believes he has been sent to save the world.

When this phalange is short, compared to the tips of the other fingers, criticism will be resented. Although the subject is continually finding faults within himself, woe betide anyone else who tries to do the same.

Salesmen, teachers and lecturers have a common need to inform others. To be successful and happy in their work they should possess long and fine, or conic Jupiters. A tip like this indicates a probing, inquiring type of mind with a desire to pass on to others what the subject himself has learnt.

If Jupiter has a square tip, its owner will be attracted by ritual, formality and pomp and circumstance – provided the ceremony is conducted with 'proper' decorum and respect. Perhaps this is why people with square Jupiters are often drawn to work as lawyers, solicitors, judges, mayors and the like.

A spatulate-tipped Jupiter is a rarity and denotes a fussy, old-womanish type who is never able to see the wood for the trees. Obsessed as he is by the minutiae of life, the vastness of the overall picture escapes him completely.

When the second phalange of Jupiter is long, the subject earns his position of authority by application of brainpower. He is a great planner, and a first-class organizer. A goodly proportion of the big white chiefs of industry, banking and business have long second phalanges on this finger.

When the third phalange is large and firm, domination is of a more physical, direct nature. A good example is the sergeant major who holds the ranks in check by use of brawn rather than brain. The same applies to the factory charge-hand, the animal trainer, and even the rabble-rouser standing at Hyde Park Corner. Their influence, however, owes as much to a rather unsubtle personal magnetism as to the strength of their vocal cords.

A flabby third phalange is an indication of over-indulgence, with quantity, not quality, being the primary consideration. Other signs may confirm a problem with weight or heart following on from these dietary indiscretions.

Should one phalange be markedly shorter than the average, the positive strengths and qualities represented by that phalange will be lacking, or markedly absent. A short middle phalange on Jupiter, for instance, means that its owner is happiest in a subordinate role, without responsibilities, and would fail miserably in an executive position.

Rings worn on the Jupiter finger

A ring worn on any finger is significant, though most of us would be hard put to give a logical reason for choosing a particular finger. It can be ascribed to fashion, custom or tradition, but once you have learnt the significance of the fingers you will be constantly amazed at the aptness of the choice made by the subconscious mind.

A ring worn on the right, or objective, Jupiter finger broadcasts its message loud and clear – this person wants to be in charge, and he will go all out for power at whatever cost. If Jupiter is small, no matter; the message is the same and the ring is compensating for the finger's lack of stature. If it is large, the ring is a means of emphasizing the statement still further. Examine the paintings exhibited in the National Portrait Gallery, paying special attention to those portraits depicting popes or dignitaries. Note the incidence of rings worn on the first finger of the right hand.

Worn on the left, or subjective Jupiter, a ring is telling anyone who cares to listen that its owner, whether male or female, likes to be the undisputed boss at home.

THE SATURN FINGER

The Saturn, or medius, finger (see Figure 82) is the most firmly rooted of all; it is readily seen that it has virtually no ability to move sideways, and that there is little muscular activity in it. This very rootedness represents man's function in society as provider and founder of the family. The owner of a long Saturn finger is constantly seeking to consolidate his position and establish a base providing security and shelter.

Benham pictures the Saturnian type – one with a dominant middle finger – as tall, thin and stooping, dour of mien, with black hair and a sallow complexion. An over-long Saturn does tend to breed a nature that verges on the depressive, which is quite unable to see the bright side, let alone look on it.

When the fingers at either side seem to withdraw from Saturn, its

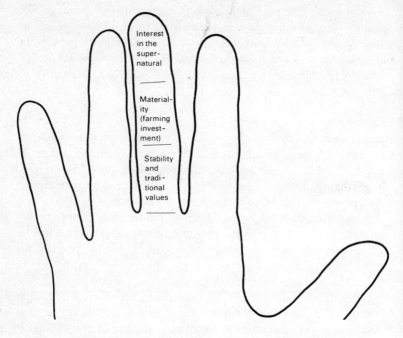

Figure 82 The Saturn finger

owner is likely to be extremely anti-social. If he marries at all, it is late in life rather than early, for he does not seem to need people at all.

Incongruously, in view of their serious outlook, many Saturnians become comedians, and brilliantly successful ones at that! Classic comedy routines often depend on keeping a deadpan face, no matter what, and the Saturnian has no trouble doing this because, very often, he is quite unable to see the joke anyway.

When the complexion has a yellow tinge and the hands are dry, a long Saturn signifies an individual who is avid for knowledge, but has no desire to impart that knowledge to others. He hoards it in the same way he hoards everything else, for he is unable to share it.

If Saturn measures less than seven-eighths of the palm's length, it is short, and the other fingers probably follow suit. In this case, caution and routine are words that have no meaning for him, and the subject will prove to be the complete antithesis of the usual Saturnian type.

When it is of average length, there is a good balance 'between vacillating instability, and an inflexible, deep-rooted fixedness: between the libertine and the stay-at-home'.[35]

Long first phalanges, particularly if the tip is flexible at the joint, indicate a keen interest in the occult and are found on the hands of practising psychics, mediums, clairvoyants and spiritualists. People with short ones have a more superficial, shallow approach. They do not concern themselves with profound discussions on the deeper meaning and purpose of life, preferring to enjoy it. Why spoil it all by worrying about an after-life that may or may not come to pass?

When the second phalange dominates the finger, expect a strong bent for the scientific and mathematical. If this person were also involved in farming – another Saturnian activity – he would be likely to use modern and up-to-date methods which have been fully tried and tested. A good second phalange also means a love of the countryside and Mother Earth.

When the third phalange is the longest of the three, there is always a great respect for traditional values, parents and the older generation. Someone with a long third phalange is inclined to forgo the dubious pleasures of present and future for the, to him, far more enticing past. It sits easily on this finger and goes with a love of antiques, and history. If its owner does not collect period furniture, jewellery or other more specialized antiquities, he may work as a historian, auctioneer or restorer of such artefacts.

When the third phalange is long and thin, the subject has a penchant for expensive and exclusive period furnishings. Whether such a phalange is a feature of the objective or subjective hand, all available resources are spent on the home, and the subject will wait and budget for the 'real thing' rather than making do with cheap imitations. Shoddy, modern, veneered 'rubbish' makes him wince. If the phalange is long and broad, the subject amasses antiques like a kleptomaniac secreting his spoils. The desire is for quantity as well as quality. If the third Saturn phalange is short and fat, discrimination is cancelled out altogether, and the subject is avaricious and greedy. He wants more and more without regard for quality.

When gaps are observable at the bases of these fat, third phalanges (see Figure 83), the individual has the greatest of difficulty holding on to his cash. It is almost as though it drains away through the gaps, which are apparent even with the fingers close together.

It is important here not to confuse the spendthrift with the aesthete. In the case of the latter, the gaps are the result of thin third phalanges, and the hand is unmistakable by virtue of its knotty joints.

In the normal way, Saturn stands upright and erect. If there is any leaning, it is the other fingers that bend towards the middle finger. Occasionally, the tip is found to lean over slightly towards the ulnar side of the hand, and the subject will have a degree of introspection in his character. If the finger itself seems to bend towards Apollo, the subject may be liable to liver, intestinal or gall-bladder problems.

A square tip is frequently found on the Saturn finger, regardless of

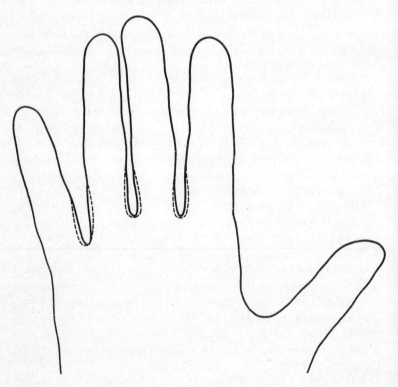

Figure 83

the shape of the other fingertips. It indicates an interest in, and understanding of, legal matters, plus great respect for the institution of marriage. It can be seen on the hands of solicitors, barristers and high-court judges and officials, or indeed anyone with a strongly developed sense of justice.

A spatulate tip tends to underline the sombreness of the Saturnian character. It also adds a dash of inventiveness to the mix so that this individual is not quite as hidebound as his square-tipped brother. He enjoys delving into the abstract and the unknown but tends to do it in a methodical and organized manner.

A fine or rounded tip means that the subject has an affinity with numbers and would make an excellent accountant, mathematician, financial controller or the like.

Rings worn on the Saturn finger

A ring on this finger, whether objective or subjective, is a *cri de coeur*. The subject has a desperate yearning for security, as represented by a stable and enduring marriage. I see it often on the hands of young girls, who tell me at the age of eighteen or so that they are afraid of being left on the shelf! For them, each and every boyfriend is a prospective husband, with the emphasis on his ability to provide security.

THE APOLLO FINGER

The finger of Apollo is the first finger to appear on the 'subconscious' side of the hand (see Chapter 9). It represents our instinctive, as opposed to considered, response to environmental stimuli, and to the people we meet from day to day (see Figure 84). It is interesting to speculate on the underlying social and cultural pressures that resulted in the Apollo finger being chosen to signify marriage or engagement. From the palmist's point of view, it is the prime indicator of our ability to find happiness and fulfilment.

I have observed that many divorced clients transfer their rings from the left to the right Apollo. This can be both a conscious action, finalizing and setting the seal on the separation, and an unconscious signal that they are now free and looking for another partner. Such rash haste may well result in another mistake, and in these cases I would expect to find that the Saturn and Apollo fingers tend to cling together, as though for support. By placing a ring on the right

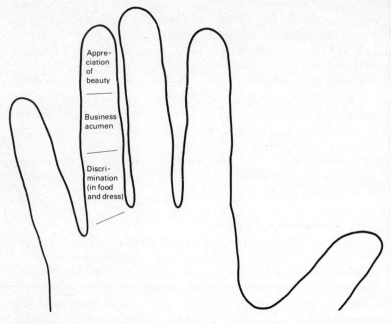

Figure 84 The Apollo finger

Apollo, the individual is advertising his need for a strong, meaningful and totally satisfying relationship.

Should Apollo pull away from the finger of home and stability, the subject enjoys a more unorthodox and solitary life-style, which may or may not bring him satisfaction, depending on other signs in his hands.

The size, shape and dimensions of Apollo hold important clues to our basic attitudes, and tell the hand analyst whether the subject feels the fates are working for or against him.

Overconfidence is reflected in an overlong Apollo, which may reach the very tip of the Saturn finger. In this exaggerated form, it is known as the 'gambler's finger', but it is comparatively rare. I see it on the hands of men who are ready to chance their arm on speculations – risky or not. They may be in business, backing a sure-fire winner at the race track, or even taking a gamble with their own life. Each of them has a common belief in the power of divine providence, and counts on the blessing of the gods.

Success as a gambler, or a bookie's dream, will depend on the existence of a good Sun line striking strongly up the palm on to the mount of Apollo. If he has one, the subject's confidence may be justified. If it is patchy, non-existent in parts and deeply marked in others, he can expect sunshine and showers. A millionaire one day – bankrupt the next.

Traditionally, Apollo is thought to be the measure of artistic and creative talent. In my experience, it marks the ability to appreciate beauty and harmony in all its many forms – perhaps, as through the eyes of a Lowry, seeing symmetry and meaning in factory chimneys silhouetted against a wintry backdrop, or even quite simply finding joy in the creation of order from chaos.

The Apollo, like Jupiter, should reach no further than halfway up the tip of the Saturn finger. When it is shorter, its owner has the greatest difficulty making decisions that involve risk-taking, and will have nothing to do with gambling in any shape or form even for fun.

If the fingertip section of the Apollo finger is long, artistic appreciation is well developed, particularly when accompanied by a fine or conic tip. If the Head line is forked, the subject may be drawn to express his feelings through writing, painting or other creative pursuits.

When the first phalange is long and spatulate, there may be a talent for acting or creative storytelling. A spatulate tip on Apollo also means that the subject prefers to produce something tangible, and dressmakers, tailors, carpenters and cooks – provided they enjoy their work – can be expected to show spatulacy on one or both Apollo fingers. If the spatulate tip occurs on the objective hand only, the ability to create must be studied and worked for; if on the subjective hand, the gift is instinctive and spontaneous. When it is found in both hands, it indicates a talent that forms the basis of the individual's career. Reference to other features in the hand will enable you to decide whether the subject plays Hamlet or creates exotic dishes for a living.

When Apollo's first phalange is square, and the second long and broad, the very making of money becomes an art form in itself, in a practical rather than aesthetic sense. Any valid means of financial expansion will be adopted, and there will be a Midas touch to the proceedings.

A mimic or impersonator needs a long, slender second phalange on this finger to be successful. This enables its owner to empathize to an incredible degree with his chosen 'victim'. For the straight actor, it is useful to possess a lengthy, slimly built Apollo finger, which will help him to slip into the skin of the character he is portraying. This slimness also gives a finicky eye for detail, especially round the home. If every item is not safely in its accustomed place, the subconscious sends out urgent distress signals, unhappy at the disturbance to routine.

When this form of Apollo is seen in an individual who is not expressing himself creatively, the palmist could suggest that the subject take up art in some shape or form, as a hobby, to provide the fulfilment and satisfaction that is missing from the normal working day.

A long, fine base phalange is associated with discrimination in the areas of taste and decor. If there are also whorls on the Apollo fingertip, this characteristic is especially marked (see page 132).

A short, fat third section goes with a penchant for anything that is bright and gay – the long, fine phalange would say gaudy and tasteless – and plenty of it. An individual with this feature loves to be the centre of attention, and seems to dress himself and decorate his home to that end. He often has a gargantuan and well-nigh insatiable appetite, not only for food, but for life. He puts on weight easily. This is a feature that may be accompanied by fine lines on the tip of the Mercury finger, indicating thyroid imbalance. In contrast, the thin third phalange never seems to gain an ounce, even if the subject can be persuaded to over-indulge.

A long, broad phalange that has no flabbiness about it goes with a subject who enjoys his food, but not to excess – for example, the gourmet, the wine-taster, and the latterday Mrs Beeton.

When a sturdy, average-to-long base phalange is surmounted by two short ones, and Apollo is short by comparison with Jupiter, there is little or no inclination towards culture for its own sake. Any apparent response to the finer things of life – classical music, ballet, fine art – is based on an ulterior motive, as a means to an end. This type prefers action to relaxation and for him a change is better than any rest, especially if he has a long, strong, decisive thumb. His aim is success, both personal and financial, in the eyes of the world, and all his efforts are directed single-mindedly towards that aim.

The short Apollo knows that success must be worked for, while the long Apollo is confident that his prosperity has been under-written by the gods.

A broad-based hand, combined with a powerful Apollo, is emphatically physical and its owner is likely to be athletic and extremely fit, not only in body but in mind too. He has geared himself psychologically to winning, whatever the competition. Any sportsman will confirm that this positive optimism is as important as, if not more than, a sound body. No matter how fit he is, an athlete cannot win his laurels if he is not confident of victory.

THE MERCURY FINGER

The 'little', or Mercury finger is known as the finger of expression (see Figure 85). If we have the ability to express ourselves, and communicate easily with our fellow men, problems will be few and far between. The ability to win friends and influence people is an important asset. Without it, we are destined to be alone and lonely, wherever we go.

In any field that involves constant contact with others a well-formed Mercury is vital to success. Teaching, selling, acting, politics,

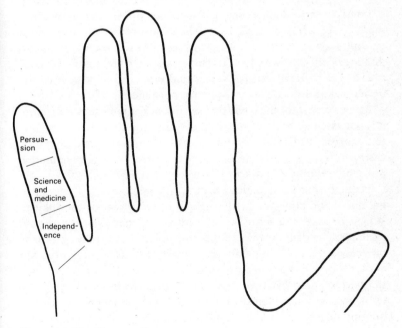

Figure 85 The Mercury finger

commercial and industrial management, public relations, music-making and love-making all rely on the powers of persuasion inherent in a strong first phalange of Mercury, while the ability to communicate ideas and needs lucidly and succinctly is suggested by a forceful, well-built digit.

Some time ago, I was invited to speak to a group of computer salesmen. They had been called by their company to a conference in order to review the past year's progress and plan a campaign for the next. My talk generated a lively, if somewhat sceptical, discussion, and it was suggested that I take three sets of prints at random and comment on them. I duly 'printed' two salesmen and the secretary, who had been making valiant efforts to minute a somewhat chaotic meeting, and who was obviously looking forward to a little light relief at my expense.

Both men, though quite different in background and temperament, possessed powerful little fingers, with lengthy and well-rounded tips. A glance around the table confirmed that every salesman there had similar Mercuries. The secretary was the exception to the rule, for her little fingers were small and thin. In direct contrast to the reps' cheerful banter, she had remained quiet and unobtrusive, scarcely venturing a word, even when spoken to. She was almost painfully shy and self-conscious, and seemed to be trying her best to disappear into the woodwork. These examples are a good illustration of the basic differences you would expect to find between the developed and the deficient Mercury personality.

As the voice is the most widely used instrument of communication, it is not surprising to find that Mercury and Jupiter fingers are likely to dominate the hands of opera singers – particularly tenors. In such cases, the first section is the longest of the three, and slightly pointed, in keeping with the quickness of response required.

The size, shape and angle at which this finger is held have much to tell about the honesty, intelligence and practicality of the subject. When it twists sideways (see Figure 86) so that first and second phalanges bend in towards Apollo, the subject is self-indulgent to the point where the division between honesty and dishonesty does not exist. He may lie and cheat to get what he wants, but he has justified the deception in his own eyes. He lives a Walter Mitty type of existence, weaving fantastic tales of impoverishment or riches – at one moment he is a second James Bond, the next the heir to a fabulous fortune he is unable to claim because his 'evil relatives have banded together to prevent it'.

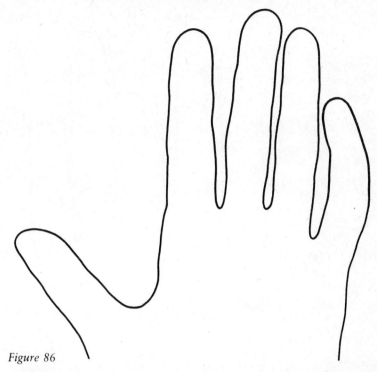

Figure 86

This phenomenon must not be confused with a little finger which leans away, with only a gentle wilting towards Apollo. The twisted finger has no conscience: the wilting finger does. Its inward turning reflects a conflict between the need for freedom and self-expression and an oppressive obligation, perhaps to an aged parent.

If Mercury's base phalange seems to huddle close to Apollo (see Figure 87), forming a sort of 'step' on the percussion, attachment to home and parents may be abnormally intense. Pity the man or woman whose partner features this setting – he or she is destined to compete, often unsuccessfully, for the spouse's affection and loyalty.

When the same 'step' is seen on a Mercury that leans away from Apollo (see (a) Figure 87), there is a never-ending conflict of loyalties. When its owner is young, he is divided between devotion to his parents and his urge to fly the nest. Later in life, the demands of an ageing parent may prevent him from seizing his only chance of happiness. If this leaning is still more extreme, he will suffer the pangs of guilt, no matter what he decides to do, thus spoiling the possibility of fulfilment in either relationship.

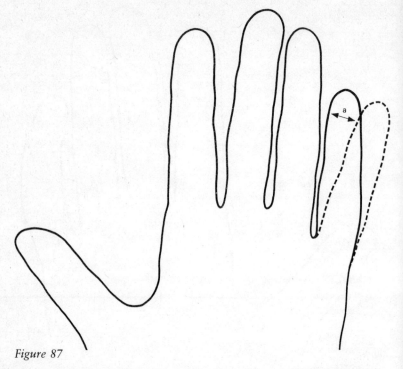

Figure 87

Knotty second joints are usually a barrier to spontaneity, as we saw earlier. When Mercury's second joint is enlarged on the inside only, it tells of sensuality and an erotic turn of mind (see Figure 88). If the third section is the broadest of the three, this quality is even more pronounced.

If the whole finger is broad and sturdy, its owner is broad-minded, with a 'live and let live' attitude to the sexual idiosyncrasies of others, especially when this type of finger is found with widely spaced Head and Heart lines (see Chapter 11) and broad palms. A long, knotty, thin-phalanged Mercury sitting on a broad palm means that the subject requires a degree of mental titillation to become aroused, while a similar finger on a lean hand suggests he is under-sexed or completely asexual.

Length of finger can only be assessed correctly by taking into account its setting. Many Mercuries appear short by reason of their position on the palm, but a good length would be equivalent to that of the two bottom phalanges and half the tip of the neighbouring Apollo (see Figure 89).

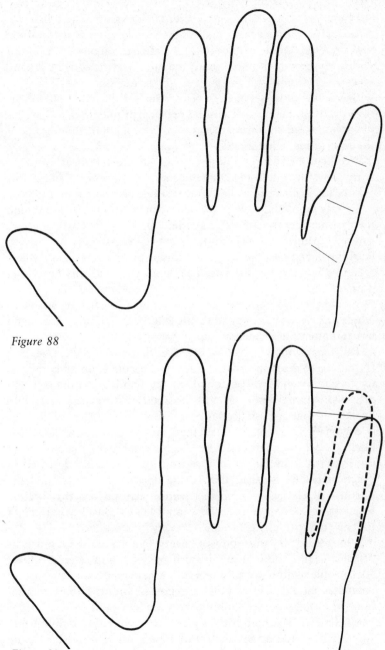

Figure 88

Figure 89

In a self-assured, confident person Mercury is always set high; if it is too high, assurance becomes arrogance and dogmatism; if it is too low, timidity, diffidence and self-deprecation are apparent. A subject with a long or high-set Mercury has no need to consult a hand analyst – he knows all the answers, or believes he does. Someone with a short or low-set one can be extremely difficult to read for. Its owner is quite unable to discuss his personal problems, or express his real feelings and, unfortunately, it is this very inability that may be at the root of his unhappiness.

A conic-tipped Mercury is never lost for a retort. It reveals a quick, witty mentality and a ready intelligence. The longer the finger, the greater the inclination to hold forth on one pet subject or another.

Sharply pointed tips warn of a sharp and cutting response should their owner feel threatened; these may be sarcastic barbs that are carefully primed with venom. If the subjective Mercury happens to be pointed, and the objective conic, this instinctive retaliation will be regretted bitterly, but too late. The damage will already have been done.

Should the finger also be low-set, the individual will be unable to admit that he was wrong, and guilt will fester long after his victim has forgotten the incident.

The square-tipped Mercury is a doer first and foremost, leaving the talking to the man with the conic tip. Spatulate tips add original-ity to action and can be found on the hands of craftsmen and artisans. Knotted knuckles add the ability to organize and build businesses that are usually successful.

Anyone with a long first phalange, of whatever shape, uses their talents to achieve their desired ends, and can charm 'the birds from the trees'. A dominant second section indicates a mind geared to practical results, such as that of the doctor, the lawyer and the scientist. If characters with this feature also possess the 'healing stigmata' (see Chapter 13), they cannot fail to consider working in the 'helping' professions in one capacity or another.

A long third phalange shows an overwhelming desire for indepen-dence; for autonomy of mind, spirit or body, and often all three. Such people seldom work for others, for they cannot abide being told what they should do and, if they also possess strong thumbs, accusa-tions of bloody-minded stubbornness are inevitable.

A balanced, well-built Mercury combined with a good thumb and Jupiter finger add up to intellect of a high order. A shorter thumb shows speedy reactions rather than quicksilver thinking – a physical response as opposed to a mental one. Jockeys, boxers, racing drivers and squash enthusiasts of any note display this combination.

A long thumb and short, deficient Mercury signify the thinker and dreamer, as opposed to the man of action. He does not have the same ability to adapt to change as the previous type, preferring to stick to a convenient set of guidelines, without which he feels lost.

If the normal position for this finger is close to, or sheltering under, Apollo, there is a narrow, perhaps even prudish outlook on life, and every movement must first have been considered from the point of view of the hypothetical Joneses next door. Those with this finger setting, particularly if Head and Heart lines run close together (see Chapter 11), pass moral judgement on others with impunity but from behind the safety of their net curtains.

Rings worn on the Mercury finger

A ring worn on the right Mercury, in a right-handed individual, unconsciously reflects his innermost feelings and inhibitions about sex. All too often, the driving force behind the acquisition of wealth and social standing is transmuted sexual energy, which would otherwise remain as pure and simple corrosive frustration. It is interesting to note how many dynamic executives fighting off all the opposition in the highly competitive world of business wear large rings on this finger. And the larger the ring, the greater the problem, as its owner is advertising if he did but know it!

Enticing consumer goods – the latest car, a yacht, a villa on the Algarve – are a tangible but not altogether satisfactory substitute for a natural, warmly loving relationship.

Worn on the subjective hand, a Mercury ring suggests that the individual has a problem acknowledging his sexual nature at all. Psycho-analytical help may be required to help him face up to his needs and accept that they are reasonable and even commonplace or, in the case of perversion, to normalize the urge.

Homosexuals who wear this ring are saying, in effect, that they are having difficulty in coming to terms with their sexuality. Partners in a stable relationship, homosexual or not, have no desire to embellish their fingers in this way.

It must be noted that wearing the ring may only be a temporary phase, coinciding with a woman's post-natal depression, the after-effects of rape, or even debilitating illness, and the hand analyst must assess each and every case on its merits, without jumping to conclusions.

9

Divisions of the Hand

All of us, in our multiplicity of ways, are seeking the same goal. Whether or not we are consciously aware of the fact, the best part of our allotted time span on this earth is spent looking for that elusive pot of gold at the rainbow's end – harmony and fulfilment.

The very concept of harmony implies that there are discordant forces to be reconciled. To perceive Yin one must first be able to identify Yang. In order to achieve physical and mental equilibrium, we have to work towards a rough balance between these opposites. The measure of our current success is reflected in the hands.

A fine balance between fingers and palm implies that the task of harmonizing will not be too onerous but, all too often, there is an imbalance which indicates problems in life. A wide, self-sufficient palm, for instance, surmounted by thin, inadequate-looking fingers suggests a capable individual (broad palm), who is quite unable to believe in his ability (narrow fingers).

Narrow palms with broad fingers are rare. The nearest approximation to this is the Dynamic type of hand, whose owner lacks not confidence but physical resources. It is a clear case of the spirit being willing, and the flesh weak. Unless he can reduce the demands he makes to a reasonable level, this individual is in danger of not only physical but mental breakdown.

If he makes a conscious effort to work with the tools he has been given, rather than those he wishes he had, the danger will be averted and his hands respond by taking on a more symmetrical appearance. I have had clients return to me after as little as six months manifesting such improvements.

As we saw in Chapter 7, the mounts show how vital energies have been, or are likely to be, utilized and how they are a useful index to individuality. Palmistry assumes that specific areas of the hand are linked with specific qualities. A more fundamental way of assessing

general capacity or the potential of the human 'battery' is to divide
the palms, and then the digits, into three imaginary sections. The
palm, thus divided, represents potential energy resources, and the
digits represent the extent of the demand that is likely to be made on
the available supply. The weak-fingered individual referred to earlier
is held back by his lack of self-confidence. He has the ability, but is
afraid to fly the nest for fear of tumbling to earth with disastrous
consequences (see Print 3).

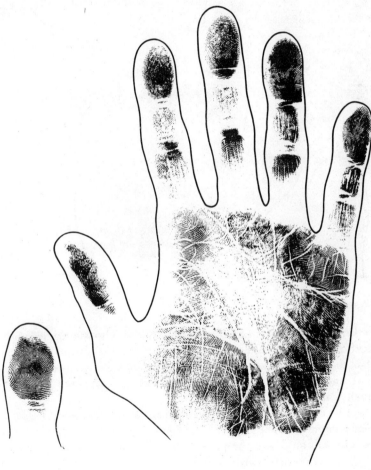

Print 3

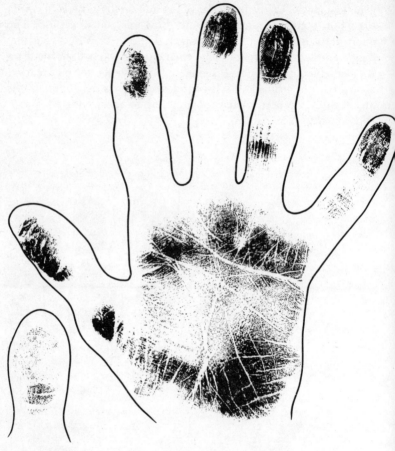

Print 4

Print 4 is the hand of a woman of eighty-two who was riddled with arthritis. Her indomitable spirit would make no allowance for the fact that her physical debility was undoubtedly caused by the excessive and unremitting demands she had placed on a frail body for many, many years.

In a happy and fulfilled person, fingers, thumbs and palms balance and complement one another. The digits show how confident we are in our abilities, with the palm revealing their degree and extent. Imbalance results in instability of temperament.

An individual who is aware of, and can make allowances for, his limitations is far stronger than the incompetent whose confidence is mistaken, or the genius whose light is destined to remain forever hidden under the proverbial bushel as a direct result of his hesitancy and self-doubt.

For the palmist, each of these types is as difficult to deal with as the other, for somehow he has to demolish their misconceptions and get them to acknowledge their wrongheadedness, without alienating them. Then he must make them see through his own unprejudiced eyes the actual foundations on which they may build. A course of positive thinking can work wonders, for there is no doubt that, 'What the mind can conceive and believe, the mind can achieve.'[36] If this potent principle can be accepted and acted upon, inadequate fingers soon start to flesh out and thin, emaciated palms broaden.

Few – if any – practising palmists are found to disagree with this first and most basic of divisions into fingers and palms, though there are minor differences when it comes to deciding what, specifically, the fingers and palm represent. Some analysts equate the whole finger with man's spiritual needs, and divide the palm between mental and physical requirements.

The system that makes the most sense to me, both in theory and in daily usage, is illustrated in Figure 90. The palm represents physical energy waiting to be drawn up into the mental zone, where it will be transformed by synthesis with emotion into readiness for action.

The fingers, in their turn, stand for physical, mental and emotional needs, dependent for their fulfilment on the state of the palm's three 'reservoirs'. In similar fashion, a tree draws up sustenance through its roots, taking it via the trunk to the branches, where, in the fullness of time, it is metamorphosed miraculously into blossom, fruit and flowers (see Figure 91).

Any part of the hand that appears small and under-developed by comparison with the remainder provides a valuable clue to its owner's weak spots and to the reasons behind failure or lack of progress.

The next important division, agreed in principle by the majority of modern hand analysts, is a vertical one. Its actual limits are not quite so easy to define, and are the subject of endless discussion and controversy. I have tried and tested them all at one time or another,

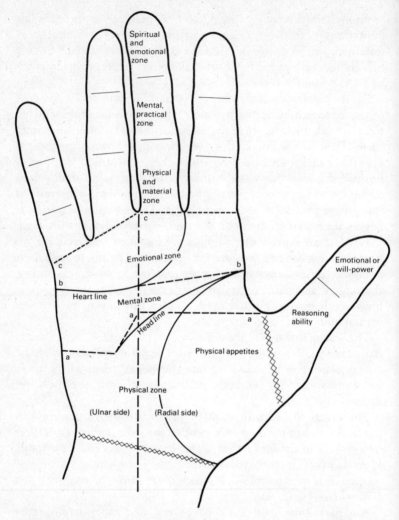

Figure 90 Divisions of the palm – the 'Three Worlds'

but always return to the method set out in (a) Figure 92. The unconscious self is shown in the percussion, ulnar (or outer) edge of the hand, and the conscious or objective self in the thumb or radial side of the hand. It is when we try to agree upon a common frontier that the arguments start!

Some palmists accomplish the division quite simply by bisecting the hand, so that the mid point occurs exactly two and one half fingers in, thereby splitting Saturn into equal halves. I see no logical reason for this and, furthermore, it is a method which reduces the status of the thumb to that of a mere finger (b). As we have already

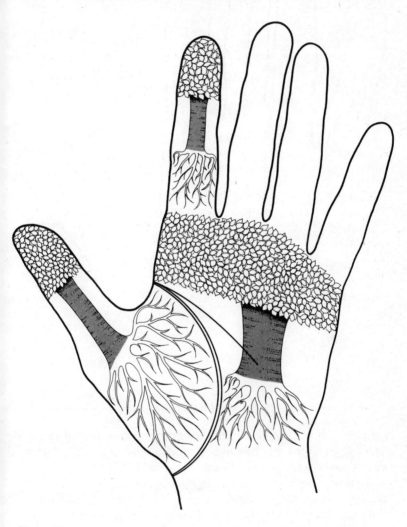

Figure 91

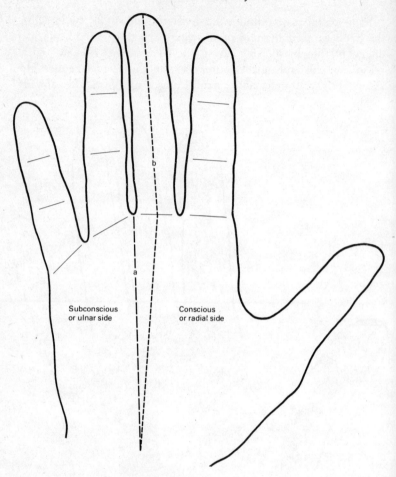

Figure 92 Divisions of the palm

seen, in man, the thumb's ability to oppose and counterbalance the other digits is the supremely important difference which gave him an evolutionary start over the beasts of the field.

Another system of division uses the physiological distribution of the nerves in the hand as a natural boundary. Figures 93 and 94 show the paths taken by the median and ulnar nerves. The Apollo finger, using this method, is a meeting place for both the conscious and the instinctive energies, which relate to the two branches of the nervous system.

Though undeniably sound from a physiological point of view, this theory falls down in palmistic practice. Index and second fingers are basically concerned with mundane relationships and man's considered *actions* within the environment, while the ring and little fingers reflect a far more personal, subjective *reaction* to that environment.

The thumb is the indisputable conductor of this little quartet. If it is strong and capable, inspired and inspiring, music will be produced.

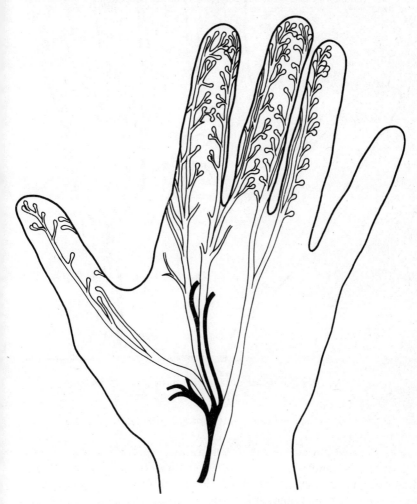

Figure 93 Distribution of the median nerve in the palm of the hand

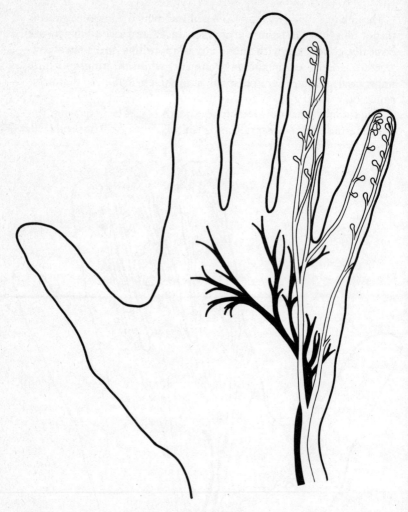

Figure 94 Distribution of the ulnar nerve in the palm of the hand

If the direction is weak, the musicians will all want to play at once, or not at all.

I myself am quite unable to agree that Apollo represents man's subjective and objective outlook simultaneously. My work convinces me that this finger represents a purely instinctive appreciation of one's surroundings. It is unable to be objective and impartial.

The next step in our analysis is to look at the handprint or outline, and to decide whether these two sections are in balance, or if one is over- or under-developed at the expense of the other. Draw a line across the top rascette, and use your ruler to divide this into two equal halves (see (a) Figure 95). Next rule another line, taking it from between the fingers of Saturn and Apollo down to this mid-point (see (b) Figure 95). Now draw a parallel line from the point where the thumb and palm join, following the index finger (see (c) Figure 95).

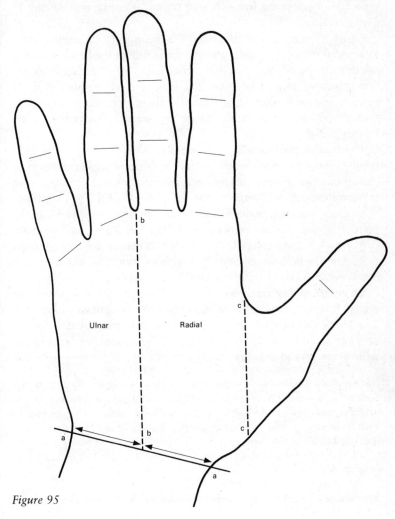

Figure 95

It should now be comparatively easy to decide which of the two sides of the hand is the dominant one – the ulnar or radial half. Most of my clients' hands are on the radial side. The remainder are obviously over-developed on the thumb side of the hand. Very rarely does the ulnar side dominate at the expense of the radial.

Our urban life-style nurtures a pragmatic, down to earth attitude and tends to be suspicious of the more primitive sixth sense, or intuition. Unless a theory can be judged by empirical testing, and measured against the five accepted senses, it is just not worthy of consideration.

Figure 95 is an outline of a hand that belongs to someone greatly influenced by this life-style, and the ulnar side of the hand is unmistakably atrophied. We are taught to disregard and suspect 'notions' whose source cannot be immediately identified or quantified. In general, it is only when we are faced with an emergency, an out-of-the-ordinary life-or-death situation, that we allow ourselves to act on our initial gut reaction.

Those who unashamedly rely on their intuitive powers to help them in daily life often reach the top, no matter what their field of endeavour. Success prevails because the instinct for self-preservation is strong enough to overcome the disapproval of the pragmatists.

Intuition is as invaluable to the sportsman or woman as it is to the politician, the military tactician and the competitive businessman. Anyone who has to compete with his fellow man in any way, or finds himself in the position of having to pit his wits against the elements, needs – not luck – but timely and reliable hunches.

Survivors of any war, past or current, can describe occasions on which, had they not heeded an inner voice, they might well have been killed. The following extract is from a novel written by two American war veterans, and the incident described should strike a chord with many an old soldier:

Dana started to rise, but Mungo pressed him down again. 'Keep your ass down. There's a fifty-seven coming in any second.' Dana stared at him in astonishment. It was impossible to hear the shells coming – the gun fired at such a velocity that the projectiles outsped the sound of their passage. The gun was hidden somewhere up the road, around the bend; Mungo couldn't possibly see the muzzle-blast. An instant later a shell crashed in and crumpled the wall of a house beside the bridge.[37]

When questioned by an incredulous and disbelieving Dana about this ability, Mungo uses the example of Joe di Maggio, the world-acclaimed baseball player, who was able, somehow, to

turn around at the crack of the bat and tear off maybe fifty yards, his back to the plate, and then stick up his hand and catch the ball.

Neither di Maggio himself nor the sceptical Dana had any idea how this was accomplished, but any consistently successful tennis or football star does the same. And I am sure a cursory inspection of their hands would reveal equally strong development of both ulnar and radial halves.

The palm is further subdivided into three transverse segments, representing the physical, the mental and the emotional disposition of the subject, with the fingers following the same pattern (see Figure 90).

The physical zone is bounded at its base by the top rascette at wrist level (see (a) Figure 90). Its upper limits are set by drawing an imaginary line from the point where thumb and palm meet across to the ulnar/radial border in the centre of the hand. The line is then extended from the lowest point of the Head line to the outer edge of the hand, and completed by joining the two portions together.

The middle, or mental, zone is next and has for its upper boundary a line drawn across the outline or print between the highest point on the Head line and the lowest on the Heart line (see (b) Figure 90). The emotional zone takes up the remainder of the palm, up to its junction with the fingers (see (c) Figure 90).

It will be found that one, or even two, of these areas stands out at the expense of the other(s) (see Figures 96 and 97). To find a perfect balance is almost unheard of. When the thumb is low on the hand, as it is in Figure 96, the physical zone is reduced on the radial side. In this example, it is the mental/practical zone which dominates, and the individual is primarily a thinker − a conscious, reasoning machine, a man with little or no time for romance or recreation of a physical nature.

On the ulnar side, the end of the Head line is high set, giving its owner a strong subconscious urge to lay down secure material foundations. Without these, he feels vulnerable and uneasy, and channels all his mental energies into the task of building an unassailable fortress.

Because of the narrowed mental zone on the ulnar side, and the

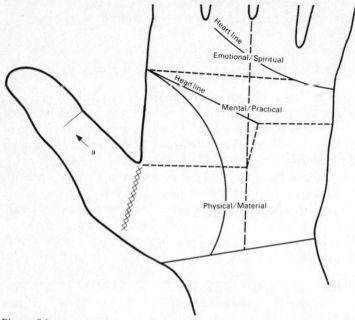

Figure 96

reduction in the entire emotional area, this man is not likely to find a loving relationship. By the same token, however, he will not hanker after one, for he has the mind of a computer and would take it as a great compliment if you told him so! The thumb (see Figure 96) tells the same story, with the logical, thinking second phalange very much longer than the tip.

In this type of hand, the fingers are usually found to be long, lean and well knuckled. By contrast, those accompanying the palm shown in Figure 97 should prove to be short, broad and smooth sided, and often spatulate. In this example, the subject is dominated by his physical needs and aspirations. He has a boisterous and ebullient love of life, and cannot do without his creature comforts. He is creative and enthusiastic, but utterly impractical. Unless his vitality can be guided and channelled constructively by someone a little more practical than he (note the limited area of the mental zone), it could become negative and disruptive.

The enlargement of the emotional and mental zones on the ulnar side of the hand means that this man can be demonstrative, affec-

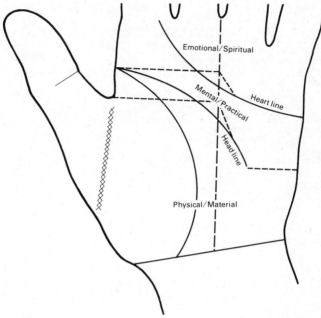

Emotional/Spiritual

Mental/Practical

Heart line

Head line

Physical/Material

Figure 97

tionate and romantic. His Achilles heel is his readiness to fall head over heels in love – and deeply, too. Rejection of his uninhibited and overly exuberant advances cuts him to the quick. He will crawl off like a kicked puppy to lick his wounds, but let anyone speak a kindly, sympathetic word, and he will be off again, tail wagging energetically.

By applying the principles that have been outlined in the first part of this book, it should be possible for the reader to give a full appreciation of any individual's hopes and fears, the reasons underlying success or failure, and a list of talents that have been developed or are still latent.

The framework enabling the hand analyst to describe fundamental characteristics and temperament, using only an outline and observation of the shape, size, and form of the hands, has been laid down. We will now go on to look at the lines and signs that make the individual unique.

Part Two

Lines, Signs and Skin-ridge Patterns

10

Taking Handprints and Using a Data Sheet

Outlining is a simple and uncomplicated method of recording and preserving the shape of the hand, but is insufficient when we begin to study the lines. Something more comprehensive is required, and this is where a handprint is invaluable.

If you have built up a small collection of outlines to compare and contrast as suggested, you will probably have discovered for yourself the necessity of keeping a data sheet with each of them. The one that I use is considerably more complex than that shown in Figure 98, but each of us works in his own particular way, and what is significant to one may be less useful to another.

Design your own questionnaire or data sheet, and incorporate those facts which will help you to gather together the relevant information as easily as possible. Then attach the data sheet to your print or outline, where it can be referred to at will.

A handprint has many advantages over reading directly from the flesh and blood hand, especially when it comes to reading the lines. Many hands seem to exhibit major lines such as Head, Heart and Life lines when viewed with the naked eye, but a print reveals the existence of numerous tiny lines running hither and thither on the palmar surface. An assessment that does not take these peripheral markings into account only gives half the story.

Hand printing

EQUIPMENT

Very little more equipment is necessary to take a full set of hand-prints than was required for making outlines. As before, you will

Subject's Name _____ Date Prints Taken _____

Age _____

Date of Birth _____

1 Is he Right-handed __ Left-handed __ Ambidextrous __

2 Is the hand shape Primary __ Useful __ Energetic __ Dynamic __ Practical __ Analytical __ Intellectual __ Sensual __ Lively __ Egocentric __ Intuitive __ Composite __

3 Is the skin at the back of the hands Fine: L __ R __ Medium: L __ R __ Leathery: L __ R __

4 Is the hand Hairless: L __ R __ Finely covered: L __ R __ Thickly matted: L __ R __

5 Is the palm Soft: L __ R __ Very soft: L __ R __ Springy: L __ R __ Hard: L __ R __

6 Is the Plain of Mars Well-padded: L __ R __ Medium: L __ R __ Thinly padded: L __ R __

7 Is the skin temperature Cold: L __ R __ Normal: L __ R __ Hot: L __ R __

8 Is the colour Pink: L __ R __ White: L __ R __ Red: L __ R __ Yellow: L __ R __ Blue: L __ R __

9 Are the nails Long: L __ R __ Short: L __ R __ Wide: L __ R __ Narrow: L __ R __ Rounded: L __ R __ Square: L __ R __ Shell-shape: L __ R __ Ridged (horizontally): L __ R __ Ridged (vertically): L __ R __

10 Is the nail colour Pink: L __ R __ White: L __ R __ Red: L __ R __ Yellow: L __ R __ Blue: L __ R __

11 Which mounts are Well-developed/Deficient (indicate below):
Venus: L __ R __ Neptune: L __ R __ Luna: L __ R __ Upper Mars: L __ R __ Lower Mars: L __ R __ Jupiter: L __ R __ Saturn: L __ R __ Apollo: L __ R __ Mercury: L __ R __

Additional Comments _____
_____
_____
_____
_____
_____

Figure 98 – Data Sheet

need some sheets of good quality A4 paper. My personal preference is for glazed paper similar to that used on some photocopying machines, for it gives better definition to the skin ridges.

A variety of substances can be used to coat the hands, but I carry with me a tube of water-based lino printing ink which is less trouble-some to remove than an oil-based printing ink, or, in an emergency, lipstick.

The next requirement is a small four-inch rubber roller of the kind used in photographic or art work. At a pinch, it is possible to co-opt any easy-to-handle, non-porous cylindrical object for the purpose; even a large, round, medicine bottle will do at this stage, while you are still practising.

Now find a ten-inch square of glass or Formica – or any other non-porous, easily cleaned rigid material on which to spread the ink. The last item you need is the inside of the ballpoint pen, with which to outline the handprint.

Before you start, it is a good idea to modify the rubber ink roller by filing down the ends (see Figure 99). This will make it easier to cope with well-developed palms. Many hands have large mounts and the standard, shop-bought roller simply cannot cope with the valleys and crevices presented by such a palm.

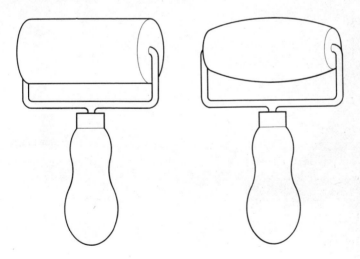

Figure 99 Rubber ink rollers

PROCEDURE

Squeeze a few beads of ink on to the sheet of glass and spread the ink with the roller until the latter is evenly coated. Should an excess of ink build up at the ends of the roller, remove it with a piece of old rag or tissue.

Make sure that the hand is perfectly relaxed and, starting at the wrist, roll on the ink until the whole hand is finely covered. The entire palmar surface – fingers, thumbs and all the nooks and crannies – must be coated with a thin sheen of ink.

This is a technique that needs a fair amount of practice to perfect, especially when dealing with the hollow type of palm, but the more prints you take the easier it will become.

Necessity is certainly the mother of invention; my own difficulties prompted me to design a hand-printing box (see Figure 100). The flexible, yet tough rubber pad inserted into the top of the box is rigid enough to allow for the hand to be outlined, yet pliable enough for

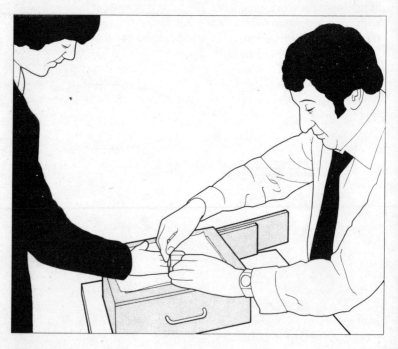

Figure 100

my own hand to be placed inside and pressed firmly against the rubber, ensuring that the subject's handprint is clearly committed to paper.

In the absence of this piece of palmistic furniture, position a small pad of tissue paper or cotton wool under the sheet of printing paper in an area corresponding to the palm. Now press your subject's hand down firmly with your own, starting at the base of the palm and finishing at the fingertips.

You may find you can avoid using the cushion of cotton wool, but only if the hand is lean and flat. Large mounts will cause the print to become smudged, as will the slightest degree of muscular activity on the part of your subject.

Extra pressure may need to be exerted on the hollow centre of the palm, and care must be taken here if you are not to be confronted with a blank space where the Plain of Mars should be. Now, mark round the hand, as instructed in Chapter 3, and hold the end of the sheet of paper gently while your subject carefully disengages the hand to reveal, hopefully, a beautifully clear and unblemished hand-print. If it isn't perfect, don't despair, keep practising.

The thumb is treated separately, as befits its important status. Ensure first of all that there is a good clean film of ink from base to tip, then place the paper at the extreme edge of the table in such a way that both phalanges of the thumb will appear next to the main print. Position the thumb carefully, roll the tip gently with your index finger, then outline the thumb and remove the sheet of paper. Repeat the whole process with the other hand.

If the water-based ink shows a tendency to dry out, as it may do rather quickly in centrally heated or air-conditioned areas, add a couple of drops of water and roll until the correct consistency is restored. If oil-based ink is being used, squeeze a few more beads from the tube and roll.

Now the subject may be allowed to wash off the ink. When the hands are clean and dry, I ask my client to sign and date each print, and to supply their date of birth. Should the intention be to return for a check print a few months later, this information is essential. In any event, the subject's date of birth must be known in order to pinpoint important dates in their life.

When you have a large number of prints it is necessary to have some means of identifying and classifying them, especially if you wish to compare a specific print with one taken at a later date. Which brings me indirectly to a question many people ask in astonishment, 'Do the hands and the lines change, then?' And the answer to that is, 'Yes, indeed. They are changing minutely every second of the day.'

The hands of an energetic, ambitious, lively person possessed of an open mind can change very quickly indeed. Lines come and go, strengthen and fade, and a check print taken six months or so later will reveal new lines growing and old ones throwing out little branches, reflecting personality growth or even illness.

Lines change most rapidly under the influence of impending disease or breakdown, only to improve as rapidly in response to the appropriate treatment. There have been several recorded cases of accidents resulting in concussion, deep coma or shock, where the lines have disappeared entirely, only returning when the patient regains consciousness and mental powers.

The Society for the Study of Physiological Patterns documents many cases where hands have changed radically, including one where the crooked fingers of a pathological liar were observed to straighten and normalize after prolonged psychological retraining. The hands of mentally subnormal or retarded adults and children show little change in either lines or shape. Lack of mental activity is reflected in a dearth of markings.

Skin ridges and fingertip patterns never change; though they may be obscured by the ravages of ill-health. Hands that have been severely burnt and subjected to painstaking skin-grafting operations, have reverted to their original patterning after a very short period of time.

I have many examples on file of dramatic changes, taking place sometimes over a matter of three to four months. Hands have grown broader and more confident, and stress and worry lines have faded away. Suicidal tendencies caused by an imbalance in the sodium/potassium ratio have disappeared, and the tell-tale marks erased from the hand, as if by magic, in a matter of weeks.

It cannot be too frequently stressed, in the light of this, that 'bad' signs in the hands should not be looked upon as totally negative. Read the signs, and act on them. Prevention is infinitely better than cure.

11

Life, Head and Heart Lines

The Primary hand (see Chapter 3) has very few lines, as we have already noted. At the other end of the scale is the Intuitive type, which exhibits a veritable plethora of essential and superficial lines. The Primary is distinguished mainly by his lack of sensitivity, while the Intuitive individual is highly sensitive to atmosphere, pain, odours and visual appearances. The former would not turn a hair at the thought of spending a night in a pigsty, as long as it happened to be warm and dry. The latter is nauseated when he even passes a farmyard!

On this basis, there would seem to be a direct link between the number of lines displayed and inherent sensibility. Research has confirmed that hands and feet contain a larger proportion of nerve endings than anywhere else in the body. It follows, therefore, that changes in the intensity and direction of thought patterns, and radical alterations in the environment or in the body itself are more than likely to provoke modification of the palmar patterns.

The lines of the hand are commonly referred to as 'flexure' lines by the uninitiated and credulous, although a moment's reflection should be enough to discredit the idea that constant opening and closing of the hands could ever produce some of the complex combinations that occur – stars, squares, circles and triangles, for instance.

Brainwaves and thought patterns have the effect of stimulating the nerve endings. Those concerned with

. . . knowledge, memory, acceptance, considered action, etc., go forward to the front part of the brain or 'dark area' as it used to be called, thus crossing the area of the terminals of nerves to the hand.[38]

If the same nerve endings are stimulated again and again by repetition of particular thought patterns, habit causes a mark to be made on the palm.

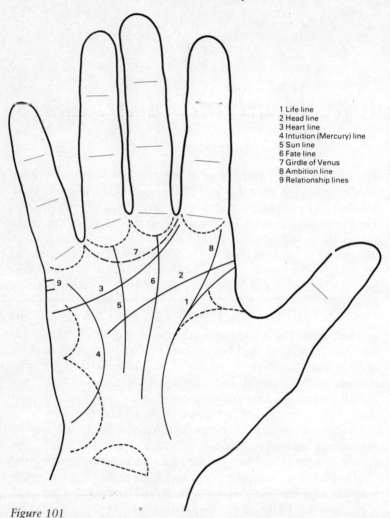

1 Life line
2 Head line
3 Heart line
4 Intuition (Mercury) line
5 Sun line
6 Fate line
7 Girdle of Venus
8 Ambition line
9 Relationship lines

Figure 101

Science tells us that, by the eighth week, lines begin to appear on the hands of the human embryo: first the Life line, then the Heart line, then the Head line (see (1), (2) and (3) Figure 101). According to Professor Wood Jones:

They develop early, soon after the fingers, and appear upon the palm before this is the site of any active movement. In the individual they are therefore not caused by actual movements of the joints of the developing hand, but are developed as a heritage which may be used and modified by the individual.[39]

This 'heritage', in the vast majority of cases, is replaced as the years go by with the subject's own personal philosophy. As he sloughs off these inherited patterns of thinking and modes of behaviour, his hands and the lines thereon alter too. If he is adaptable and mentally flexible, this process will continue throughout his adult life. The patterns on the hands of a normal mature individual should bear little relation to the patterns imprinted on his hands at birth.

The Life line

I agree absolutely with nature when it gives first place to the Life line. It is the measure of vitality – the very will to win through and to surmount difficulties, instead of going under. It depicts the life force from birth to death, and on the strength of this line depend the quality and strength of our fleshly existence.

The Life line commences at the very edge of the hand, and directly beneath the mount of Jupiter (see (1) Figure 101). If the Life line is at all thin or wavy and attacked on every side by minor lines cutting through, the life itself will be without depth and purpose, with the subject condemned to wander aimlessly through a barren wasteland, afflicted by fear and despair.

The Life line should be clear and clean-cut, a sharply etched valley that is neither wide nor narrow, shallow or fine, but prominent and well defined both to the naked eye and on the palm print. Any crossing line represents an obstacle, ready to disrupt life's even tenor, and putting a stumbling block in the way – tripping the unwary traveller.

POINT OF COMMENCEMENT

The line may start high up under Jupiter, or lower down and closer to the thumb. It may start at the extreme edge of the hand, or further into the palm, leaving a gap. It may, at the point of commencement and for a short distance thereafter, form chains, islands, or a mess of criss-crossing lines. It is unusual for the Life line to start smoothly – just as it is rare for a child's early years to be unmarked by trauma or difficulty.

The closer the starting point of this line to the finger of Jupiter, the more ambitious and single-minded its owner. The pride and self-centredness inherent in Jupiter will be intensified and the Lower

Mars mount area enlarged, indicating a very strong desire to get on, and an abundance of natural aggression and determination.

When the line starts close to the thumb, the opposite will be the case. Lower Mars will be weak, with drive and self-interest at a low ebb. This type of person is quite content with his lowly station, and hates to draw attention to himself by causing ripples on the pond.

The ideal is, as always, to strike a balance between the two; the line should commence midway between the bases of Jupiter and the thumb, thereby avoiding the twin pitfalls of self-aggrandizement and self-abnegation. Free will obtains, because the scales are not weighted too heavily in one direction or the other.

THE LINE'S DIRECTION

The Life line marks out the boundary of the Venus mount. When it cuts in close and curtails the area available to Venus, the warmth and passion it represents are also limited (see (a) Figure 102). Should this apply to the subjective hand only, domestic life – especially up to the age of thirty-five – will be restricted and often regimented. I have observed this feature in the hands of those whose development was dominated by a harsh, overbearing and bigoted parent. They felt it an obligation to look after those same parents until, at the age of thirty-five or so, they were able to make the break and belatedly spread their wings.

When the Life line veers out, curving widely round Venus as though heading for the base of the Luna mount, the spirit of adventure is strong. Even if the line should revert to a course that is less extreme, the desire to travel and break new ground will have prevailed during the early years (see (b) Figure 102).

Whenever the Life line terminates by tucking itself away under the ball of the thumb, you can be sure that, no matter how far this subject roams, he will start to yearn for the familiarity of his own dear and comfortable hearth after a few weeks away – there to plan and dream of his next adventure (see (c) Figure 102). But, if the arc is restricted all the way from beginning to end, holidays, evenings and weekends will all, for preference, be spent at home.

When the line forks at or near this extremity and the most powerful and vigorous branch is the one that turns outwards (see (d) Figure 102) emigration is a strong possibility. The forking of the Life line means that the final decision will be a difficult one, and the subject

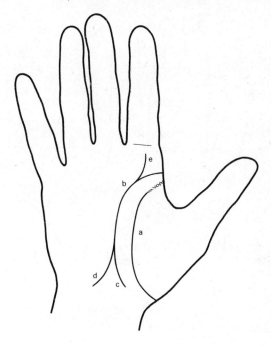

Figure 102

will be torn between staying in his adopted country and returning to the land of his birth.

If the inner line is stronger (see (e) Figure 102) the subject, rightly or wrongly, returns home. Detailed instructions for timing these and other important events on the Life line are given at the end of the chapter.

It is a common misconception that a short or interrupted Life line invariably forewarns of an early or a violent death. There is no truth in this whatsoever, but it is an old wives' tale that has been reponsible for more than its fair share of distress and pain. A woman client with this formation (see Figure 103) wasted four years of her life making contingency plans for 'when she died'. She had just told her husband that she would not emigrate with him, but could not tell him that a seaside fortune-teller had implied that she would suffer a fatal accident at the age of thirty-five. She was thirty-four when she came to see me – the latest in a long line of mediums, spiritualists, card readers and palmists.

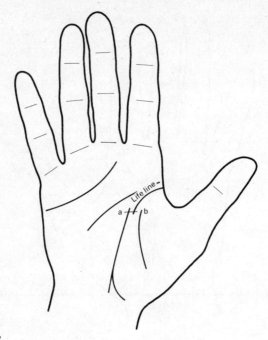

Figure 103

I innocently asked her whether there was any chance of a trip to Australia or the United States. At this, she burst into floods of hysterical tears and accused me of hiding the truth from her. Fifteen minutes' hard questioning uncovered the whole story, including her dread of leaving her husband a widower with young children to bring up on his own in a strange country.

It took another three-quarters of an hour to allay her fears and convince her that a split Life line is a common occurrence. Frequently, in the absence of a continuing line, the Fate line takes over, and the individual can continue along this line quite happily.

What the split Life line suggests is a dramatic change of life-style at the time indicated. In this particular woman's case the continuing line forms a wider arc than the earlier portion (see (a) Figure 103) and is quite consistent with an opportunity to emigrate or to take a massive step up in the world.

Occasionally, after such a break the line will take a narrower course (see (b) Figure 103), limiting the area of the Venus mount and indicating restrictions and narrowed horizons. Whether the ensuing arc is wider or narrower, there is generally found to be a tiny line bridging the gap between the two. If you can imagine an escape route in the form of a flimsy rope-bridge spanning a deep chasm, you will begin to get some idea of the true significance of the split Life line.

Though the opportunity may exist to make a change, there are always certain risks involved. In the example given (see Print 5) there was a chance to clamber out of a secure, well-paid rut which was, above all, safe. It was infinitely boring, but it paid the rent and the bills and had a good pension and fringe benefits. The new job involved meeting famous people – stars of stage and screen – and

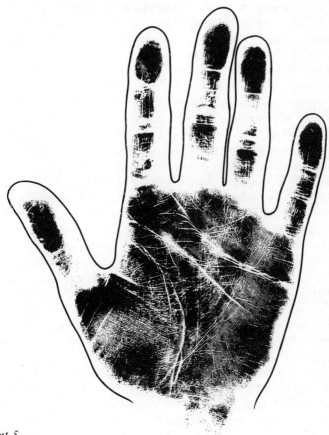

Print 5

opportunities to travel the world, but on a tight budget and for peanuts. It was an uncertain and risky speculation that might not have paid off at all in terms of financial security, but five years proved it had been a risk that was worth taking.

The further out into the hand the Life line travels, the greater the potential and innate vitality – the closer it comes to the thumb the weaker and more inadequate the individual's resources when it comes to fighting either adversity or disease.

THE DOUBLE LIFE LINE

Very infrequently, you may come across a double Life line. This may occur in one or both hands, though, in my experience, the latter is rare indeed. Look at the example shown in Print 6. The inner line has a separate beginning and a separate end, and runs along throughout its length parallel to the main Life line. Be careful not to confuse it with the Mars line (see (f) Figure 104), which is much shorter and far more common in both hands.

I have no more than a dozen examples of the double Life line in my collection of prints but, in each and every case, the owner seemed destined to lead a dual existence. A typical example of this was the shy, quiet, unassuming lady who came to see me on the verge of complete exhaustion and nervous debility.

She had, it appeared, turned a flair for making soft toys into a thriving cottage industry. Her local television station had featured her because, quite unbeknown to her, she had become the principal employer in her own tiny community. This had resulted in a flood of orders from which had come business from Europe, Japan and America. The 'cottage industry' was big business now and she felt she could no longer cope with it and the demands of a growing family.

The dual Life line was a feature of both hands, and she agreed wholeheartedly when I explained that she was fated to initiate ventures that swept her unwillingly on the crest of a tidal wave of interest and success. All she had ever wanted was to earn a little pin-money, but all her little enterprises seemed to grow and grow out of all proportion to her abilities, and far beyond her aspirations.

I warned her that, unless she made allowances for her limitations, similar situations would continue to arise. If, however, she looked around for someone who was willing and able to work with her and take the strain, she could be happy and successful at the same time.

She did the next best thing and sold the company, lock, stock and barrel at a comfortable profit, remaining employed in an advisory capacity. When I next saw her, a few months later, she gave the impression of being a far more contented and fulfilled person.

By opting to live out her days on the comfortable yet limited inner Life line, she had given up a wonderful opportunity that would have enabled her to grow and break away from the confines of insular domesticity. However, the lure would always be there, waiting in the background, represented by the other, outward-looking, infinitely more adventurous Life line.

In the case of Print 6, the opposite happened. This subject was a career woman first and foremost. Note the strong, well-defined Fate lines (see Chapter 12) and the general capability of the hand as a

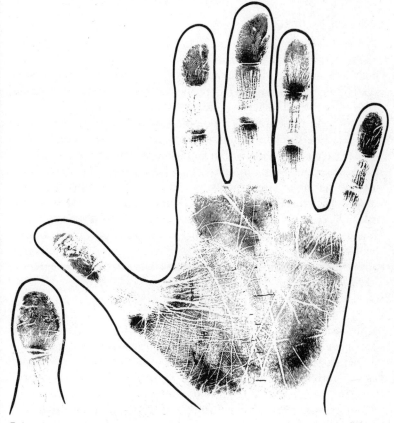

Print 6

whole. Indeed, were it not for the inside Life line, there is no doubt that she would have been content to remain an independent bachelor girl.

Unfortunately, it seemed that her karma required that she marry and raise a family, though she was basically not the marrying kind. She had come to see me because she had just become pregnant, and was concerned about her ambivalent attitude to what all her friends thought should have been a 'happy event'. I reassured her that, for her, this response was quite natural, and advised her to look for a nanny or mother's help as soon as the baby was born. In this way she was able to have the benefit of both worlds without feeling trapped and restricted, and the child was assured of a happy and fulfilled mother.

AMBITION LINES

A line that branches off from the Life line and heads up the hand in the direction of the Jupiter mount is known as an Ambition line. It marks the point at which some heart-felt ambition was realized, such as fulfilment of a desire to marry and settle down, or to bear a child, or even to take a yacht round the world single-handed. What it cannot, and does not, do is pinpoint the precise form these Great Expectations are going to take in any particular instance.

Experience suggests that the ambition will only be realized if the line reaches the Jupiter mount (see (a) Figure 104). If it stops short, outside the Jupiter area, success is said to be unlikely. In my experience, though this is true in some cases, it is certainly not an infallible rule. I have often noted a series of such short lines on the palms of student and graduate nurses, doctors, dentists and other professional people. In these individuals, the lines signify a series of examinations passed or promotions achieved during the course of their careers.

EFFORT LINES

A line rising from the Life line in similar fashion to an Ambition line but finishing near the mount of Saturn is known as an Effort line (see (b) Figure 104). It is a line that seldom encroaches on the mount and usually terminates near the Head or Heart line. It marks a record-breaking endeavour, a mighty attempt to face an upward move. When its owner finally wins through, it is only after a good deal of

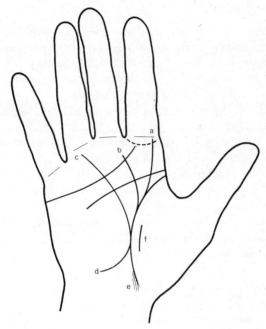

Figure 104

hard work, and he may feel as though he had been trying to lift himself up by his bootlaces. His efforts have been rewarded, but he can expect nothing to be handed to him on a plate.

I have seen this line in the hands of women whose adult lives have been sacrificed on the altar of unhappy and destructive marriages. It represents the decision to leave and make a fresh start. A successful move is recorded by a positive, outward swing of the Life line.

SUCCESS LINES

When a line heads off from the Life line in the direction of Apollo, efforts or ambitions are assured of success. The sun seems to shine benevolently on its owner's whims and fancies during the time indicated by the length of the Success line (see (c) Figure 104). It is almost as though he has only to express his desire for it to be granted.

INFLUENCE LINES

Lines leaving the Life line on the *inside* and travelling down the mount of Venus (see Figure 36) by a vaguely parallel route are known as Influence lines. Each of these proclaims the advent of a dominant and influential personality at a time corresponding to the point at which it separates from the Life line.

The effect of the relationship may be good or ill, but it is always intense. In many hands the influence is that of a husband or wife to be. In others, the individual's life will be altered drastically by the birth, or adoption, of a child. I have even found it in the hands of lonely women representing the purchase of a much-loved pet!

A lengthy Influence line suggests a long-lived relationship. When the Influence line is as deeply, or more deeply, etched than the Life line, the incoming influence will be a forceful one. A lighter line implies that the interplay of personalities will not have such a dramatic and far-reaching effect on its owner.

TRAVEL LINES

Lines veering off from the Life line in the direction of Luna (see (d) Figure 104) are known as Travel lines. In my experience, they herald an opportunity to make a voyage which may or may not be taken up. The individual's response varies according to his state of mind and predominating attitudes.

A Travel line that results in positive action is normally accompanied by an inner restlessness – this will be mirrored in minor lines elsewhere on the palm, (see Chapter 13).

Do not confuse a small phalanx of fine lines dropping away from the Life line (see (e) Figure 104) with Travel lines. This feature is sometimes found at the very base of the line, signifying a weakening of the life force. Vitality will be at a low ebb at the time indicated and, in the hands of a man or woman who has just lost a dearly loved partner, could imply loss of the will to carry on alone.

MARS LINES

Another 'minor' line which may cause confusion is the Mars line (see (f) Figure 104). When it occurs, it runs alongside and parallel to part of the Life line, and acts in the same way as a guardian angel, providing a protective barrier against knocks and bumps.

A Mars line suggests that help is going to be needed during a specific period, which corresponds to its length.

In spite of tragedy and upheaval, people survive and carry on – and are strengthened by their experiences, especially when they possess this line. I have heard tales of the most terrifying narrow escapes from physical danger, in times of both war and peace, when seeking confirmation of the effects of a Mars line from a client.

WORRY LINES

If the Life line is apparently under attack from inside the Venus mount by a host of transverse lines (see (a) Figure 105) you can be sure that the owner of the hand is a worrier. Mountains are made out of mini-molehills – particularly when the fingers are heavily knuckled at the second joint.

This kind of person worries because there is nothing to worry about and, if her husband happens to be ten minutes late home from work, has already worked herself into a state approaching hysteria. In that time, she has envisaged an accident, with bodies strewn grotesquely all over the road, her husband's funeral and the ensuing problems of bringing up a family single-handedly.

It is almost an anti-climax when he arrives – a victim of heavy homebound traffic. My advice to her involves taking a step back from the problem and analysing her reactions minutely. How often does the situation occur and how much unnecessary friction has been caused by it?

Indications on the Head line might suggest that the root cause lies in a simple chemical imbalance in the bloodstream. If the sodium/potassium ratio is out of kilter, due to years of faulty eating habits, only a complete reversal of the trend can put matters to rights. In these cases, the advice of a reputable homeopath or acupuncturist should be sought.

When the lines crossing Venus cut through the Life line, the tendency to worry is more intense, and that much more difficult to deal with, because more deeply entrenched. There may be associated emotional disturbances resulting from an unhappy marriage. The individual may find himself unable to come to terms with a

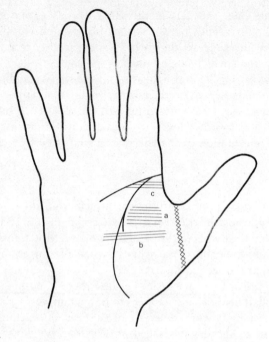

Figure 105

bereavement or apply his mind to resolving a particular difficulty. The thicker the line, the more deeply affected the owner will be (see (b) Figure 105).

Worry lines crossing the lower mount of Mars (see (c) Figure 105) speak of traumatic early years where the subject has had to call upon the Martian qualities of fortitude, tenacity and endurance to survive. All the more so when the lines terminate at the Head line, as they do in this example.

LOYALTY LINES

A deep crease cutting through the Venus mount can often be clearly seen in a print, though seldom with the naked eye (see Print 7). It is known as a Loyalty line, but it is not a line at all, in the true sense of the word. If it actually hits the Life line it implies a conflict of interests at the time indicated on the Life line, and a choice must then be made between desire and duty.

The dilemma may involve making a decision that benefits the individual, but only at the expense of parents or family. A new job in another part of the country, for instance, may mean that an aged parent has to be placed in care. Or leaving a cold, emotionally sterile relationship for a more fulfilling one may mean leaving children behind.

Whatever the final decision, a Loyalty line always marks a period characterized by indecision and self-doubt.

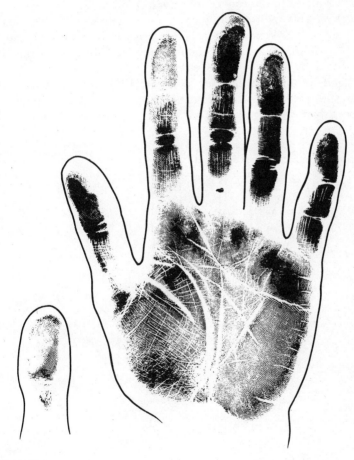

Print 7

IRREGULARITIES ON THE LIFE LINE

Breaks in the Life line can be a sign that ill-health is building up in the near, or distant, future (see (a) Figure 106). If it is repeated in both hands, the individual may have inherited a predisposition towards a particular ailment. Preventative measures started soon enough may ward off the possibility, in which case the broken line will knit together, quickly in the right or objective hand, and more slowly in the subjective. Alternatively, a protective square may form (see (b) Figure 106). In either case, the danger has been averted and energy reserves are sufficient to meet the crisis.

Occasionally, a broken Life line is found with a small line lying next to it on the Venus mount. This acts as a bridge or a splint and has the same effect as the square – the vital flow of energy is unaffected by the detour (see (c) Figure 106).

Islands on the Life line (see (d) Figure 106) represent bouts of depression, ill-health, confinement in hospital – or even in prison! Obviously a warning to be noted and acted upon.

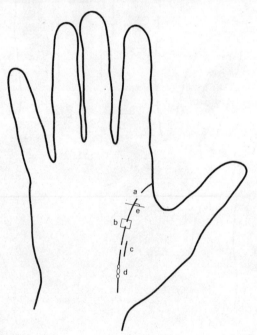

Figure 106

Islands on lines crossing the Life line (see (e) Figure 106) are also bad news. When they are found on a worry line, anxiety is intense. It is held in some quarters that, if an islanded line rises towards Saturn, it indicates financial distress; if it rises towards Apollo, it means, a loss of face in the eyes of the world. Whatever the case, it is important to remember that a feature which shows up as an island today may revert to separate lines in a month or two. A change of attitude could result in the threat being averted.

When the Life line shows on the print as a broad, white band (see (b) Print 7), an over-acid stomach, leading to heartburn, flatulence and an assortment of aches and pains can be expected. Acidity of the blood has resulted in a thickening of the Head line (see (c) Print 7) and is confirmed by a number of fine lines rising along the percussion edge of the hand, in the area of Upper Mars (see (d) Print 7).

A thin, fragile-looking Life line signals a lack of vitality and lowered resistance both to illness and the debilitating effects of life. A strong Head line and thumb might encourage the individual to rely on nervous, rather than physical, resources, thus paving the way for a breakdown. Should common sense prevail, however, productive steps aimed at rebuilding health will soon cause the Life line to deepen.

A line that is deep as opposed to thick carries the Life forces along on a strong, positive current. The owner of this line is not easy to deter. Once his mind is set on a course of action, he will not be dissuaded from it lightly.

Any Life line (or indeed any line) that is subject to one or more of the above irregularities can be transformed once the problem or deficiency is understood and a conscious decision has been made to take positive action.

Weaknesses can be turned into strengths, but weak desires cannot bring results. Persistence can. Those who keep on trying

. . . receive, as their compensation, whatever goal they are pursuing. That is not all! They receive something infinitely more important than material compensation – the knowledge that every failure brings with it the seed of an equivalent advantage.[40]

And a change of philosophy will very soon be reflected in the hands.

MEASURING TIME ON THE LIFE LINE

Another vexed question for the would-be palmist is how to judge time on the lines. Cheiro's method involved dividing the Life line and the Fate line into periods of seven years. It was his belief that

This division into periods of seven is the most natural one of all, as the entire nature changes every seven years.[41]

Mrs Robinson, in her much-vaunted book *The Graven Palm* insists that, as our early years are so much fuller in every way than our old age, the lines should be marked up to allow for it, with carefully graduated segments – wide ones representing the years up to middle age, and shorter ones thereafter.

Julius Spier inspired C. G. Jung to take up the study of hands and had many revolutionary theories, including some on the measurement of time. He held that the Life line should be read from the bottom up, as it were, but died before he could explain his reasoning.

In days of yore, the Life line allowed only for the biblically sanctioned three score years and ten. Nowadays, life expectancy in

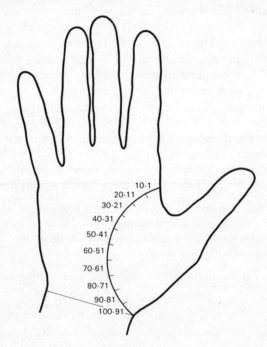

Figure 107

the West can be as much as a hundred years, and the Life line should be marked accordingly. In a few years, if cryogenic research is successful, and suspended animation become commonplace, we may have to think yet again about the nature of time and how it is represented in the hand of man. Until then, I shall continue to use the following system which works for me in the majority of cases.

Take the print and follow the path indicated by the Life line, whether this is short or normal in length. Measure the total distance from the edge of the hand to the point where the first rascette meets the ball of the thumb (see Figure 107). Divide this distance into ten equal sections. Each of these represents, very roughly, ten years. I must emphasize here that, when we are using such relatively clumsy tools as protractor and rule, absolute accuracy is out of the question. The most that can be hoped for is a fair approximation. Only access to a high-powered or electron microscope could bring us anywhere near absolutely precise results.

If the line measures, say, 120 millimetres, each 12 millimetres will approximate ten years, and the Life line should be divided into ten equal segments of 12 millimetres each. For ease of reference, it is helpful to indicate these lightly with pen or pencil. It is then a relatively simple matter to cast a glance at the print from time to time, checking significant dates with your subject as you proceed with the assessment.

The Head line

There is a popular misconception that the Head line can indicate the quality and scope of its owner's mental capabilities. It cannot. What it can and does do is to reveal to the hand reader in no uncertain terms whether his subject is inclined to be creative and imaginative, prosaic and pragmatic, romantic or matter-of-fact.

IQ levels may be indicated both in the hand generally and in the lines, or lack of them. The Head line can only show when mind power is temporarily reduced through a biochemical imbalance in the bloodstream; potassium insufficiency, for instance, can lead to forgetfulness and woolly thinking. This results in islands appearing on the line (see also Chapter 14).

The state of the brain, and its efficiency from a physiological point of view is reflected in a clear Head line that is neither too thin nor too broad. A thin line goes with an unstable, highly strung personality –

the type who goes to pieces in an emergency. The possessor of a wide Head line finds himself unable to work up more than a passing enthusiasm for anything, though he may be very interested at the time. His thinking is shallow and lacking in dynamism. In similar fashion, a wide river meanders along tranquilly, but when it reaches a narrow channel it rushes forward as though possessed. Once harnessed, its energy can be transformed into electricity, and the healthy Head line uses mental energies in much the same way.

POINT OF COMMENCEMENT

Like the Life line, the Head line has a variety of starting points. It may rise close to the index finger or lower down, actually inside the boundary enclosing the Venus mount, or anywhere in between (see (2) Figure 101). It may accompany the Life line for part of its journey, or be widely spaced from it, and it can start some distance into the palm, or at the extreme ulnar edge.

When the line commences high on the mount of Jupiter, the thinking processes are characterized by drive and aggression – because this effectively extends the Lower Mars mount (see (a) Figure 108). The higher the Head and Life lines, the greater the

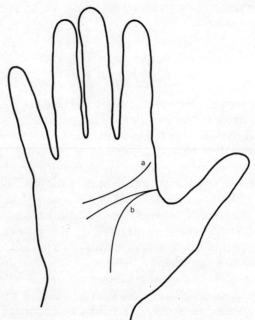

Figure 108

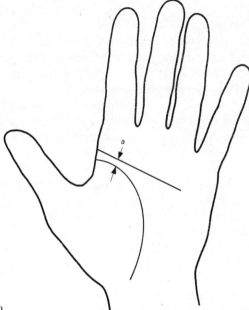

Figure 109

ambition and pride in self-reliance. If the two lines are tied for any great distance (see (b) Figure 108) – or even for the entire width of the Jupiter mount – self-confidence is lacking and there is doubt and confusion in the subject concerning his own abilities. Any success must be achieved in spite of these limitations, and he will need a persistent and strong-willed thumb, when he will spur himself on to the winning post in an attempt to prove both to himself and the world at large that he is not afraid.

Look at the hand of the dependent, over-cautious son or daughter. He or she is bound to have these tied Head and Life lines, especially in those not infrequent cases where emotional blackmail is brought to bear, to ensure filial devotion. Over-emotionalism is always a weakness and, if reinforced by a full Girdle of Venus (see Chapter 13), impossible to beat. Such extreme sensitivity is a burden and, when confronted with the problems of others, the subject is so overwhelmed by his own sympathetic reaction, he is incapable of giving practical assistance.

Wide separation of the Head and Life lines (see (a) Figure 109) predisposes the subject to seek independence at an early age. As a child, the individual will have been impulsive and self-willed. As an

adult, he may inspire criticism for being outspoken, extravagant and
foolhardy. A planned approach to a project is alien to his nature, for
he is unpredictable and acts according to the whim of the moment.
When accompanied by a weak thumb and an overlong Apollo finger,
this feature can indicate an excessive gambler. Its owner is inclined to
suffer from the delusion that fortune cannot fail to shine on him, and
substantial and repeated losses do little to disabuse him of the
fallacy. The most favourable position for the Head line is when it
travels along with the Life line for no more than a fraction of an inch.
The individual is then neither too audacious nor too wary in his
response to life and to his fellow man.

If tiny bridging lines are found to link the two lines (see Figure
110), the subject will be characterized by spurts of confidence,
followed by periods of hesitancy and self-doubt. Only self-
knowledge and a liberal dose of common sense will help him to
overcome his ambivalence. When this happens, the lattice-work
effect may fade away and the lines can be interpreted in the normal
way.

A Head line that starts from a point inside the Life line (see Figure
111) is a strong indication of a belligerent and irascible temper. In

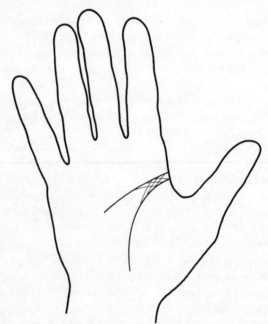

Figure 110

Figure 111

this case, however, squalls and stormy weather are based on the philosophy that attack is the best form of defence; and not on aggression for its own sake. The individual lacks confidence and frequently (often unjustifiably) feels as though he is being unreasonably criticized.

A formation that is rare in both hands, and rather more common in just one, is the Simian line (see Figure 112). Here Head and Heart line merge to form a composite stretching from one side of the hand to the other. Effectively, the emotional zone is enlarged at the

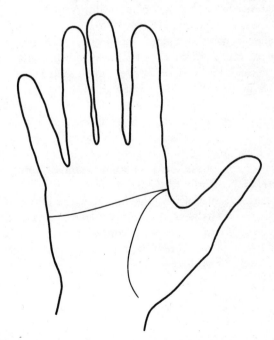

Figure 112

expense of the mental, suggesting that the individual is totally self-centred and subjective in his dealings.

When the Head line is positioned high on the hand, the Heart line too is inclined to be somewhat higher than normal, thus narrowing considerably the area of emotional expression. As we saw in Chapter 9, a Head line that travels horizontally across the hand can mean an almost overwhelming desire for secure material foundations. The Simian line is, in effect, a high-set Head line combined with a low-set Heart line. The subject could become selfish, suspicious and demanding. Its owner can concentrate his mental energies and apply them with laser-like intensity – but only on one project, thought or person at a time. He never does anything half-heartedly, and it is impossible to speak to him when he is totally absorbed in a task. He won't even hear you!

In relationships, this becomes a failing. He is either totally for, or totally against, a person, which makes him extremely vulnerable when it comes to love and marriage. His 'love' is the kind that has to possess, body and soul, for hasn't *he* given his all? The Simian mentality is not content to live and let live – it tries to absorb the partner into itself.

This desire can be translated into jealousy and suspicion, and such possessiveness is seldom tolerated for long. The possessor of a Simian line is easily hurt, and the scars take a long time to heal, if they heal at all. For a marriage to be successful, his wife must identify totally with all his aims, never ever look at another man and turn a blind eye to any affairs he may have.

If found in the subjective hand only, the Simian line indicates more trouble in the domestic sphere than outside it. In both subjective and objective hands, home and working life are affected. The subject cannot trust anyone and is constantly looking for evidence of perfidy. As a result, he often surrounds himself with weak, insipid characters who won't challenge his authority.

The best possible form for this line to take is shown in Figure 113. Here, single-mindedness is an asset, rather than a failing and, instead of projecting his own base motives on to others, as is the case with the example shown in Figure 110, the subjects approach is leavened with a degree of sympathy.

THE COURSE OF THE LINE

The ideal Head line terminates about three-quarters of the way into the palm, and under the finger of Apollo (see Figure 114). If it ends under Saturn, it is considered short and, if it travels beyond Apollo, long. We look to the Head line for information on the subject's creative or practical abilities.

Figure 113

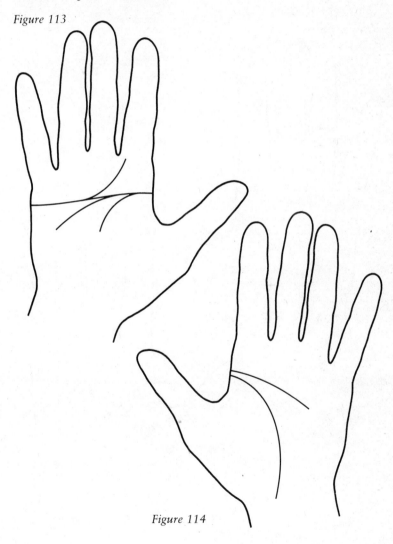

Figure 114

A short Head line that plunges downwards in the direction of Luna suggests that the subject is both imaginative and pragmatic. He is able to visualize a completed project in his mind's eye, anticipating and eliminating all possible snags (see Figure 115).

When the short Head line is reasonably straight, taking an almost horizontal path across the hand, the subject is less inclined to be an initiator but, without looking at the rest of the hand, it is impossible to be specific about this.

Figure 115

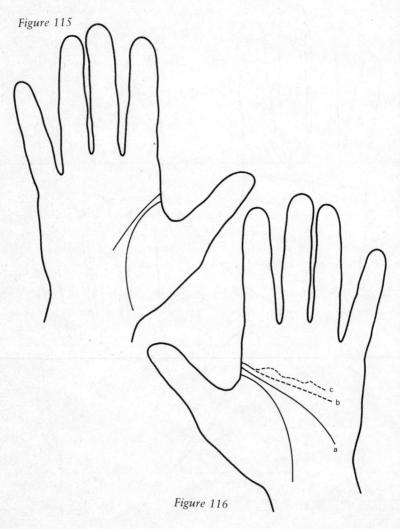

Figure 116

A short Head line always shows a desire for security. Those with a Luna-oriented line seek emotional fulfilment as a priority; those with a horizontal line go all out for money and the reassurance that comes from owning a home, a car and a holiday villa in the South of France.

A long, sloping Head line, terminating deep down on the Luna mount, suggests someone who is far less practical. Its owner trusts his feelings implicitly and, to the amazement of those whose actions only follow careful, logical planning, his 'irrational' behaviour brings results! (See Figure 116.) If the Head line veers too sharply towards Luna, the world of imagination will be its owner's natural habitat. This type is easily affected by negative vibrations and, to survive, needs constant guidance from someone just a little more worldly to survive. He is often referred to in rather disparaging terms and classed as 'artistic' or eccentric, or both.

When the line is long and straight, the subject is inclined to be inflexible and fixed in all his doings. He will throw the baby out with the bath water time and time again, for he is literal-minded and understands nothing unless it is phrased in good, old-fashioned, common-sense terms (see (b) Figure 116).

A wavy line (see (c) Figure 116) is generally thought to indicate a mind that is easily distracted and easily changed. The deeper the line, the greater the ability to concentrate – provided it is also relatively straight. When the line is lightly etched on the palm, thinking deeply and studying tend to be a strain. The basic cause of this may be general ill-health particularly if all the lines are similarly affected.

If the line appears to vary in depth, with one part deep and another faint, the subject usually proves to have experienced periods when he found it almost impossible to concentrate, followed by times when, it became easier. If the line is also chained, look for potassium deficiency, especially if Heart and Mercury lines are similarly affected.

An island on the Head line may indicate an extended period of worry, or the possibility of a nervous breakdown. If one appears in the same place on both hands, there may well be an hereditary tendency to suffer from nerves. Dots on the line are also thought to be a sign of nagging worries, but are rather difficult to identify. Lines crossing the Head or any other line represent obstacles. When the Head line continues along confidently the problem has been success-fully overcome. A little branch coming off the end of the Head line in

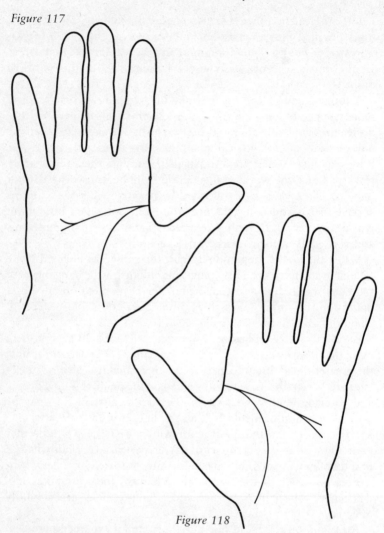

Figure 117

Figure 118

the direction of the Mercury finger (see Figure 117) seems to indicate acute awareness of what money will actually buy.

A forked ending to the Head line has come to be known as the 'writer's fork'. The upper branch remains in the more material, practical zone of the palm, and is usually horizontal, while the lower branch is rooted in Luna, the area related to inspiration and imagination (see Figure 118). The result is often a commercially successful melding of a creative talent – not necessarily concerning the written word – with good business instincts. The subject may be drawn to portrait painting, acting, or producing wickerwork furniture or soft toys. But, whatever it is, there must be a practical, useful end to his labours. Tradition has it that, when one fork extends to the extreme edge of the palm, whatever the individual's occupation, word of it will sooner or later be noised abroad. Apart from the unconscious mind, Luna also represents water and the oceans of the physical world.

If the two branches diverge at an extreme angle – between sixty and ninety degrees – the subject may have great difficulty when it comes to reconciling the two opposing sides of his nature and the result is often a wearing, and unremitting, internal war of nerves.

A three-pronged fork is rarely found. It is thought to denote extraordinary mental abilities, and success is based on an unbeatable combination of business acumen (the fork to Mercury), an unyielding, dogged determination (the fork to Upper Mars) and inspiration (the Luna fork). Barbara Cartland has it (see Figure 119).

A very good example of this tridentine formation can be seen in Chapter 11 of *Your Hand and Career*.

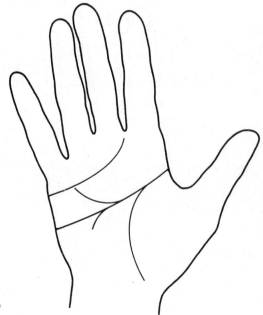

Figure 119

THE DOUBLE HEAD LINE

I have several examples of doubling of the Head line in my collection, yet it is a feature that is seldom if ever mentioned in contemporary books on palmistry. Cheiro was proud that his own hands displayed this phenomenon and he does not fail to refer to it often in his many works (see Figure 120). The following is a typical description:

A double line of Head is very rarely found, but when found it is a sure sign of brain power and mentality. Such people have a perfectly double nature – one side sensitive and gentle, the other confident, cold and cruel. They have enormous versatility, great command of language, a peculiar power for playing and toying with human nature, and generally great will and determination.[42]

There is no doubt that a double Head line indicates a duality of nature and a gift for seeing both sides of any argument, but when found in an otherwise negative hand the individual ums and aahs, dithers and shilly-shallies when it comes to making a definite decision. Friends and relatives are constantly bemused by his ability to convince both them and apparently himself of the benefits of a

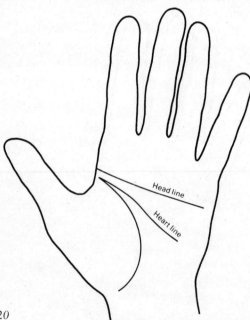

Figure 120

particular option, only to change his mind minutes later. The only successful way to interpret the double Head line is to assess each line according to its individual merits, and then incorporate the information gained into the composite whole.

MEASURING TIME ON THE HEAD LINE

There have been many ingenious schemes put forward for accurately measuring time on the Head line. I have tried most of them without success. In my opinion, there is no effective means of measuring time on this line.

The Heart line

Some palmists refer to the Heart line only as a guide to the subject's emotional and romantic make-up. Others see the state of the physical organ reflected in the line, and yet others decree that that part of the line between Apollo and the percussion stands for the heart, while the remainder of the line on the thumb side of the hand relates to the affections.

In my own experience, it is the direction and length of the line that relate to the individual's sexual and emotional disposition, while the actual quality of the line tells of the strength and general condition of the physical pump. It is important to point out at this stage that, if the subjective hand suggests a weakness and the objective hand is clear and unblemished, your subject can be reassured that, though there may be a well-documented family history of heart disease, he or she is unlikely to suffer in this way. Provided a reasonable amount of care is taken of the body, the threat will remain just a threat. If care is not taken, however, the inherited tendency could raise its ugly head and strike. Even if both hands show early signs of ill-health, it is still not too late to initiate a regime of positive health, thereby reversing the trend.

POINT OF COMMENCEMENT

Although we are in the habit of talking as though the Heart line started at one end of life and ended at the other, there is no real reason for this. It is quite impossible to read time on the line of Heart, and one part, as far as is known, does not develop in advance of the other. However, the convention is a useful one for reference and identification, so, for our purposes, the line 'starts' under the first or second finger, or more rarely, under the third.

When the Heart line commences under the index finger, and curves gently downwards towards the percussion (see (a) Figure 121), the emphasis is feminine and romantic. This type of line is not exclusively found in the hands of women, and in a masculine palm is a strong indication of emotional vulnerability. Because of this, he may overcompensate and appear to be hard and ruthless, but watch him on flag days and during films like *Love Story*. He is a push-over for a hard-luck story, too.

The line starting under the first finger absorbs from Jupiter pride, self-awareness and a sense of honour and fair play. When it also lies low on the hand (see (b) Figure 121), there will be a streak of idealism in the subject. Unfortunately, this causes him to place his loved ones on an impossibly high pedestal. He expects too much and is always disappointed.

When the long Heart line is set higher on the palm, the effect is somewhat reduced, and common sense may prevail occasionally. Nevertheless, many of my clients with lines starting under the Jupiter finger have marital problems stemming from their extreme sensitivity.

In the female's hand, this type of Heart line can result in its owner being unable to face reality and she may compensate by taking refuge in dreams. A case in point was a woman who admitted that the love of her life was a Catholic priest who was not even aware of her existence. And that, of course, was the way she wanted it. She had no desire for a flesh-and-blood relationship and would have been appalled at the very thought of transforming her dream into reality.

A line starting from a point between Jupiter and Saturn, or directly under the Saturn finger (see Figure 122), curving sharply downwards before levelling off towards the percussion, is classed as masculine, dominant and demanding. The owner of this line, whether male or female, is an out-and-out sensualist, and gratification of his or her physical needs does not necessarily require emotional involvement.

When such a line appears in a hand that is also broad and capable, the individual will not take offence when the subject of sexuality is broached. Many women with this form of line have latent or fulfilled homosexual tendencies, and some find it refreshing to be able for once to speak openly about themselves.

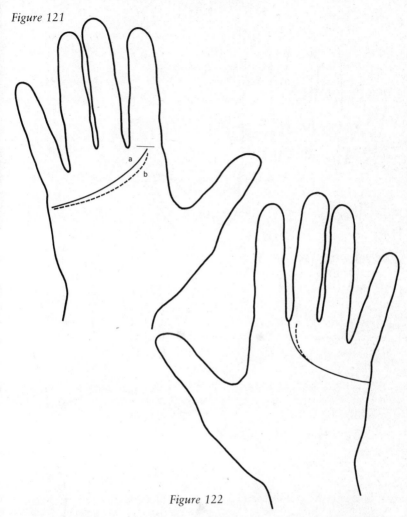

Figure 121

Figure 122

The 'masculine' Heart line always means bluntness and directness, unlike the long, emotional one whose owner would die at the very thought of unconventional sexual activity, let alone indulge in free and open discussion of the matter. If a man with this type of line is foolish enough to marry or get involved with a woman possessing a long Heart line, both parties will regret it. The wife will suffer agonies as a result of her husband's constant betrayals. Yet, to him, they have no deep significance. In his own eyes, provided he is not

Figure 123

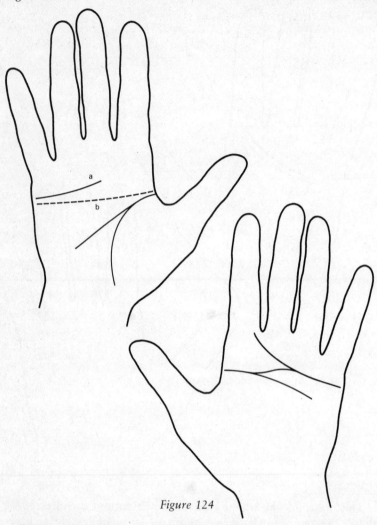

Figure 124

tempted to leave home for good, he remains faithful and true. A more basic problem arises from the couple's totally opposed attitudes to sex. To respond at all, she must be treated like a piece of Dresden china – reverently and gently. He has no time for such finesse, and the rift between them can only become wider with time.

A very short Heart line, lying high up the palm (see (a) Figure 123) is representative of a nature that is nothing less than amoral. The only acceptable course is the expedient one, and loyalties, morals and other niceties are expendable. His own needs and desires are all that count where this type is concerned and, if he has to take what he wants from someone else, he does not give it a thought.

A short, low-lying line presupposes a certain amount of difficulty, for the individual's instincts and moral code are constantly at odds. His ambivalence lies in his desire to 'have a girl in every port', while the pangs of a guilty conscience would never allow him to even behave flirtatiously if he thought it would hurt a more permanent relationship.

A line that cuts directly across the hand from one side to the other (see (b) Figure 123) gives the individual a great sense of purpose in life. Though not to be confused with the Simian line referred to earlier, there is similar intensity here, and all projects are attacked with tremendous zeal. If his interests lie in community service, as they very well might, a family crisis could put a strain on loyalties and emotions. The rest of the hand will tell whether he is capable of fulfilling both demands.

An interest involving head and heart simultaneously may give rise to an Intensity line linking the two major lines together (see Figure 124). 'Head over heels in love' describes the feeling when it applies to another human being, but passionate commitment to one's work or to an all-absorbing hobby may have the same effect.

A branch linking Head and Heart lines below the Jupiter finger suggests that the subject will not rest until he is happy and contented at home and at work (see Figure 125). The majority of people are satisfied merely to have a job at all, and fulfilment is a bonus. To this type, it is essential, and his mental and physical well-being suffer when it is lacking. The upper prong of the fork represents the need for a warmly loving, totally trustworthy mate, and the lower his demand for job satisfaction.

Any differences between the two hands should be carefully noted. For example, a long Heart line in the subjective hand and a shorter one in the objective, implies that hard experience has taught the subject to avoid hurt by making a conscious effort to hide his innate sensitivity. His outwardly cynical and worldly attitude successfully fools all except those he allows to become his intimates.

THE QUALITY OF THE HEART LINE

The Heart line should be fine and clearly marked throughout its length, without islands, chaining, breaks or lines cutting through it. Thickening of the line may be a warning of a high cholesterol level

Figure 125

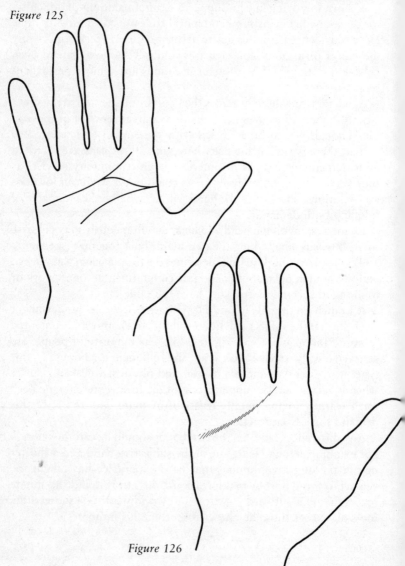

Figure 126

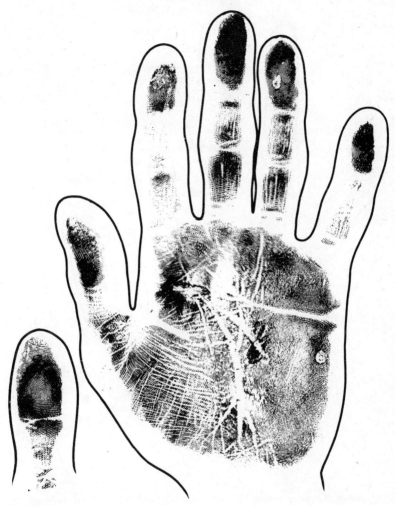

Print 8

and its attendant dangers. Nutritional guidance can be of value here and the sooner it is sought the better (see Print 8).

Fraying of the line (see Figure 126) is characteristic of nervous heart action. It is often the result of unremitting stress over a prolonged period. Yoga or transcendental meditation have helped many to cope with the accelerating demands of everyday life, efficiently and without flagging.

Figure 127

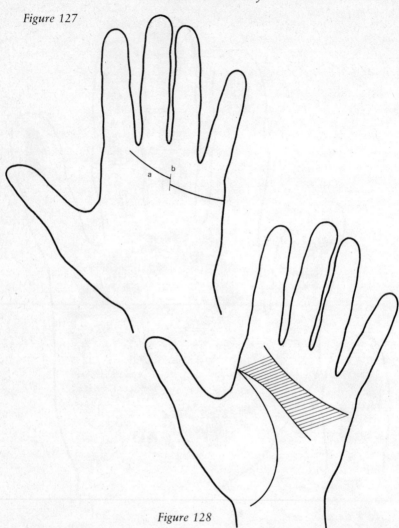

Figure 128

A split in the Heart line in both hands can signal a more serious heart condition (see (a) Figure 127). If there is a bridging line (see (b) Figure 127), the condition will not be fatal, but the warning should be heeded. As soon as corrective treatment is begun, and the heart well on its way to being restored to health, the bridge will start to form.

If the lines are pale, and the palms themselves are colourless, iron deficiency may be a problem, causing dizzy spells and a thumping heart. Ask a doctor to arrange a blood test, or consult your naturopath or homeopathic practitioner, but do not dose yourself with iron supplements – it could make matters worse! Not all anaemia is directly attributable to a lack of dietary iron; sometimes it is the result of inefficient metabolism.

A blue tinge to the line indicates circulatory difficulties, in which case the nails too will have a bluish look about them and the line will also be unhealthily broad. Once again, dietary faults and omissions may be to blame.

Man is what he eats, and the moral is clear. Respect your body as you do any machine. A car, a washing machine, a television set all need regular servicing if they are to serve you well. Why expect to treat the human body any differently?

The Quadrangle

Another area of the hand that was given particular significance by traditional palmists was the Quadrangle, or space between the Head and Heart lines (see Figure 128). Ideally, this formation should be evenly spaced and, of course, clearly marked. Narrowing of the area at any point suggests an equivalent narrow-mindedness. If the Quadrangle is narrow throughout its length, the subject is introspective and almost totally concerned with self. His attitudes are strongly individualistic and he is more likely to influence than be influenced by others. In matters such as religion, he is naturally bigoted.

Widely spaced Head and Heart lines indicate an outward-going, confident, generous and sympathetic type with a live-and-let-live philosophy. This feature is usually found in broad, capable hands softened by the addition of some conic features.

When the Quadrangle narrows or broadens under a specific finger, the above guidelines should be modified according to the significance of the nearest mount.

12

Fate, Sun and Mercury Lines

Any or all of these lines may be missing from a subject's hands, though this is unlikely, except in the most basic types.

The Fate line

The Fate line can start from a number of points on the palm, and may be short or long, well marked or fragmented, double, single or broken – all of which help to make it one of the most confusing and difficult lines to identify in the hand.

It may start from the mount of Neptune, from the Luna mount, from a point on the Venus mount, on, above or below the Head line – or even, if creativity has been submerged till late in life, on the Life line (see (6) Figure 101). The one common factor in each case is the direction of the line. Whether or not it actually completes its journey, its destination is the mount of Saturn.

The shape and form of the Fate line, wherever it appears in the hand, reflects a determination to realize a certain hope or dream, and to devote oneself absolutely to the desired end. If the line fades out later on, look for a change of emphasis and objective.

A firm, straight line marching up the hand uninterrupted from the mount of Neptune to the Saturn mount is unusual. The appearance of such a line signifies that the individual has always known what he wanted to do in life; it is often found in the hands of doctors and nurses, policemen and soldiers (see (a) Figure 129).

Like a man who buys a ticket in advance for a one-way journey on a non-stop, long-distance train, the danger here is that, if he changes his mind, it's often too late to get off! He may then be forced into a narrow, severely limiting rut which he soon learns to hate, but which he is forced to follow, in the manner of a bullock on a treadmill, for the rest of his days.

More frequently, the Fate line is broken and split (see (b) Figure 129) into a series of overlapping fragments. The suggestion here is that, when the individual starts to become bored or frustrated with the daily grind, he decides to do something about it. He is not irresponsible or impetuous in his moves, however, and may even take a course of higher education to achieve the desired results. The length of the overlap often reveals the length of time he has been mulling over the possibility of a move – and weighing up all the pros and cons. If he changes his mind and decides to stay put, the line will consolidate and the overlapping portion fade away.

An uneven line, deep in places and fainter in others, tells a similar story. In the first instance effort or interest flags from time to time, and then the subject reverts to renewed struggles to succeed. In the second, intensity of effort is followed by a complete lack of interest;

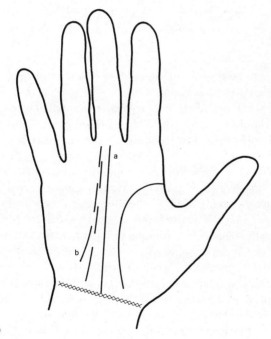

Figure 129

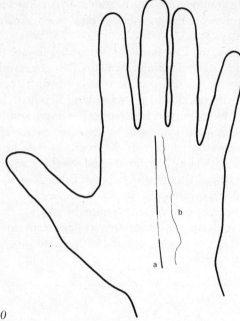

Figure 130

interest may be sparked off again later by the same or a completely different goal (see (a) Figure 130).

A wavy, indistinct Fate line suggests an individual who is unable to work without motivation; he is like a reed blowing in the wind when it comes to having, and standing up for, his own beliefs (see (b) Figure 130).

When this line starts from the mount of Venus, or from a point on the Life line (see (a) Figure 131), family commitments have been important, especially during the early years. This is likely to appear on the hand of a son whose father wanted his children to follow him into the family business, without a thought to their own needs. If the Fate line continues strongly without let or hindrance, the father may have achieved his aim. If, however, it collides with another, sturdier Fate line (see (b) Figure 131) and stops, an inner struggle will have been resolved that puts paid to the father's selfish hopes and dreams.

A line commencing on the mount of Luna (see (a) Figure 132) suggests a persistent desire for public recognition. This may be satisfied by taking up a career in entertainment, or working directly with or for the public. Being in the public eye and appreciated by those who do not know them personally seems to be essential for the self-esteem of such subjects.

Occasionally, a line will be found between the Fate line and the Life line (see (b) Figure 132). This intruder has been called the 'Line of Milieu' and means that its owner will be thwarted in all his aims and ambitions during the period of its influence. He may be

Figure 131

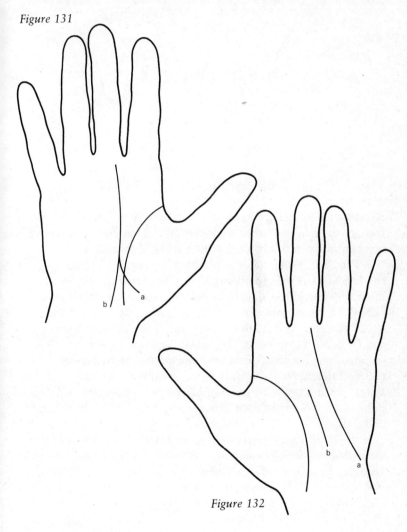

Figure 132

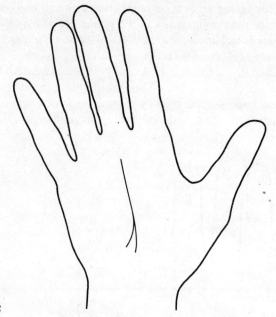

Figure 133

restrained by ill-health, financial restrictions or whatever but, when the Line of Milieu vanishes, so do the limitations, and there is often a compensatory and highly successful surge forward.

A Fate line is sometimes joined by a shorter line driving up from the direction of Luna (see Figure 133). Like that attaching itself to the inner Life line, this is known as an Influence line. Here, it need not • necessarily be an influence that engages the affections; if the individual is fortunate enough to have a stable and contented marriage, the influence is probably connected with his career, or even an all-absorbing hobby. Taking on a new partner, moving into a completely different field of work, or being inspired by an author or artist to see life and one's purpose on earth from a completely different point of view – any of these influences can radically affect attitudes and outlook.

If the main Fate line seems to have been reinforced and strengthened after the junction, the influence is a fortunate one. If it becomes weak and indistinct, a new partnership should be avoided, if at all possible. Forewarned is forearmed, and no good is likely to come of it.

Should the main Fate line grow another shoot that branches off towards Apollo immediately after the junction, the new partnership, liaison or friendship will be happy and successful. A branch in the direction of Mercury is a strong indication that the influence is favourably connected with business or scientific interests.

If the Influence line crosses, rather than joins, the Fate line, its effect can be expected to be transient and of little importance (see (a) Figure 134).

A Fate line that stops dead when it meets the Head line (see (b) Figure 134) suggests a sudden and dramatic ending to the subject's previous way of working. Other signs in the hand will tell you if he has won the pools and retired early to a life of leisure, or made a rash, spur-of-the moment decision to resign. If another Fate line takes over almost immediately, provided the new line is more robust than the old one, the move will be for the best.

If the Fate line terminates on the Heart line, the subject is unlikely to leave his employment before he has claimed his long-service

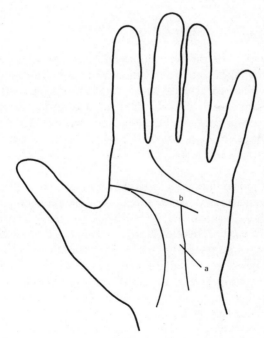

Figure 134

award. A new and vigorous line beginning after this point could indicate a fresh start, furthering a long cherished dream (see Figure 135).

A budding executive, apart from having a long Jupiter finger, may exhibit a Fate line that either veers in the direction of the Jupiter mount or sends an offshoot in that direction. Ambition, pride and a desire to promote himself as the best man for the job come naturally to him (see (a) Figure 136).

A Fate line that is doubled throughout its length implies two careers running simultaneously. It could be a feature in the hand of a housewife coping with a business of her own, or a champion jockey who is equally interested in a career as a novelist or farmer.

A number of short Fate lines bunched together (see (b) Figure 136) shows a diversity of interests. If all stand out with equal clarity, there is the danger of the individual over-extending himself and having too many irons in the fire. Far better to concentrate on perfecting one than gaining mediocre results, or worse, from them all.

The Sun line

Some palmists see the line of the Sun (or Apollo) as a channel provided to make creative expression easier and more fluent. Others equate it with physical well-being and a vigorous constitution. In my view, it expresses the individual's conviction, or lack of it, that his wants, whatever they may be, are being met. His sights may have been set on wealth, fame or prestige. Whatever the prize, the degree to which he feels he has succeeded is shown in this line (see (5) Figure 101).

A fledgeling millionaire may have no Sun line if he is plagued with financial insecurity. Years of struggling and making do have effects that are not wiped away overnight, and he may never be comfortable with his riches. In a man to whom personal fulfilment and public recognition are important, as they were to the late Bing Crosby, Sun lines need not relate to the acquisition of wealth at all. To Crosby, money was a fringe benefit of the main task of pleasing his fans. His first Sun line emerged at the age of thirty-eight, and was closely connected to a Fate line.

A hand that is devoid of Sun lines is certainly no indication that an individual is doomed to be unhappy and poverty-stricken, as has

Figure 135

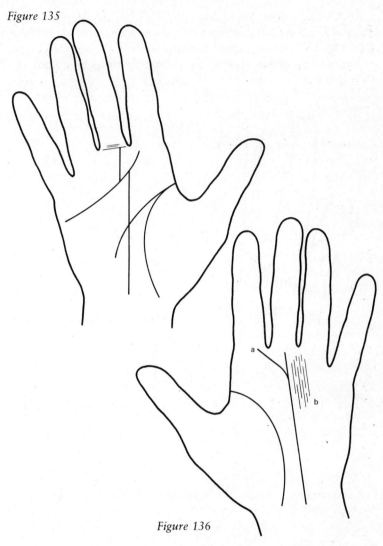

Figure 136

sometimes been suggested. For the vast majority, fulfilment and making good are judged in terms of financial reward, and a dearth of Sun lines could mean: (a) that salary goes out almost as fast as it comes in; (b) the individual is indeed poverty stricken; or (c) that he is a carping, niggardly type who is never happy, whatever the situation.

The Sun line is seldom seen below the Heart line. When it is (see Figure 137), it is probable that a long-desired ambition has not been realized until after the subject's middle years. If the line rises on the Mercury or percussion side of the palm, then turns in towards the mount of Apollo, satisfying work with, or for, the public is a distinct

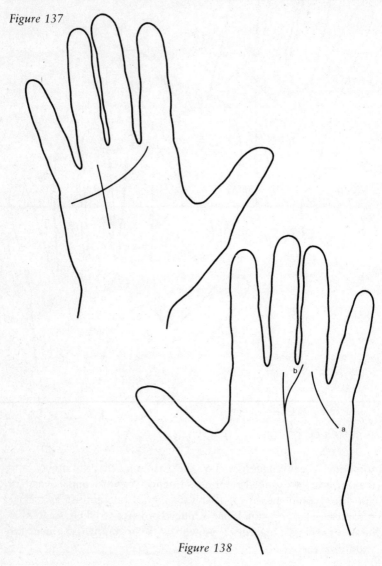

Figure 137

Figure 138

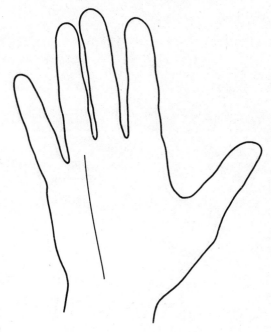

Figure 139

possibility bringing with it kudos and prestige (see (a) Figure 138). If it comes in from the Saturn mount (see (b) Figure 138) his sense of achievement comes from a job done well, thoroughly and painstakingly. To gain satisfaction at all, he must work hard.

It has been suggested that, to be meaningful, the Sun line should start at the wrist and finish at the apex of the Apollo mount (see Figure 139). I have never seen this and do not expect to, though I have read the hands of many successful individuals. Such a man would be fortunate indeed, 'for happiness shall follow him all his days and he shall dwell in plenitude for ever'.

The next best thing would, of course, be to have a guaranteed, underwritten hedge against inflation! Traditionally, three lines above the Heart line (see Figure 140) do just that. No matter how close the workhouse looms, or how near the coffers come to being empty, the gods relent – albeit at the very last second.

It is impossible to be either objective or specific when assessing Sun lines. Remember always that they may represent material well-being

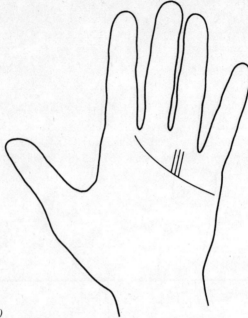

Figure 140

in one case, and spiritual fulfilment in another, depending on the basic make-up of the individual. In an artistic hand, the Sun line may stand for admiration and acclaim. The rest of the hand will show what the underlying needs are in any particular instance.

The Mercury line

Minor lines appearing on, or in the region of, the mount of Mercury, or terminating in that area, have been and still are the subject of controversy and heated argument. Many and varied are the names and associations given these lines – Health, Liver, Hepatica, Business and Intuition being the most popular (see (4) Figure 101).

A good deal of research needs to be carried out before the definitive meaning of the Mercury line is brought to light. In my view, there are only two certainties about this mystery line: that it directs itself towards the Mercury mount (it makes no difference where from, or even that it does not always complete the journey), and that it is connected very definitely with the unconscious mind. Here I agree with Beryl Hutchinson when she says:

Remembering that any engraving on the percussion must be some awareness of knowledge that is in the mind from the instinctive nervous system, there seems little point in an argument about names.[43]

In my experience, the point of origin is the significant thing about the Mercury line. A line forking away from the Fate line (see Figure 141) suggests that the subject has a career or business whose prosperity and success depend heavily on insight and inspiration. Most businessmen of my acquaintance vehemently deny the suggestion, but the fact remains that decisions are made not so much on facts, figures and sales-graphs, but at the urging of that 'still, small voice within'. The stronger the Mercury line, the greater the reliance on this subconscious ability.

The line generally known as the Intuition line is a Mercury line starting from the Luna area, and curving up and round the mount of

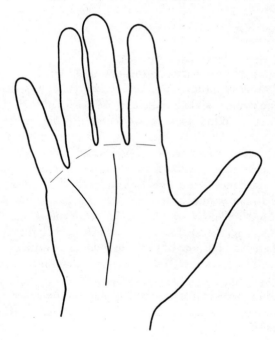

Figure 141

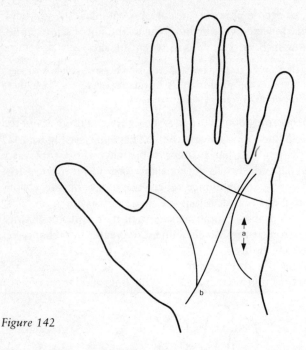

Figure 142

Upper Mars to terminate near the mount of Mercury (see (a) Figure 142). Powers of intuition and manifestations of a 'sixth sense' are heightened when this line emerges from deep within the boundaries of the Luna mount. This, as we learnt in Chapter 7, stands for imagination and psychic awareness, and seems to lend the line of Intuition additional impetus and power. It is a line that is frequently seen in the hands of mediums, psychics, psychometrists and dowsers – and in the hands of those doctors, nurses and charity workers who are said to be 'born to it'.

If a Mercury line starts its journey from the Venus mount and appears stronger than the Life line it leaves behind (see (b) Figure 142), there may be a threat to the individual's health at that time. I have noted that, when the Life line continues weakly or stops where the Mercury line cuts it, there may be the threat of terminal illness.

If the lines are equal in strength, or Mercury is weaker than the line of Life, the danger can be averted. A weakened constitution has sometimes been known to take on a new lease of life after the junction of these two lines.

Mercury lines may be clean and clear, islanded, chained or broken. Some remain low on the palm and never actually reach the base of the mount for which they are named. With this particular line, there is an imponderable factor, a missing piece of the jigsaw, that upsets and makes nonsense of many of the unequivocal definitions ascribed to it.

I have seen long islands on the Mercury line that, according to most reference books, are sure indications of ill-health, yet their owners have never suffered a day's real illness. Firm, confident lines – normally looked upon as auguring good health – have been found in the hands of those whose lives have been blighted by the effects of a 'delicate' constitution.

It is a line that is wide open for investigation and scientific research. So far, the surface has barely been scratched and much work has to be done before its true significance comes to light.

——— *Measuring time on the lines* ———

Since the Fate line represents one's life work or mundane preoccupation, it is logical to assume that it will not show quite as many years as the Life line does. By its very nature, in many hands the Fate line is broken, or grows branches, islands or reassuring squares. Timing on this line, therefore, cannot be relied upon and, if the Life line indicates the age of thirty-eight as being important and the Fate line suggests thirty-four, I would be more inclined to trust the former.

To measure both Fate and Sun lines, divide the palm into eight equal portions, as we did in Chapter 8 (see Figure 57). Reading from the base of the hand, up to the fingers, each portion stands for one ten-year period.

Many ingenious methods have been devised to ensure that time is accurately assessed on the other lines in the hand. To date, unfortunately, none has been very successful, making this yet another area of palmistry that would benefit from a programme of research.

13

Minor Lines and Signs

The 'minor' lines and signs are so called not because they are any less relevant than the 'major' lines, but because they appear less often. They are not standard, and are important for that very reason. They individualize the personality and add precision to an analysis.

The Girdle of Venus

The Girdle of Venus is found in the emotional zone of the hand, between the finger bases and the Heart line (see (a) Figure 143). It may be fragmented or, more rarely, appear as a single unbroken line, and it bridges the gap between the conscious and unconscious areas of the hand as represented in Figure 95 (Chapter 9).

Anyone with a completed Girdle of Venus would be useless as a doctor or nurse. Instead of getting on with the job of healing the sick, he would be inclined to suffer along with his patients, for all incoming impressions are personalized. Sympathy becomes empathy and two people suffer instead of one, for such a subject cannot help taking on every passing problem and hurt, and making them his own. Let a passer-by or acquaintance happen to glance in his direction while conducting an innocent conversation, and he immediately concludes that the discussion is about him. No matter that the parties concerned were merely admiring the dahlias behind him – he would never be convinced.

If the line strikes downwards, crossing the palm to join forces with a relationship line (see (b) Figure 143), these nagging doubts and feelings of insecurity will eventually sour the most promising friendship. Personal relationships are always a problem, for this type invariably interprets a headache as an excuse. Even if his partner is genuinely under the weather, he imagines he has offended her in some way and she is sulking – or worse.

With a broken line, the effect is somewhat dissipated and common sense occasionally prevails. Nevertheless, there is always the danger that:

Such a one will suffer from any slight or inattention, will be easily depressed, and in the world of today, when even people with the best intentions have not time to humour the eccentricities of nervous humanity, he will soon come to think that he has no place in the world, and that no one cares for him.[44]

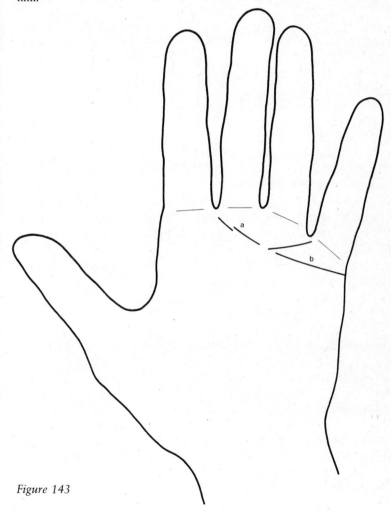

Figure 143

The Ring of Solomon

This is a semi-circular formation round the mount of Jupiter and rising between the Jupiter and Saturn fingers (see (a) Figure 144). As its name suggests, it is a line that, traditionally, was thought to bestow wisdom on its owner. It is rarely found as a fully completed ring, being more often made up of two or more curving lines.

Both Cheiro and Benham saw it as indicating a deep interest in the

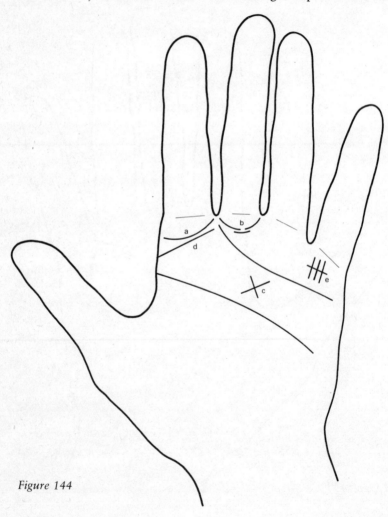

Figure 144

occult, sometimes leading to the subject becoming a master or adept of the magical arts. Clients of mine who had this feature certainly admitted to a great interest in the supernatural and in psychic phenomena, but none admitted to having a degree from an 'occult university'!

Other signs in the hand should be checked to see if there is any latent ability in the occult field. Every course of study needs intelligence, perseverance and self-discipline, and the occult is no exception.

The Ring of Saturn

A completed Ring of Saturn is even more uncommon than the Ring of Solomon. Whether completed or made up of two or more lines, it encircles the mount of Saturn (see (b) Figure 144) and seems to isolate and over-emphasize the negative Saturnian qualities, leaving its owner sober and morose.

It may be a temporary manifestation following a deep personal tragedy that has thrown the subject in on himself. When, or if, he recovers his equilibrium and his outlook becomes once more outgoing and social, the line should disappear.

Cheiro regarded it as 'the most unfortunate mark ever to find' and baldly states that he had never 'come across any person with this mark who succeeded in life or was able to carry any one of his plans to a successful termination'.[45]

Our approach nowadays is a more positive one. For every failing shown in the hand there is always an equivalent strength. It is the task of the hand analyst to point to the ways in which his client can overcome his weaknesses, and not be overcome by them.

The Mystic Cross

This is a cross found in the Quadrangle, or narrow area between Head and Heart lines (see (c) Figure 144). It is usually encountered on the upper reaches of the Plain of Mars, and only occasionally to one side or other of the Quadrangle.

There are often crossing lines in this area, but the true Mystic Cross is always separately marked. It should not be confused with a Fate line or part of one.

Once again, there is an interest in the occult, which may be the result of discovering a psychic gift. Indeed, the individual should be naturally talented as a clairvoyant or spiritual medium. Sixth sense, highly developed intuition, or feelings that consistently prove to have been correct after the event, often signal early development of such talents. When a Mystic Cross is found in close proximity to a Fate line, or near the Saturn mount, study of the occult may become a major preoccupation, even an obsession.

Sympathy lines

A Sympathy line follows the same general direction as the Ring of Solomon, but it is not curved and lies diagonally across the mount of Jupiter (see (d) Figure 144). In my view, this straight line reliably indicates a sympathetic, wise and universally applied understanding of one's fellow men. I have noted it in the hands of nurses, doctors and those who are inspired with a desire to alleviate suffering.

Healing or Medical stigmata

Another feature that frequently appears in the hands of the healer, both orthodox and non-orthodox, is the Healing stigmata. This is formed from no fewer than three small vertical lines, linked by a crossing line, and is found on the Mercury mount (see (e) Figure 144).

A modification of the stigmata is to be found on the palms of those who mistakenly allow their partners and families to 'put upon' them. The cross-bar is usually missing, along with the sense of proportion that would allow them to see that no useful purpose is served by their becoming a doormat. Both marks, nevertheless, have the same basic meaning. An individual possessing one always wants to help and has a genuinely generous spirit.

Relationship lines

Apart from the Head, Heart and Life lines, this must be one of the most well-known features in the hand. The line, or lines, will be found coming in from the outer edge of the palm, under the Mercury finger (see (a) Figure 145). They are also known as lines of Marriage or Affection and are connected with the individual's capacity for giving and receiving affection.

A Relationship line may or may not refer to husband, wife or lover. To my certain knowledge, it has, in at least one case, indicated a lonely lady's fondness for a beloved pet.

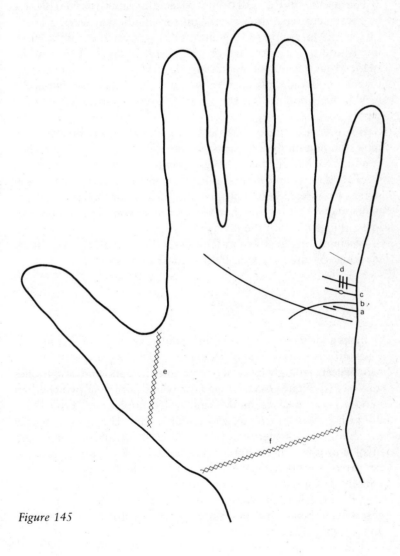

Figure 145

It is not possible, as I know to my cost, to rely on these lines alone as predicting marriage or the start of a long-term relationship. In several instances, I have mistaken a later line for the start of a new affair, only to be told, in no uncertain terms, that there was never anyone else in the world for that particular lady but her partner. What the second line represented, in fact, was a rekindling of affection resulting in a sort of second honeymoon!

The lines should be read from the Heart line upwards, and divorce or permanent separation is thought to be indicated when a line is broken (see (a) Figure 145). A line dropping down towards the Heart line is said to suggest a bad marriage (see (b) Figure 145), and an islanded line a period of separation (see (c) Figure 145). Lines cutting through symbolize a sudden ending of the marriage or affair and a fork' at the end of the line suggests that the two parties will go their separate ways.

However, experience has taught me not to place too literal an interpretation on these endings, for often the individuals concerned continue to live together. Though there may be no marriage in real terms, and the couple may be united only in the sense that they live in the same house, there is tacit agreement that, as long as the cracks are papered over, all is well – but heaven help anyone who attempts to bring things out into the open!

When looking at Relationship lines, take account also of critical markings on the Life, Sun, Health and Fate lines.

Children lines

In times gone by, reading these lines was regarded as an easy matter. Lines dropping down on to a Relationship line represent children – broad, deep, strongly marked ones meant boys, and fine, fragile ones girls (see (d) Figure 145). Nowadays, when more than two children may be a great financial burden, and birth control is the accepted rule, it is rather more difficult to read Children lines. They may appear in the hands of a spinster teacher and stand for her dedication to and involvement with her pupils. In the hands of a woman dedicated to her career, they may indicate the number of children she could have conceived had she not been on the Pill.

In my experience, these lines are accurate in about 50 per cent of cases. Even then, a fine line may represent a sensitive or sickly boy, and a strong one a tomboyish girl.

The Family Ring

While not usually a line in the true sense of the word, the Family Ring continues the theme set by the previous lines. It separates the mount of Venus and the second phalange of the thumb (see (e) Figure 145). There may be one or several – or one main one and two or three incomplete lines. A chained formation is quite normal and ties in well with the general theory that chains and islands mark periods of difficulty and emotional tension. As any parent will tell you, raising a family is no easy task!

A strong, emphatic line, particularly when it encircles the thumb, shows deep family commitments. An uncompleted arc suggests an unsuccessful alliance or an unfulfilled desire to have children. If family ties are of no great importance, the line may be hardly visible.

The rascettes

Like the Family Ring, the rascettes, or bracelets as they are some-times called, do not normally take the form of straight, clear lines but appear as criss-cross patterns (see (f) Figure 145). They are rarely consulted by contemporary palmists, and even Cheiro was rather scathing when discussing their importance. The rascettes were

. . . called by the Greeks the Bracelets of Health, Wealth and Happiness [but] experience in life does not give much hope that these three much sought-after possessions can ever be found together on this side of the grave.[46]

Strangely enough, another finding of the Ancient Greeks is currently being confirmed by the new science of dermatoglyphics – biological research based on signs in the hands and feet (see Chapter 14). If the Ancient Greek priests found the first rascette arching up on to the base of the palm itself, a woman was not allowed to marry but was made a vestal virgin at the temple instead. The arch was thought to indicate 'some internal malformation that would prevent her bring-ing children into the world'. Cheiro goes on to remark:

Perhaps the old Greek Priest was right in his idea, for if this first Bracelet is found rising into the hand in the form of an arch, both men and women possessing it are delicate internally, and especially so in matters relating to sex.[47]

I have noted personally that a split rascette with a sort of prong heading into the area at the very base of Luna (see (a) Figure 146) often accompanies difficulties in conceiving or carrying a baby to full term. Once again, the fault often lies in faulty or inadequate nutrition. When this is rectified and the glandular system restored, the line heals and resumes a more normal course.

Frustration lines

Periods when ambition or desire have been consistently thwarted show up on the fingers and thumbs as crossing lines (see (b) Figure 146). Since very few of us are fortunate enough to be able to have our own way all the time, these are extremely common.

In subjects with the selfish, Egocentric type of hand, frustration results from virtually anything that prevents them from ful!lling their innumerable and – to them – urgent aspirations.

People with the full, soft Sensual type suffer from their own laziness and indolence. Their longings fail to bear fruit for they hate hard work and lack persistence.

Many wives and mothers have great hopes and expectations for their husbands and children. Their frustration may result from being let down when the family insists on 'doing its own thing' (and being a lot happier!), or not living up to the high standards that have been set for them.

Restlessness lines

Another indication that the individual is not 100 per cent happy with the pattern of his life comes in the form of Restlessness lines. These fine lines appear on the percussion edge of the hand (see (c) Figure 146), on the Luna mount.

Restlessness lines go with a love of change and hatred of routine. Consequently, if the Life or Travel lines (see Chapter 11) stretch out towards the mount of Luna, frustration may be assuaged by travelling widely or emigrating.

When the lines cover the percussion side of Luna and Upper Mars from top to bottom, the individual is not likely to settle anywhere for long. Boredom starts to set in and he is frequently found staring

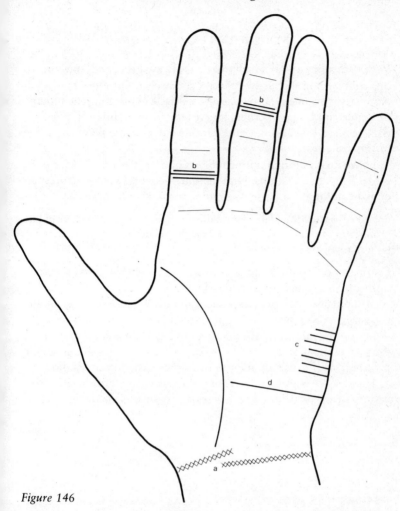

Figure 146

longingly into the far distance, instead of getting on with his work. Challenges are bread and meat to this type and, if he cannot follow his natural inclinations as an explorer and globe-trotter, he is almost as happy travelling on the wings of imagination into uncharted areas and unplumbed depths.

Look at the rest of the hand to discover whether he will make a successful pioneer and pathfinder, inventor or science-fiction writer, or settle for being a mere dreamer.

————— *The Via Lasciva or Poison line* —————

Yet another line about which there has always been, and continues to be, controversy is the so-called Via Lasciva. In some books on palmistry, this line is shown as a semi-circle connecting the mounts of Venus and Luna; in others it takes the form of an ascending line, rising up the Luna mount and slanting towards the percussion (see (d) Figure 146).

I have no doubt that, in the fullness of time, these will prove to be quite distinct formations, with definite meanings. Cheiro states unequivocally that, in its semi-circular form, it indicates:

unbridled sensuality and passion, and where it cuts through the Line of Life it indicates death, but one usually brought about in connection with the licentiousness that it denotes.[48]

Doom, gloom and certain self-destruction were the fate of anyone unfortunate enough to bear this line.

Benham also sees the same effects, but his Via Lasciva 'is generally supposed to occupy a slanting position'.[49] Be that as it may, modern books on the subject see the line as showing an awareness of what, in the way of medicines or foods (or any other substance that might be ingested), will cause an adverse or allergic reaction in the body.

The subject with this line is often hypersensitive to the effects of certain drugs or drinks and has learnt to steer clear of them.

14

Skin-ridge Patterns and Health in the Hands

Palmistry has had a long and chequered history and is still far from respectable. The 'new' science of dermatoglyphics is not a recent innovation at all and it is hardly surprising to learn that it, too, has been fighting for acceptance by the medical profession for many years. The study of the ridged patterns peculiar to human hands and feet dates back at least three hundred years, yet its significance in the measurement and regulation of mental and physical health is only just being acknowledged.

In his book *Mind Map*, Anthony Masters gives an excellent potted history of the science, from the work of Dr Nehemiah Grew, whose findings were published in 1684 in the *Philosophical Transactions of the Royal Society*, to the brilliant work of Sir Francis Galton (1822–1911) which was summarized in his book *Fingerprints*, published in 1892. It is a pity that Mr Masters's book, as a whole, lacks accuracy.

The Czech doctor and scientist, Dr J. E. Purkenje (1787–1869), is credited with originating an objective and well-researched approach to the developing science:

To Dr Purkenje we owe the observation of the spiral sweat glands in the skin, the patterns made by their alignment, the classification of those patterns and his conjectures about their genetic and diagnostic importance.[50]

In England, Noel Jaquin was an early pioneer. His efforts were concentrated on establishing how fingerprints and skin-ridge patterns related to character and to the physiological and psychological condition of the individual. In 1945 he founded the Society for the Study of Physiological Patterns (SSPP). The stated aims of the society were, and are:

[to] further the study of, and research into, the meaning and value of the Physiological Pattern as diagnostic evidence in psychological and pathological connections, [and to] prove and stabilize the scientific importance of those studies.

The society's scope has since broadened to include, amongst other patterns, astrology and graphology, and it is alive and flourishing.

Recent research has proved systematically and conclusively that medical hand analysis deserves all the backing that scientific resources can provide. Unfortunately, the popular and scientific approaches to the subject seem destined to remain at odds, for both the scientific jargon and the abstruse mathematical formulae with which the researcher cloaks his findings are unintelligible to the average layman.

Revolutionary work is currently proceeding in Germany, Switzerland, America and to a lesser extent in the British Isles – handicapped as we are by financial stringencies. It may soon be possible to replace much of the more conventional diagnostic machinery with experts trained to analyse minutely the prints of patients through a high-powered electron microscope.

Dr Alexander Rodewald, another pioneer, working at the University of Munich, reports that he is able to pinpoint a remarkable range of congenital abnormalities with 97 per cent accuracy and predict with 80 per cent accuracy a new-born infant's chances of developing cancer, diabetes, heart diseases, leukaemia or mental illness during his or her lifetime.

In Germany, more and more GPs are able to get in touch with an expert dermatoglyphic technician, for a training programme in Dr Rodewald's methods has been instituted at every major German university. The question is how long will it take for these methods to be adopted world-wide?

Jaquin's description strips away any mystique, and the principles are easy to understand:

From the brain to even the most distant area of the epidermis, as well as to the most deep-seated of the internal organs, there runs an elaborate telegraphic system – the nervous system.

In the hand are millions of nerve endings, or eyes, each nerve fibre ending in some part of the brain. In response to stimuli, the nerve reacts, causing a measurable movement in the nerve endings.

Its position in the hand betrays its type and quality by correspondence with the area of the brain which has been affected [see Chapter 5]. Thus the emotions connected with our amorous impulses are shown in the formation of the Cardiac or Heart lines, while the logical abilities and the degree of will power are indicated by the formation of the Cerebral or Head line.[51]

I have been convinced, through my own limited researches into the hand and health, that it is possible to diagnose with incredible accuracy the current and future fitness and vitality of any individual. And, most important of all, that it is possible to detect abnormalities in time to instigate preventative measures well before symptoms appear in the rest of the body.

Prevention is more efficient than repair, and good health is founded on fulfilment. Wholeness is the well of happiness, and happiness flows from health. Mental and physical well-being are two sides of the same coin, and therefore inseparable.

Biochemistry monitors pathological changes at cell level – the sort of changes that result in the patient 'looking' ill. Complexion, pallor, feverishness, darkness under the eyes, skin temperature and texture are all important indications to the orthodox doctor and helpful to him in his diagnosis. But, if tests are carried out at an early stage, in response to minute alterations and deterioration seen in the skin ridges, there would often be no need for the patient to suffer at all.

The sooner we see Positive Health centres in every neighbourhood, where handprints are taken every few months as a matter of course, the better. One of the first observable signs of ill-health is a disturbance of the endocrine system, reflected in the lines of the hands and in the fingernails.

Sudden violent emotions, such as terror, fear, and anger, stimulate an equally violent response from the ductless glands. Since the alternatives of 'fight or flight' are not always socially acceptable, this response has to be contained. The danger of toxicity is high, especially when it is fashionable to sit in front of a television or cinema screen artificially inducing these emotions night after night:

[It is] logical to assume that a continued state of fear, an apprehensively anxious state of mind, would result in an excessive production of a normally defensive secretion which, if continued over a number of years, would ultimately result in a state of auto-intoxication. An unnatural state of mind will produce an unnatural, which is unhealthy, state of body.[52]

The inevitable consequence of this is to lower the body's powers of resistance to the point where hostile and unfriendly bacteria are welcome to take up residence without being challenged! When this happens, the individual starts to feel below par and, if nothing positive is done, he will go downhill at an ever-increasing rate. The weakest link in the chain will break, and he will suffer a heart attack, kidney failure, a mental breakdown, or whatever.

The endocrine orchestra is also thrown into confusion by an inadequate diet, particularly one lacking in essential vitamins. There is a vital link between vitamins and hormones and, when they are in short supply, hormone secretion decreases in direct proportion to the lack. Unfortunately, allopathic medicine traditionally concentrates its energies on the treatment of symptoms rather than on the identification of underlying causes, and even a thorough grounding in dermatoglyphics would do little to change this emphasis.

How can you judge whether a hand is healthy or not? Take a copy of your handprint and a magnifying glass, and compare it with Print 9. The skin-ridge pattern in Print 9 stands out clearly and sharply, and is easy to see even without the glass. There are no superfluous vertical or horizontal lines and, though there are a few stress lines on the fingers, the owner appears to be a remarkably well balanced and healthy individual.

Life has not been a bed of roses for this woman (see the lines crossing the Life line), but she has the advantage of being a trained dietician and practises what she preaches. The benefits of plenty of fresh fruit and vegetables daily are obvious here. My client was lucky enough to have inherited a good constitution from her forbears, and was wise enough to play squash or tennis daily, which helped to discharge harmlessly much of the tension and worry that beset her. Many are not so fortunate, or so aware.

As we know, the left hand reveals hereditary tendencies. If, therefore, there are any signs of rheumatism, arthritis, thyroid imbalance or any other functional disorder, the individual concerned would be well advised to take particular care. Some of us are born healthy, but most of us could be far healthier than we are right now.

Print 10 shows the hand of a senior nursing officer, a woman suffering under the pressure of responsibility for running six wards in a psychiatric hospital for months on end without a proper break. The skin-ridge patterns are almost indistinguishable, and the fine, cobwebby lines running up the side of the palm, on and over the

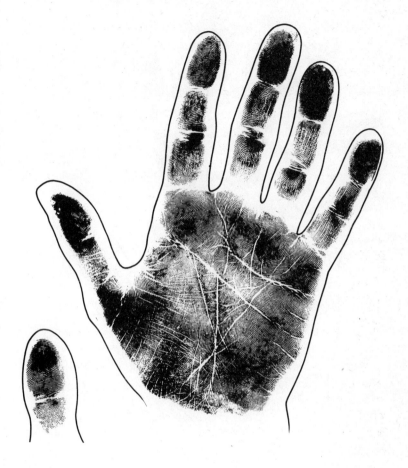

Print 9

mount of Luna, show a build-up of uric acid in the bloodstream. The next stage would have been arthritis and rheumatism – she had already noted the first few twinges – but she took up my recommendation and consulted a nutritionalist and homeopath. When we last spoke, she was feeling much improved and better able to cope with the demands of her work.

Vitamin deficiency and stress both cause body cells to break down, releasing uric acid from their nuclei. Provided the diet supplies

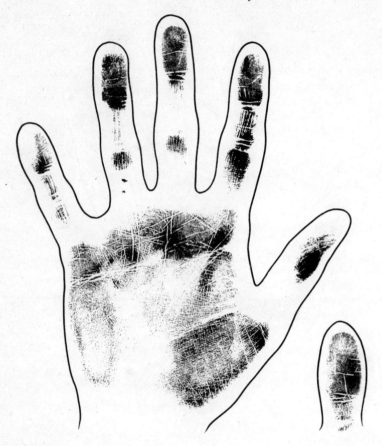

Print 10

enough of the vitamin-B complex, this will be broken down efficiently and excreted in the urine in the normal way. If it does not, or there is a lack of B5, the excess builds up in the bloodstream, and an inexorable chain reaction is set in motion.

In the case of the nursing officer, there were signs of kidney trouble building up. A clearer example of this is shown in Print 11. Note the large phalanx of lines rising towards the Mercury finger. A 'flame' effect like this is often the first sign of damaged kidneys or kidney stones. Once again, precipitated uric acid, combined with calcium and other improperly metabolized acids, was to blame.

In this man's case, over-prescribing of oral antibiotics had destroyed the intestinal bacteria which, in the normal way, 'mop up' much of the body's waste. Unfortunately, antibiotics cannot differentiate between these ecological refuse-collectors and hostile organisms. As a result, uric acid was flooding my client's system, which was already weakened through faulty eating habits, and forming stones.

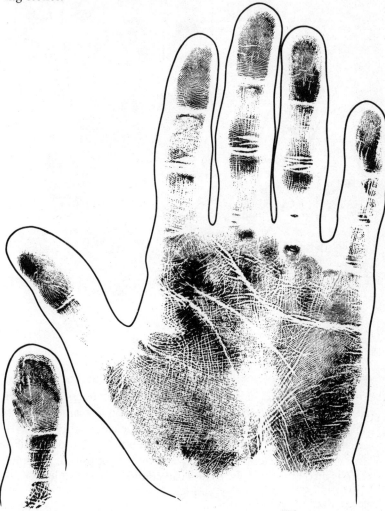

Print 11

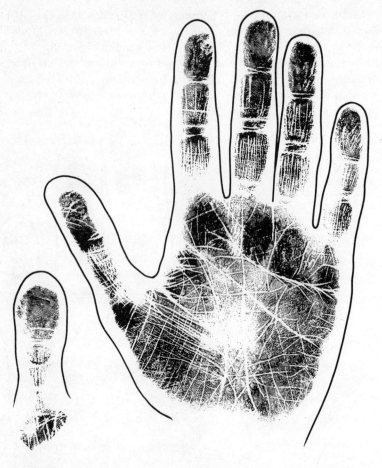

Print 12

Other side effects of indiscriminate prescribing of antibiotics can be constipation, wind, thrush, internal bleeding and other ailments related to B-vitamin deficiency. A few enlightened doctors are advising patients, young and old, to take a couple of tablespoons full of 'live' yoghurt or acidophilus milk with their prescriptions. Intestinal flora is then quickly replaced and can continue its valuable work of synthesizing the B-complex vitamins.

Incidentally, fresh, natural yoghurt is not nearly so unpleasant as it sounds! With a little imagination, it can be transformed into delicious salad dressings and desserts. At present, it can only be found in some delicatessens or your health-food shop. I advise many clients to get into the habit of taking some daily, especially if there are already signs of a family tendency to rheumatism or other uric-acid-induced ills.

Thyroidal imbalance is extremely common, and signs of it can easily be seen in the hand. Print 12 shows the hand of a woman who came to see me in great distress. She had been trying unsuccessfully to lose weight for years and her morale was low. She felt unattractive and depressed and her marriage was suffering. Her doctor had reassured her that her thyroidal imbalance was so slight as to be almost non-existent and that there was nothing he could do 'unless or until it got worse'. He prescribed Valium, which she was reluctant to take.

She had the classic symptoms of an under-active thyroid. Her hands were cold, dry and rough and, apart from her depression, she suffered periods of extreme lethargy. For the hand analyst, the most important clues to under- or over-activity of the thyroid gland are the vertical lines which appear on the tip of the Mercury finger. These will be closely followed by a deterioration in the clarity of the skin-ridge patterning, showing that the other glands are being affected too.

Over-activity of the gland is seen in lines on the Mercury tip, accompanied by warm, unpleasantly moist hands, and perhaps a slight trembling. Hyper-activity and tension are common, and being underweight is more of a problem than obesity.

Print 13 is typical of adrenal over-activity. The skin is dark and sallow, and the palms and skin-ridge patterning are almost obscured by the heavy veiling of superficial lines. This client complained that he was haunted by a continuous fear of impending doom, which caused him to be constantly 'looking over his shoulder'. The reaction was quite illogical and accompanied by insomnia, high blood pressure and palpitations.

Stress turns on the tap, and adrenalin flows into the bloodstream. Constant tension is equivalent to leaving the tap running all the time. Once again, instead of the hormone being used to facilitate fight or flight, as intended by nature, an excess of adrenalin builds up and causes havoc. In this case, the fingertips, too, were veiled, showing that a breakdown in health was imminent. I recommended that he consult an accredited homeopath without further delay. It is not

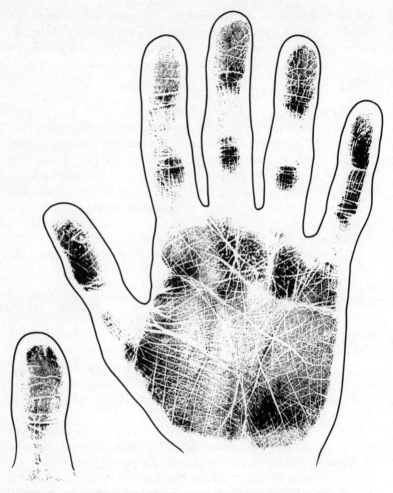

Print 13

generally known that some GPs offer homeopathic treatment on the NHS.

When the base of Luna is disfigured by a host of criss-crossing lines, cystitis or thrush may be a recurring problem. There may be trouble with the bladder, testes, uterus or ovaries, and expert help should be sought to get to the root cause and eliminate it. It is interesting to note that reflexology, or finger acupuncture, treats exactly this area of the hand in cases of genito-urinary ailments.

It has been known for centuries that a simple chemical imbalance can cause depression and personality changes. The ancients extracted curative essences from plant and herb, and minerals from rock and soil and mountain stream. The elements that were effective then are as abundant today, but the knowledge of how to use them has been lost to all but a small minority.

The causes of depression are many and varied. It can be brought on by emotional, psychological or chemical factors, or an interaction between the three. To the trained hand analyst the point of breakdown is clearly visible in a handprint.

Whether it is the depression that causes the imbalance, or the imbalance the depression, the net result is the same. A timely and informed analysis of the sufferer's dietary sins and omissions could be enough to point up a solution. A common error is the lavish and indiscriminate use of salt. Too much sodium in the blood stream causes mental confusion and disorder. It can also result in high blood pressure, heart trouble and a variety of skin disorders.

When we are low and out of sorts, we tend to feel irritable, frustrated and 'weepy', and there is the danger of bursting into tears at the slightest provocation. If our conditioning precludes the luxury of tears, we may perspire profusely. In this way, the body is attempting to rid itself of the sodium that has been allowed to build up, for whatever reason.

Long-term sodium/potassium imbalance shows up in the chaining or islanding of the Head, Heart and Mercury lines already referred to. One answer is to cut back on such foods as salted nuts, crisps, etc., and substitute potassium-rich foods such as almonds, oats, bananas, spinach and fresh fruits and vegetables.

If the deficiency has been a long-term one, even the adoption of a full and varied diet may not be enough, for the stage may have been reached where the body is unable to utilize the mineral it so urgently needs. A plant will only thrive and grow according to the quality of the soil it is rooted in. In the same way, man cannot regenerate or replace dying cells without the appropriate nutritive material, and disease will result.

The process can only be reversed by supplying the necessary mineral, or minerals, in homeopathic potency. The mineral can then enter the cell directly, without having to go through the digestive process in the normal way. It is absorbed into the blood and intercellular fluids through the mouth and oesophagus, immediately

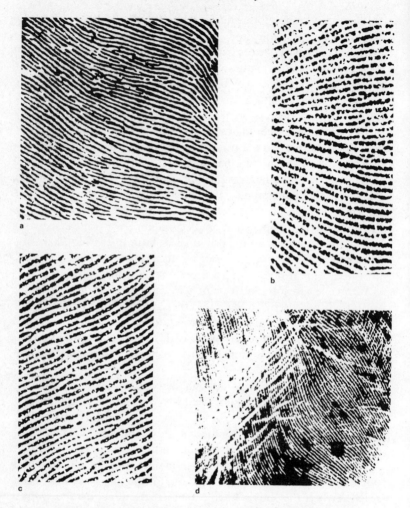

Figure 147a: A healthy hand, showing normal clear ridge lines

   b: Bacterial infection. Imprint of palmar skin, showing the typical malformation of the ridge pattern in the case of an acute bacterial infection of the intestine

   c: Malaria. Imprint of the hand of a man suffering from malaria. Observe the minute white dots in the ridge lines

   d: A number of fine lines running slantwise down the hand indicate gastric disorder and acidity of the digestive tract, generally the result of faulty feeding

restoring equilibrium at molecular level. Illness can be said to have abated when the handprint one again shows clear, unbroken skin-ridge formations.

Urgent research is required to correlate specific indications in the hand with particular mineral deficiencies. Beryl Hutchinson, in *Your Life in Your Hands*, has succeeded in identifying many of these. The relationship of mineral imbalance to disease has already been scientifically and empirically proved, and at least 'fifty ailments are positively related to signs in the hands. Twenty congenital diseases have been correctly pinpointed by palmar abnormalities, and twenty-four disorders can be detected from the fingernails alone.'[53]

Apart from major requirements for calcium, phosphorus, sodium, potassium, sulphur, chlorine and magnesium, optimum vitality depends on minute quantities of at least fourteen, and possibly as many as a hundred, trace elements: when it comes to food, variety isn't the spice of life, it *is* life.

The hand analyst has a duty to use his knowledge to guide and direct those who come to him, but he must also be discreet. Suggestion is a powerful and potent weapon – and double-edged. It can be used for positive or negative ends, and the palmist who voices his client's fears without showing him how to overcome them is guilty of betraying a trust.

If suffering, [whether mental, physical, or spiritual] can be alleviated and understood by so-called unorthodox methods, then those who recognize these truths must struggle for their acceptance.[54]

Appendices

References

1. Christine Smith, *Divination*, Rider (1978).
2. Mir Bashir, *Art of Hand Analysis*, Muller (1973).
3. Cheiro (Count Louis Hamon), *Palmistry for All*, Barrie & Jenkins (1915).
4. Fred Gittings, *Book of Palmistry*, Hamlyn (1974).
5. Comte C. de Saint-Germain, *Practice of Palmistry*, Weiser (New York, 1974).
6. Saint-Germain, *Practice of Palmistry*.
7. William G. Benham, *Laws of Scientific Hand Reading*, Hawthorn (New York, 1946).
8. Noel Jaquin, *The Hand of Man*, Faber (1934).
9. Julius Spier, *The Hands of Children*, Routledge (1955).
10. Stanislas d'Arpentigny, *La Chirognomie* (1839).
11. Cheiro, *Language of the Hand*, Barrie & Jenkins (1975).
12. Cheiro, *Language of the Hand*.
13. Heron Allen, *Science of the Hand* (1886).
14. Alexis Carrel, *Man, the Unknown*, Burns and Oates/A. Clarke Books (1968).
15. Beryl Hutchinson, *Your Life in Your Hands*, Sphere (1977).
16. Cheiro, *Language of the Hand*.
17. Mark Brown, *Left Handed: Right Handed*, David & Charles (1979).
18. Brown, *Left Handed: Right Handed*.
19. Benham, *Laws of Scientific Hand Reading*.
20. Dr F. Wood Jones, *Principles of Anatomy as Seen in the Hand*, Bailliere, Tindall & Cassell (1946).
21. Saint-Germain, *Practice of Palmistry*.
22. Saint-Germain, *Practice of Palmistry*.
23. Cheiro, *Palmistry for All*.
24. D. Robinson, *The Graven Palm*, Edward Arnold (1911).
25. Hutchinson, *Your Life in Your Hands*.
26. Hutchinson, *Your Life in Your Hands*.
27. Benham, *Laws of Scientific Hand Reading*.
28. Noel Jaquin, *Signature of Time*, Faber (1950).

29. Hutchinson, *Your Life in Your Hands*.
30. Jaquin, *Signature of Time*.
31. David Brandon-Jones, *Palmistry of Love*, Arrow (1980).
32. Hutchinson, *Your Life in Your Hands*.
33. Adelle Davis, *Let's Get Well* . . . , Allen & Unwin (1966).
34. Brandon-Jones, *Palmistry of Love*.
35. Brandon-Jones, *Palmistry of Love*.
36. Napoleon Hill and W. Clement Stone, *Success through a Positive Mental Attitude*, Prentice-Hall (1960).
37. Delano Stagg, *The Glory Jumpers*, Mayflower (1964).
38. Hutchinson, *Your Life in Your Hands*.
39. Wood Jones, *Principles of Anatomy as Seen in the Hand*.
40. Napoleon Hill, *Think and Grow Rich*, Wilshire (Los Angeles).
41. Cheiro, *Palmistry for All*.
42. Cheiro, *Language of the Hand*.
43. Hutchinson, *Your Life in Your Hands*.
44. Benham, *Laws of Scientific Hand Reading*.
45. Cheiro, *Palmistry for All*.
46. Cheiro, *Palmistry for All*.
47. Cheiro, *Palmistry for All*.
48. Cheiro, *Palmistry for All*.
49. Benham, *Laws of Scientific Hand Reading*.
50. Hutchinson, *Your Life in Your Hands*.
51. Jaquin, *The Hand of Man*.
52. Jaquin, *The Hand of Man*.
53. Jaquin, *The Hand of Man*.
54. Eugene Scheimann, *A Doctor's Guide to Better Health through Palmistry*, M. D. Parker (USA, 1969).

Recommended Additional Reading

Palmistry

William G. Benham, *Laws of Scientific Hand Reading*, Hawthorn (New York, 1946).

Beryl Hutchinson, *Your Life in Your Hands*, Sphere (1977).

Eugene Scheimann, *A Doctor's Guide to Better Health through Palmistry*, M. D. Parker (USA, 1969).

Positive Health

Ruth Adams and Frank Murray, *Body, Mind and the B Vitamins*, Larchmont (New York, 1979).

Ruth Adams and Frank Murray, *Minerals: Kill or Cure?*, Larchmont (New York, 1974).

Adelle Davis, *Let's Get Well*, Allen & Unwin (1966). (Published in paperback by Unwin, 1979.)

Martin Ebon, *Which Vitamins Do You Need?*, Bantam (New York, 1974).

Walter M. Germain, *Magic Power of Your Mind*, Wilshire (Los Angeles, 1977).

Malcolm Hulke (ed.), *The Encyclopedia of Alternative Medicine and Self-Help*, Rider (1978).

Ivan Illich, *Limits to Medicine*, Pelican (1977).

Brian Inglis, *Fringe Medicine*, Faber (1964).

Lelord Kordel, *Health the Easy Way*, Tandem (London, 1973). American edition: Award (New York, 1973).

Useful Addresses

The Acupuncture Association,
34 Alderney Street,
London SW1
For a small fee, they will send a register of qualified practitioners.

The British Homeopathic Association,
27 Devonshire Street,
London W1
Provides lists of homeopathic practitioners, including doctors who have taken a course in this form of treatment.

National Institute of Medical Herbalists,
22 Osborne Avenue,
Jesmond,
Newcastle-upon-Tyne NE2 1JQ
Gives details of nearest practitioner.

British Naturopathic and Osteopathic Association,
6 Netherhall Gardens,
London NW3
Send 50p and a large SAE for Register of Practitioner Members, or look in your local library.

General Council and Register of Osteopaths,
16 Buckingham Gate,
London SW1E 6LB
Send 70p for list of registered osteopaths.

New Era Laboratories Ltd,
39 Wales Farm Road,
London W3 6XH
Will be pleased to help if the biochemic tissue salts are not available at your health-food store.

'Earthlore',
Tunnel Cottage,
Symonds Yat East,
Herefordshire HR9 6JL

They will forward, by return, their excellent vitamin and mineral supplements. The B-complex is a good insurance policy and guards against the debilitating effects of prolonged stress.